T0322022

# TAKE
# MY
# GRIEF
# AWAY

# TAKE MY GRIEF AWAY

## VOICES FROM THE
## WAR IN UKRAINE

Katerina Gordeeva

Translated by Lisa C. Hayden

I

WH Allen, an imprint of Ebury Publishing
20 Vauxhall Bridge Road
London SW1V 2SA

WH Allen is part of the Penguin Random House group of companies
whose addresses can be found at global.penguinrandomhouse.com

Penguin
Random House
UK

First published by WH Allen in 2024

www.penguin.co.uk

A CIP catalogue record for this book is available from the British Library

ISBN 9780753560594
TRADE PAPERBACK ISBN 9780753560860

Typeset in 12/14.75pt Dante MT Std by Jouve (UK), Milton Keynes
Printed and bound in Great Britain by Clays Ltd, Elcograf S.p.A.

The authorised representative in the EEA is Penguin Random House Ireland,
Morrison Chambers, 32 Nassau Street, Dublin D02 YH68

Penguin Random House is committed to a sustainable future
for our business, our readers and our planet. This book is made
from Forest Stewardship Council® certified paper.

MIX
Paper | Supporting
responsible forestry
FSC® C018179

*To my grandmother Roza, who was born*
*in Mykolaiv and died in Rostov-on-Don.*
*To my grandmother Katya, who was born*
*in Moscow and died in Kyiv.*
*To everyone I love on both sides of the war.*

# Table of Contents

Only hatred flies from South to North,
Overtaking spring.

Joseph Brodsky

# Translator's Note

The book you're holding in your hands, *Take My Grief Away*, first came into the world as a documentary film called *Humans at War*. To make the documentary and to write this book, Katerina 'Katya' Gordeeva, a prize-winning independent Russian journalist, travelled to dozens of locations in Europe and Russia, where she conducted interviews with people whose lives had been upended by the war in Ukraine. The film has been viewed over 3 million times. The resulting book has been translated into many languages, including German, Dutch, Italian, Finnish, Polish and, now, English.

*Take My Grief Away* isn't a history book or a book about the war itself. It's a book about how history and war have affected people in Ukraine and Russia. When Katya asks questions of her interviewees she sometimes admits to us, her readers, that she has no idea what she could or should ask. Once she – or her interviewee – finds something to say, she makes space for them to speak, giving them silence that's palpable on the page.

Katya's questions and comments guide her interviewees as they tell their stories. The interviews reveal patterns. We hear from people who'd been satisfied with their lives before Russia's initial invasion and the annexation of territories that followed in 2014. They also tell of how their lives changed on 24 February 2022, the date Russia's full-scale invasion began. There's even sometimes confusion about which country's army some soldiers were fighting for; anyone with a weapon is a potential threat to a civilian.

As a translator, I can say that the interview material in *Take My Grief Away* is linguistically intriguing. At times people seem to contradict themselves or speak in fragmented sentences. Given the ebb and flow of nerves, stress, and emotions during wartime, those apparent oddities are completely natural, even normal, as speakers attempt to express their own thoughts and feelings about absolutely unthinkable events.

We decided to include brief footnotes and a small glossary in this English edition to help readers orient themselves. Although each interview in the book tells a human story that's comprehensible with very little historical or political context, you may find it helpful to check news archives and Wikipedia for additional details. Much may have changed between my writing of this note, in late January 2024, and your reading of it, later in 2024 or beyond.

Significant differences between Russian and English present challenges when translating a book with so much oral speech. Like French, German, Spanish, and other languages, Russian has two forms of 'you'. In very over-simplified terms, one form ('ты' or 'ty') is for only one person, generally someone you know well. The other form ('вы' or 'vy') is used for one person if it's not someone you know well, or for two or more people. Age and respect can also be factors. I've called the 'ty' form the 'familiar you' in the book. Katya notes sudden changes in usage when some interviewees unexpectedly begin using 'ty' with her. We've used bold text to mark portions of quoted dialogue that are in Ukrainian. Some speakers blend occasional Ukrainian words and phrases into their Russian.

We've used transliterated Ukrainian spellings for all place names in Ukraine. Russian place names have been transliterated from the Russian. I never use any one transliteration system, preferring to combine loose rules, sometimes shuffling my options so the anglicised spelling is relatively easy to pronounce. Personal names were far more difficult to handle. Since many names are open to seemingly infinite diminutive forms, we decided to use just one version of a name for each person in the book. Some interviewees' names are anonymised.

Translating *Take My Grief Away* was an exceptionally emotional process. Despite being much, much further removed from interviewees than Katya, their words and emotions all flowed through my head – in both Russian and English – with every draft of the book. I grieved for strangers I'd never met as I considered words, choosing English versions that felt most fitting for their thoughts and feelings. They, along with their stories, will always be with me. I'm beyond grateful to Katya for writing this book and for recording these interviews, often in multiple forms, so that we and future generations can read about the horrors and the grief that this war has brought.

# Introduction

I was asked to write an introduction to this book, to briefly explain how it came about. I tried to honour the request before my deadline, but instead I found myself sitting in front of a blank document for weeks.

I'm a journalist. I worked for Russian television for many years, where I was a reporter who went to places where there was unrest. I had to leave TV when propaganda began replacing freedom of speech, and loyalty to the authorities took the place of professionalism. After the annexation of Crimea and the outbreak of war in southeastern Ukraine in 2014, I left Russia.

I became an independent journalist. I have my own YouTube channel with 1.5 million subscribers; the videos have tens of millions of views. Even after leaving Russia, though, I've been filming and reporting about Russia. No matter how you look at it, I have no other motherland and never will.

On 24 February 2022, it felt as if that had all lost its meaning.

I never thought I would have to tell my children, 'Don't shout, kids. A war started this morning.' And I certainly never thought I'd have to tell my children that the country that we call our motherland had started the war.

Half our family lives in Ukraine, in Kyiv: my brother and sister, their families and children, and my elderly uncle who was born in 1939.

That means that my state – both formally and acting in my name, too – went to war against people I love.

My work as a journalist helped me pull myself together. We'd all ended up on the very darkest pages of a history textbook, so I decided to document what was happening to people during the war.

I've hardly been home since February 2022. I've travelled, had conversations and filmed. I planned business trips and scheduled meetings but some of the people in this book came into my life in inconceivable ways: at a border crossing, on a train, on the street, through friends or friends of friends, and from unintentional eaves-dropping and random questions.

The war has taken away lives and spun all of us into a spiral of perpetual hatred but I managed, step-by-step, to make my way through a landscape that seemed absolutely unendurable, unforgiv-able and disastrous. I know how difficult it was for some of the people in this book to meet and talk. Sometimes the problem lay in speaking with me in particular. For some that was because I'm from Russia. For others it was because I'm a 'foreign agent' in Russia.* But these tremendous people always found the strength within to do so. And we talked.

That's how a film came out in summer 2022 on my YouTube channel. To be honest, I thought I'd feel relieved when the film came out. I'd stop living with everything I'd heard and seen that remained in my head, and then I'd release the stories from my heart. I'd exhale.

But the film came out and my people – the ones in the film and the ones whose stories hadn't made it through the final editing – weren't letting me go. I dreamed about them. Their voices sounded in my head constantly. I realised I wouldn't be able to cope and that I needed to write everything down. And so I began writing this book during summer 2022. And new figures kept coming into my life as I was writing it. The war wasn't ending. It was, however, getting more and more difficult not to let myself grow accustomed to it. But I wrote everything down. That's how this book came into being. And so, when I was asked to write an introduction, I sat for several weeks in front of an empty screen. I didn't feel quite right, I just

* Russia's foreign agent legislation went into effect in November 2012. The designation 'иностранный агент' ('inostrannyi agent', which means 'foreign agent') has been applied to hundreds of organisations and individuals, including the author, who was added to the list in September 2022. [*translator*]

couldn't grasp what was happening to me and why I couldn't write a single word.

I was saved by a note from one of the women in the book who wrote to me after reading the manuscript. She wrote: 'Each of us went through our own terrible and tragic but unique story. You went through them all.'

Yes, that's right.

The train ride from Berlin to Naumburg runs three hours or so, with a transfer in Halle. I'll need to wait 28 minutes in Halle for the next train. What a big station. Glass roof. I crane my neck. There's an airplane flying in the sky. For some reason I think about what will happen if it drops a bomb right on the station. I think about that all the time now.

I can't watch videos taken by drones. This gets ridiculous. Someone I know sent me a story about an elk cow, in Russia's Ivanovo Oblast, that gave birth to elk calves and lives with them there in the forest. My acquaintance used a drone to film the elk cow's story, showing the cow, the calves and the forest. And I can't watch. I'm scared. It seems as if someone will run out of the forest and start shooting, then he'll be shot; he'll die; a drone will film that death and the death is what I'll see instead of some elk calves. I don't cry. During a year of war, I, like everybody else, have taught myself not to cry.

But I'm standing in Halle station in Germany. Everything's good. Nobody's planning to bomb us, nobody here is afraid of drones. I'm trying to exhale my fear along with my breath, without anyone noticing. I go to buy orange juice. How much does it cost? Three euros? Four? Two and a half? I don't remember. Tanya, who's from Ukrainian Mariupol, a seacoast city hundreds of kilometres from the Russian border, wrote to me just as the price appeared on the cash register.

Tanya wrote:

*Since early March, when constant bombings began on Sea Boulevard, where our apartment was, my children and I had been living in a bomb shelter in my mother's building on Meotyda Boulevard. Every three or four days we* walked a kilometre home to our place because our two cats were left in our apartment. On 11 March, I came home to feed the animals. The bombing started when I was getting ready to leave. The military had put a mortar on the roof of our building. The building shuddered and there was a shroud of cement dust in the rooms. One of the shells landed very close, destroying the Baptist church. The shards and shockwaves made glass and window frames fly into my apartment. There was automatic rifle fire outside. Bullets whistled in the apartment, flying in the windows and getting stuck in the walls. I lay on the floor in the area between apartments. The neighbours weren't there. Bombing, darkness, cold and total desolation. Towards evening, there was another incoming and our building caught fire. It burned all night. There was an easterly wind so I was afraid the fire would spread to our part of the building. By morning, though, the battle quieted and the fire was almost out.

At around 4.30am I emptied a few kilos of food on the floor for the cats, poured a full basin of water and got out of the building. An apocalyptic picture appeared before me. There was a feeling of the unreality of what was happening and a strong sense that I'd die if I returned to the apartment. At the time I didn't yet know I'd never return home, that a few days later my building would burn up completely along with my beloved animals, bedridden people who were dear to me and other residents who died there . . .

I ran along broken glass and slate, and crawled over concrete slabs to reach the bomb shelter and my loved ones. I ran past the corpses of people lying by the fence at a kindergarten. I'd only taken my passport and a certificate of disability from home. In my pocket, in case I didn't make it, I had a note with my full name, my mother's address and my brother's address: whom to contact if I'm found.

I didn't run into a single living person along the way. But I made it to the bomb shelter. The first thing my daughter said at the entrance was, 'Where's Lyosha?' I felt sick. Lyosha's my son. It turned out Lyosha had gone to search for me the day before. But he didn't make it home and didn't return to the basement. The men from our shelter found him a few days later in an empty lot between buildings with his stomach ripped open. It was my fault, after all, that he'd gone to search for me. I'll never forgive myself. We buried Lyosha in the yard.

I'm on my way to Naumburg to meet with Tanya. I have her photograph: a black-haired woman standing in the hallway of a sleeping car on a train. Her arms are at her sides and it seems like there's a bag in one hand. Or maybe not, maybe there's no bag at all. A volunteer who helped Tanya leave Russia and come to Naumburg sent me that photo. That volunteer told me, 'Tanya was my most painful removal, through the whole war.'

I think about how many people that volunteer brought out. I also think about how this volunteer used to treat teeth and knit cashmere scarves in a small Russian city. And how they now know how to bring a person out of Russia without regular documents, how to convince someone who's lost everything to live on and how to pass DNA samples from Russia to Ukraine for identifying the dead. Important knowledge, by the way.

Tanya attempted to talk me out of meeting. 'I have cerebral palsy,' she wrote. 'It's not pretty.' And I'm thinking that having cerebral palsy and giving birth to two children is a tremendous feat. She ought to be proud.

Tanya herself, by the way, is from Primorye, a maritime region of Russia's Far East. Her parents brought her to Soviet Mariupol, to the warm Azov Sea, in the early 1980s. Bathing children with cerebral palsy in the Azov was considered helpful for them. Tanya's parents came to love Mariupol so stayed, to live there. Tanya grew up, married and, how about that, gave birth to two children: a boy and a girl. She also had an apartment with windows facing the sea.

I board the train. There's a little over an hour until I meet with Tanya. The train sets off and a new message from Tanya arrives.

*After the deaths of my son and husband, I sat in a basement with my mother and daughter [Lyuda], not leaving. There were about a hundred other people. We slept sitting up because there wasn't enough space. There was no electricity, no water, no connection with the outside world. We didn't just not wash during that whole time: we also didn't take off our boots and hats. It was very cold. At first we drained water from the boilers of destroyed stores, later we melted snow and boiled and drank industrial water. Then the water was gone. The snipers who'd settled in residential buildings started shooting the men who left the basement to find some water or put a kettle on the fire. We buried the killed near the building, in shell craters.*

*On 19 March, my daughter went up to my mother's apartment to get medicines, a couple of blankets and groats. She was gone for about 20 minutes. 'She probably can't find the medicine,' someone said. Just then, there was a terrible explosion, the building shuddered and cement dust and quiet hung in the air. And then people began screaming.*

*After we'd made our way out of the basement, we saw that our part of the building was burning. A neighbour ran into the entryway. But he returned soon. He said Lyuda was gone. I remember everything that happened after that in some sort of fog or slow motion.*

*I tried to go up into the building but they wouldn't let me.*

Students in the next row on the train are laughing and making a TikTok video.

I'm breathing fast so I won't cry. A message from Tanya comes in saying she'd written her story for me so as not to speak about it when we meet. Tanya writes that she's afraid of not being able to handle her emotions and she doesn't want to cry.

Tanya writes that it had only been possible to leave the part of Mariupol where she and her family had ended up by going towards Russia. That's how Tanya and her concussed mother ended up in Rostov-on-Don, my native city. Tanya's mother died soon after, but Tanya was transferred to another temporary housing facility, in Ryazan, 200 kilometres from Moscow. A year later, the management of the facility presented her with a choice: either renounce her Ukrainian citizenship and receive Russian citizenship or leave her temporary shelter. Tanya was aided by Russian volunteers who work under the threat of criminal prosecution because they assist Ukrainian refugees leaving for Europe. That's how Russian Tanya, who holds a Ukrainian passport and lost everyone she loved in besieged Mariupol, ended up in Naumburg.

Tanya greets me at the train. There's nobody else on the platform. We walk. Where are we going? At the entrance to the train station there stands a monument of a woman with a suitcase, but I'm nervous and don't have a chance to really look at it.

'The cerebral palsy's totally not noticeable, at all!' I tell Tanya.

'I'm just not tired yet,' she answers.

We have nowhere to go. Everything's closed. It's Sunday evening. There's bowling across from the train station; it's empty there. We sit at the bar and get coffee with milk. Tanya says, 'I don't have one single photograph of my children on my phone. I deleted them. I can't look at them, so please don't ask me.'

We talk about the sea. About how Tanya was made to wear a sun hat as a child. About how I came to that Azov Sea of hers as a little girl and how you can keep walking and walking in the Azov but the water's always at your knees. It's that shallow, which is why it's warm.

Here Tanya says, 'When we were sitting in the basement, we had this one girl – she was 23 – who gave birth to her first. She didn't have any milk at all, it was obviously nerves. Her mother would go upstairs and heat water on the burner for her daughter and grandson. That woman was killed during more shelling. And her grandson, that girl's son, died soon after. From hunger and cold, just imagine.'

I can't imagine. But I suddenly realise what hell should look like for whomever started this war: a basement, a child always being born and dying, all so the one housed in that hell never forgets that the war was his fault.

Tanya sees me off at my train. I return to Berlin with a transfer in Halle and Tanya goes back to Naumburg's dormitory for refugees. The dormitory houses nearly 300 people from all around the world on four storeys. That's too many for small Naumburg, which is why the dormitory's planning to shut down by the end of the summer. What Tanya fears most is having nowhere to go. Nobody awaits her anywhere.

Tanya hugs me and says, as quietly as a rustling leaf, 'I don't know why I'm alive, why I survived or how to live on. You can take my story for the book if you want.'

I say I'll tell her story, I say that for me, everything that happened to her, to Tanya, *is* this war.

Tanya sighs and says, 'I don't know if that has any point. I feel like there's no point in anything anymore. You can't fix anything.'

Tanya left Germany for England in the late summer of 2023.

My friends who saw her off sent photos from Brandenburg airport. Tanya's standing there, wearing a crimson sweatshirt. She's smiling.

At the time of writing, Tanya lives in England, not far from Grayswood, an hour from London. Tanya has her own room on the second floor of the home of an elderly woman who used to be a German teacher.

Tanya writes that she's never seen such green grass or such a long rainy spell. She also writes that she hopes to find serenity there, far from the places where she felt so much pain.

# Cockroaches

Friday, 29 April 2022. Morning. The border of Russia and Estonia. It's called Shumilkino on the Russian side, Luhamaa on the Estonian side. Four border inspection booths (three Russian, one Estonian) are lined up a kilometre and a half from the Riga–Pskov highway, which is a remnant of Soviet times. Forest all around. Sometimes a fox runs out, towards people crossing the border. The fox isn't wild but it doesn't approach closely: it comes out, watches and returns to the forest. And then it comes back again, from the other side of the border.

There's a coffee shop just beyond the Estonian border checkpoint. They usually cook up a filling breakfast for long-haul truckers: a huge plate of eggs, bacon, chips and toast.

I get coffee.

A woman comes in, one child in her arms, another holding her hand, with her husband behind her, carrying three big chequered bags and rolling a suitcase. She approaches the counter, asks in Russian for tea and a chocolate bar, and wants to know if she can pay in roubles.

'You can't.'

She asks if she can pay with a Russian bank card.

'You can't.'

She asks if she can pay in Ukrainian currency.

'You can't.'

She turns around before hearing everything.

I speak to her, asking, 'How about I buy it for you?'

She doesn't turn. The child, a girl, turns. But her mother pulls her hand. And the girl turns back around.

I buy two chocolate bars and a tea. They're standing in the coffee shop's entryway. I hold out the chocolate and tea for them; they don't take them. I say, 'Come now, why not?'

And she says, 'Why not what? What do you mean, why not?'

She's not shouting but I see she's irritated. Her hand is squeezing her daughter's hand hard.

I don't say anything.

'We don't need your chocolate,' she says, 'we have a thermos.'

I again don't say anything.

And she says, 'We're from Mariupol.'

I say I'd figured that out.

But I hadn't figured anything out. I have two Twixes in my hands. I'm standing, not moving. Because I don't know what's best. Leave or stay? And then there's the chocolate.

And so I say, 'My name is Katya.'

'Marina,' she says, then, nodding at her daughters, 'Anya, Lena. That's my husband, Sergei.'

I ask, 'How can I help you?'

'We don't need help. Somebody's coming for us now. We're going to Poland.'

I say that I know people in Poland. I'll call them if you want and maybe they can help you settle in? That works; Marina agrees.

Fortunately, my Polish acquaintances answer the phone and we agree that they'll meet Marina and her family in Krakow.

Why do I ask about the chocolate bars again after that?

She says, 'We don't need it, we have everything.'

I ask, 'Is it because I'm Russian?'

She answers, 'It's because I don't know you.'

And she adds, 'I'm sorry.'

I have a car so I offer to wait with them for the people who'll take them to Poland, just in case something happens.

Marina says there's no need. They'll wait by themselves. But the five of us stay, sitting on a bench in the entryway of the coffee shop at the Luhamaa border crossing on the Russia–Estonia border.

We're silent. And the children are silent, too. The children are silent and aren't budging, which looks very strange.

Our common silence grows stifling.

I go outside to wander around for a bit. Marina's husband follows me out, for a smoke.

He says, 'She's actually fun. She can play the accordion, she sings songs. She sang and played at our wedding, can you believe it? She was a vice principal at a school, responsible for organising large group cultural functions: concerts, events, she thought up jokes for the kids to use in KVN* competitions. And everybody laughed. Can you believe that? I can't believe it myself. It's just we sat in a basement for three weeks, we saw too much. Marina had a nervous breakdown, I thought she'd lose her mind completely. Our youngest girl turned one there in the basement. On 23 March.'

'My birthday's also 23 March,' I say, just to say something. I'm still standing there with the chocolate bars. The sun's rising. Marina and the girls come outside. To fill time, I tell them about the fox.

And then Marina says, 'The cockroaches went away after the war started. One day they just upped and disappeared. We lived on the first floor, my husband and I were always thinking about how to kill them, they really multiplied, it was awful. And then, suddenly they're gone, they're smart creatures. Where did they go, do you know?

'But we hadn't even thought about needing to escape and save ourselves. So we didn't go anywhere. Even when it was already *booming*. We didn't believe until the very end that something like this could happen. We thought that, well, it's like always, the outskirts will suffer a little and so, well, they'll shoot a little and then calm down, like all those eight years. We heard them shooting back and forth. So what kind of war could there be? No, we didn't believe it. So it turns out we're dumber than cockroaches or something?'

I keep quiet.

Marina's 28. She's very short, up to her tall husband's elbow.

---

* KVN stands for 'Klub Vesiolykh i nakhodchivikh', which is roughly 'Club of Funny and Quick-Witted People'. KVN competitions have been around since the early 1960s, when KVN was first aired on Soviet TV. KVN has remained popular in some countries of the former Soviet Union and there are teams in other countries, too. Ukrainian President Volodymyr Zelenskyy is a KVN alumnus.

She's black-haired with big hazel eyes on a face that seems perpetually surprised. Her younger daughter Anya's a year old; the elder girl, Lena, will be eight in the autumn. Lena was born in 2014, in a maternity hospital in Donetsk, to the din of the first shelling.

'We went to Donetsk, to my mother-in-law's, for the birth,' says Marina. 'She's an ob-gyn. So everything would be under control. Uh-huh, oh sure. We later rushed out of Donetsk with a newborn while he,' Marina nods at her husband, 'was beside himself for sending us to his mother's. Well, we came home. Our apartment was new, with windows facing the sea, only you couldn't see the sea because we were on a low floor. But you could smell it. The apartment was a half-hour walk from the sea. A very good apartment, I really loved it. It was nice there, cosy, he and I fully furnished it. For ourselves, you know? We recently bought a new TV. A good apartment, what can you say. Two rooms. But now it's gone. And our serenity's gone, too. And now there's no serenity for us anywhere. We won't have it anywhere. Anywhere.'

I'm afraid she'll start crying now. But she doesn't cry. She just repeats: *Anywhere. Anywhere. Anywhere.*

Anya's crying. They give her the thermos to drink some tea.

A phone rings. It's the volunteer who's supposed to meet them and take them to the Polish border. He's late, so I say, 'Why don't you come with me, we'll go and meet up with the volunteer.'

Marina doesn't want to. But she agrees to. We go.

She says, 'Nature's so interesting here, it's so northern, such tall spruce trees. Or are they pines?'

She says, 'I'll never get used to it.'

I ask, 'To what?'

She says, 'I can't get used to anything, see? I'm not a cockroach! I care about things. And I can't leave when it's dangerous and come when food shows up, do you understand that?'

Sergei touches her elbow. 'Marina.'

She says, 'Yes, everything's fine, I'm fine, I'm not nervous. I just can't get used to things, see?'

Marina either talks, saying a lot fast, or falls silent. She's now silent, after Sergei stopped her. I think she left something unsaid but she's keeping quiet, looking out the car window. There are pines, pines, pines.

We ride in silence for a half-hour. Estonia ends and Latvia begins.

Sergei says, 'The roads are so good here. They're worse in Russia. We have good roads in Ukraine, too. We did. Now there's probably no roads left. The ones they didn't bomb out were probably hacked up by tanks.'

That's what he said, 'hacked up'. Why not 'destroyed' or 'overwhelmed' or 'ruined'?

He says, 'They did a pretty good job finishing construction of our city in recent years. We were really starting to live well under the new mayor: they fixed all the old buildings, fixed the roads, the drama theatre, everything was done beautifully, then they built that new Ice Centre so the kids could play hockey. And the beach is really beautiful, too.

'Did you know that about a million people lived in Mariupol in Soviet times? And then they left when the Soviet Union broke apart. But now they'd started coming back, I mean coming back before the war. Our city'd gotten so beautiful, we had these fountains, you can't even imagine! We even thought we wouldn't leave home this summer, we'd stay and take our holiday on our sea. Some vacation.'

He lights a cigarette.

And Marina says:

'He was earning decent money working at Azovstal. Basically, everybody in the city works at either Azovstal or Ilyich, that's another big factory. Back in the 1990s they paid badly there but it got much better in recent years. But that's not what I'm talking about.

'My husband was at work when everything – all those sirens, air alerts – got started. He calls and says, "Get the kids and come, they're opening the bomb shelter here at the factory." And I run around the apartment in a rush, everything's falling out of my hands. And it was like I didn't have enough time to pack things. A stupid reason not to go, isn't it? I don't know how to explain it to you but we didn't go. And then everything seemed to get a little quieter.

'He came home from his shift that night and said, "Let's pack and go to the factory, it's safe there." And I say, "Seryozha, I have a premonition or maybe something else, that we shouldn't go there. It's a trap. We won't make it out of there if something happens." I tell him we're on the first floor, we're closest to the basement, let's stay at home, these are our own walls, they'll protect us. And then it's suddenly really booming while I'm talking. Like something fell into the room. There's smoke all around, a burning smell, it got totally dark and quiet. I ended up going deaf, something deafened me for a minute or so. And I have Anya in my arms, I'm holding her. But I don't see Lena. And suddenly some sounds are starting to get through, it's like I'm under water. I hear Anya shouting, I hear Sergei, he's calling to me, asking if I'm in one piece, and I'm shouting to him, "Lena, Lena! Look for Lena!" and the building's already falling, it's collapsing like cardboard.

'You know what they say about the earth going out from under your feet? That's how it was. It's like you're looking at yourself from a distance but you can't believe it's you. You're gripped with horror but you don't feel anything, you're doing everything fast but it seems like you're in slow motion.

'I apparently wasn't thinking straight at all and Sergei literally tossed Anya and me out the window and then went back for Lena himself. It seemed like he was gone for a long time. Anya and I were standing outside, I don't know how we weren't killed. But maybe it just seemed like it was a long time. He says he found her right away, she was scared and sitting in the kitchen behind the refrigerator, all curled up in a ball. He grabbed her and they jumped out – and that whole section of our building collapsed.

'And so we're standing in the yard of our former building, wearing only our indoor clothes. And the building's no longer a building, it's just a heap of slabs. It was freezing cold, I don't remember the temperature, but the cold was really fierce. And then for some reason I looked up. I don't know if I wanted to see God or something else in the sky. But you couldn't see the sky over us. There was this grey murk with black snow falling out of it, on our heads. The aftertaste of burning – disgusting, making you want to puke – is still in my throat. I can't get rid of it, no matter what I've done, even gargling with pure alcohol.

'I probably would have frozen in the yard if not for Seryozha. That black snow affected me like hypnosis. I didn't hear either Lena or Anya, who was crying in my arms. But my husband started shaking me by the shoulders and dragged me to the building across the way.

'They didn't exactly have a bomb shelter there – there weren't bomb shelters as such in our area, they were all new buildings, built from slabs. They had basements.

'There were two 12-storey buildings across from ours. There was a basement in each. You know, it was like fate, we chose our basement but if we'd gone to the other one we wouldn't be talking with you now. A missile fell there almost immediately.

'I now know how long it takes for a 12-storey building to burn: 40 minutes. That's it. And nobody's left. They brought a little boy from that building to our basement, already unconscious, with a head injury. His little arms and legs were just hanging, it was obvious it was over, he couldn't be saved, his face was so white. But people couldn't believe it, they crowded around, somebody did artificial respiration, somebody attempted to massage his heart or something, I'm not familiar with that. But one woman started washing the wound, she wanted to treat it somehow. And then I suddenly see this is my little boy, he's from our school, I know his name, he sang in concerts at our school. His voice was so delicate, so angelic. His voice started sounding in my ears and I no longer had it in me to hold back. I started yelling very loudly, "Sons of bitches, sons of bitches, I hate you, God damn you!" My husband was hitting my cheeks, people pulled me away. I didn't recover for a long, long time after. But something in me died with that little boy. It was like they'd pulled out my heart. It wasn't like he was my own child, my own children, they're alive, thank God. But I'll never forget his white face with such a huge wound at the corner of his forehead, I'll die with that.

'And I'll tell you it was at that point that I decided I'll survive and get out of there. And pull the children out. And my husband. We won't die. I memorised that day. It was 6 March. Later I didn't count the days. Only after going through filtration did we count that we sat in the basement for 21 days. And Anya turned one there. Sergei said you and she have the same birthday. You probably didn't celebrate yours like that.'

Anya, her younger daughter, is sitting on her sister Lena's lap and Lena is watching the tall spruce trees flash past beside the road. Sergei is smoking out the window. We're nearing the gas station, in Latvian territory, where we agreed to meet with the Latvian volunteer and move their things to his car.

I give them my phone number, just in case. We say goodbye; they leave for Poland. I'm absolutely sure we'll never see each other again. I'm feeling something akin to relief about that. It's hard for me to converse with her.

But a couple weeks later, she writes: 'Hello, it's Marina from Mariupol. I told you about cockroaches. Can you talk?'

# 2.

# The Magnet

Yulia's hair is pulled back in a ponytail, held in place by a hair slide. If you look at Yulia from the side, you can see a piece of metal sticking out of her head, just below the ponytail. It's a shard from a mortar shell. It got stuck in Yulia's head on 6 March 2022.

She and I are meeting a month and a half after her injury. She laughs. 'How about this, we put a magnet on it and it sticks!'

I ask Yulia why she's laughing. Yulia takes off the slide and slowly lets her hair down.

Then she answers, 'I've cried myself out. It's actually easy to cry, you know? When you're feeling low, it's easier to cry than not cry, did you know that? You sit down, just wringing your hands: I've got nothing, I was broken and broken again, too, they took my motherland away. Well, so they did. They took our house away, took our life away. They took away and finished off everything we loved. Everybody we loved, too . . . Finished off. And you can't bring that back, no matter what they tell us about the new life we'll start living now. There's nothing left. But they won't see my tears. I'm not crying anymore. I need to live. We need to keep on living, see?'

Yulia looks all around, as if she's choosing where, exactly, she's planning to live. Yulia was born and raised in Mariupol. She and I are meeting in May 2022 in Taganrog, in southern Russia. It's quiet all around. There are lots people near us but they're speaking in half-whispers.

We're sitting on two office chairs in the corner of a sports complex on Lenin Street.

In February 2022, even before the full-scale war started, this sports complex on Taganrog's Lenin Street was converted into a temporary housing site for refugees. Folding beds stand in eight rows, from one end to the other of what used to be a basketball court. Refugees who were brought to Russia from Ukrainian cities that were destroyed by bombing and wrecked by the war sit, lie, sleep and eat – basically live – on those folding beds. Refugees spend one to five days in these places before being sent further, deeper into Russia.

The hall for the Taganrog housing site can hold a maximum of 560 people. But there are fewer people now. Like Yulia, many have children with them. The children are looking at phones. But Yulia's son, Platon, is too small to be able to do anything by himself for long, even with a phone. He's two years, four months old.

Part of the former basketball court has been designated as a children's play area. There's a mat on the floor and toys have been tossed around: four blocks, a truck without a cab, a crane without a truck and a small red car. Platon's playing with the car.

Yulia doesn't take her eyes off her son. And Platon comes over to his mum after he hears his name in our conversation. He occasionally drinks water out of a baby bottle that Yulia's holding in her hands.

Yulia says, 'Who'll take care of him if I don't stop crying? Why would he need a mother who cries all the time and can't explain anything? Imagine how mixed up everything must be inside him: he sat in a basement for two months. Uninterrupted, see? I can't imagine what he went through. He doesn't talk.

'But I've asked myself all his questions many times: "So how is it you and I lived normally for the first two years of my life, went out to play in the park every day and walked to see Gramma and Grampa, but now we can't go outside the gate? Where are my toys and my daycare anyway? Why are you all so scared, why have you changed so much? Who are these people coming into our house, yelling and making us kneel? Why did we have such a great life – Gramma's garden, friends, fountains – but now that's all gone?"

'Maybe those aren't the questions in his head. He keeps quiet so I don't know. But I hadn't planned on my son having all that in his head instead of toy ships and balls. See?'

I ask Yulia if Platon was afraid of explosions and shooting. Yulia calls Platon over and says, calmly, looking him in the eye, 'bang'.

Platon sticks his fingers in his ears. Yulia taught him to do that in the basement. She also taught him to stay quiet and not cry if soldiers are walking past the building and to obey if Mum says 'lie down'. That means an 'incoming' is close.

'Incoming' is new language from the Russo–Ukrainian War. I first heard the word in 2014, from a refugee woman from Donetsk. Now everybody says 'incoming'. Not just refugees. There's even a definition in Russian Wiktionary: 'A hit from a single artillery shell, missile or loitering munition.'

Yulia says, 'Lie down.' Platon lies on the floor, covering his head with his arms.

I'd never seen a two-year-old child who knew those commands and obeyed them so dutifully. But as Yulia hugs Platon, she says these commands were a matter of life and death. She then turns and speaks not to me and not to Platon, but to the green wall of the sports complex's former basketball court.

'I sometimes wake up in the night, sweating, and wonder, what if he never starts talking at all? What if it affected him that way? And what will I do, how will I live? But he does say "Mama". What do you think, is that normal for his age?'

I say it's normal, that there are children who don't talk for a long time, even without a war. But I don't actually know what this two-year-old child will remember about the war. And Yulia says: 'He and I didn't go out beyond the gate in the yard for the first time until April, so we could go for humanitarian aid. I'm pulling him by the hand and he's afraid to go. He's crying. We walk past neighbours, past single-family homes where he'd been before: his godfather lived in one, his godmother in another, and somewhere nearby were my sister-in-law's kinfolk, Gramma and Grampa. It's like everything's familiar, it's spring, it should smell like spring. But it just smells like burning. Here are the buildings where our people used to live but now there's nobody: the windows are black and all smashed, the panes are knocked out and there's furniture lying around in the yards. There was a sofa hanging out a window. Dark blue, I remember that.

'There's usually a little kitchen garden somewhere in front of private homes in our area, sometimes there's a small front-yard flower garden, but here there's a stick driven into almost every one with a little sign that says CORPSE. The little one can't read but he sees it! There's corpses everywhere, sometimes just in shallow graves, sometimes rolled up in a rug with the head sticking out, other times just lying there, dried out, you can even see all the ribs. At my sister's house, there was a corpse lying in the yard, right on a bench, wrapped in a jersey, no head. It turned out to be someone we knew; they buried him later by the school.

'There's no longer either a city or people. I don't know what they show you on TV, who's living there, or why. Who are those people anyway?

'When the little one and I were walking that day, I realised we weren't staying there. We'd leave and start a new life, right, sweetie?'

Yulia nods to her son. Their gazes meet. Platon walks up to Yulia again to drink water out of the bottle. There's no more water in the bottle. But Yulia doesn't notice. Platon turns the bottle in his hands, gives it to his mum and walks off to play with the red car.

A poster looms over Platon, over Yulia and over all the rest of the people in that hall: 'Khabarovsk awaits!' I ask Yulia who Khabarovsk is waiting for and why.

She says it's a programme for refugees. Those who agree to leave Taganrog for Khabarovsk will be given relocation expenses, several hundred square metres of land, and refugee status. The Russian government is offering the programme. There are brochures set out around the former basketball court, telling of the beauty of the Khabarovsk region and how well people live there.

Khabarovsk is the Far East. It's 7,000 kilometres from Taganrog to Khabarovsk. Yulia says its seems there was one family at the temporary housing facility that agreed to go to Khabarovsk under the programme. But nobody from that family got in touch after leaving. It's unclear how they've settled in.

'I don't want to go anywhere,' says Yulia. 'I've decided to stay here. The sea is here. That's important to me. And it's somewhat similar to Mariupol here. Well, more or less.'

Taganrog is one of the oldest and most beautiful cities in

southern Russia. It's on the Azov Sea. Just like the beautiful and even more ancient Ukrainian Mariupol, where Yulia was born. The distance between them is 113 kilometres, two hours by car. As a child, Yulia rode with her mother from Mariupol to Taganrog to go to the house museum where writer Anton Chekhov lived.

But now, Yulia says, 'It took us eight hours to get here. There was more standing than riding. The main delay was filtration. All the questioning takes a tonne of time. Do I know any people who are against Russia's liberation operation? Yes, you're laughing, I guess, but they do ask questions like that. What, do you really think everybody was just sitting and waiting until they'd come to take everything away from us and shoot us all? I don't even know where people who want that live . . . Or maybe they'll expose them with their filtration?'

Yulia goes silent. She turns away from me and looks at the green wall, at the 'Khabarovsk awaits!' poster and at a basketball hoop that's unneeded, out of place and hanging over exhausted people.

'You know, of course I would have told them everything, the way it was. But I don't think they had any interest in knowing that. Why do they want details if they're not the ones being liberated? They're the ones *liberating*.'

I ask Yulia if she was scared. She shrugs.

'I haven't been scared whatsoever, not once. Listen, I worked at Azovstal as warehouse manager, I'm not afraid of anything. My mum always said I'm *trouble*. The broad with balls in the joke, yes, that's me. So when the war started I somehow realised immediately that I'm not giving up, I'm surviving. I'm going to survive and I'll pull the little one out of this, too.

'The only thing is that at the very start of the war I sat down by his bed and wondered if I should wake him up or not. It seemed then like the longer he sleeps, the longer his childhood will be. Without war. Well, theoretically that's how it came out. He was still sleeping but there was already all this . . . Apocalypse.

'But I wasn't afraid. I knew we'd be saved. When the power went out on 2 March and when the phone cut out and when there was no more water. We were sitting in the basement, our family, my mother, my sister and her husband, about ten of our relatives, they had an

eight-month-old child with them who turned nine months in the basement. Later another woman and her daughter ran to us from the
building across the way: a missile hit their building and people were
lying in the basement, dead, with their limbs ripped off. Four of the six
lay dead, the other two were alive and came to us. The little girl's hand
was burned and her mum's shoulder . . . We stealthily brought them
to the hospital during the night. I don't know what happened to them.

'And one day – I don't remember exactly what one, everything's
already blended into one endless day, actually one night – a few
APCs suddenly drove up to the dormitory just across the road from
us. Soldiers got out: harsh swearing, shooting, shouting, they kicked
everybody out of the basement and settled in to sleep there themselves. And ate people's chow. And they didn't give a shit if you had
kids or didn't have kids, they stupidly kicked everybody out into the
cold. Well, we took in the people who had children. Three people
for one night. And later, well . . . I'm sorry, but we had to live. I don't
know what happened to them either, I hope they made it.

'And we sat, we quietly sat, Katya. We put up with everything
because I knew we just had to wait it out.'

Yulia suddenly stops and asks if I want some tea. I don't, but we
leave the basketball court and go to a cafeteria that's painted blue.
We get some water from the cooler for Platon. Yulia puts the teakettle on. A woman comes in and says supper won't be until six but
she can give us some bread.

'It's like Young Pioneer camp,' Yulia says to me, winking. And she
politely answers the woman, telling her we don't need bread, everything's fine.

'Shall we go outside?' she asks, forgetting the tea.

We go outside. Children of various ages are playing some kind of
game by the front steps; Platon joins them. Off to the side, the parents are smoking. They're not allowed to go outside the fence
surrounding the sports complex. Among the scooters and bicycles
leaning against the front steps we find a big yellow plastic car for
Platon. We walk around the sports complex from the rear and settle
in by a wall.

Yulia lights a cigarette. She says, 'When combat shifted beyond our building, towards Azovstal, we started quietly going outside. To chop some firewood, get some air, have a smoke.

'And so on 6 March, four of us went out to smoke. One went out to her death. And I got it in the head, arm and my lower back.'

She takes a drag. I keep silent and look at her. There are several very strange seconds: she both wants and doesn't want to tell. I don't know what she's thinking about, but after her next drag, I understand she'll tell me.

And Yulia says, 'I didn't initially realise what happened. First we tried to get my friend ready to take her to the hospital. But in her stomach . . . There was no chance. And then I feel like I can't see anything, something's running along my eyes, from my head to my sweater. And I go into the building, to the sink, not touching anything, so I wouldn't leave marks. I lean. But there's nothing in the building: no water, no electricity, though there's blood pouring out of me, out of my head. They say it's like a river, right? But no. It wasn't flowing like a river, it was like somebody was pouring water on my hands out of a pitcher. Like that. I started losing consciousness and then I started getting scared: What is this, anyway? Will I really die now and not be able to help my kid out of this hell? I got so scared, Katya. So scared that I suddenly told myself: *Well, holy crap.*

'I grabbed the edge of the sink and told Mama, water, give me a glass of water. I'd read somewhere that you have to drink water if you're losing consciousness.

'And I didn't lose it. I stayed on my feet. My mother cleaned everything for me with vodka and we bandaged my head. Once my head was bandaged, I felt like there was something in my side bothering me: there was a hole in my sweater, almost like it went through. A shard had gone in and stayed by a rib, and only the tail end of it was sticking out. And so? Vodka again and back it went. She stuck it back. I didn't peep. We did all that quietly, too, so as not to clatter anything. The little one didn't even wake up, how about that.'

She laughs. She's proud of herself. I don't ask anymore why she's laughing. I just clarify: 'Yulia, why didn't you go to the hospital?'

'Who'd stay with the little guy? When you're sitting there in a basement, each person has their chores: wash, cook, tidy, heat . . .

This injury really laid me low, I couldn't help at full power for at least three weeks. I walked along the wall. But first thing in the morning we put a hat over the dressing so Platon wouldn't be scared.'

She lights another cigarette. I ask if she remembers where the mortar shell flew in from. She takes a drag. Lets out the smoke.

'Well, from the Vynohradne direction. Why?'

She asks that defiantly. As if I know who was stationed in Vynohradne and that answer should stagger me.

But the last time I was in Mariupol was 1989 and the Soviet Union was nearing its end, though we didn't know that at the time. My grandmother and I bought cherries at the market and swam in the sea. I don't even remember the street where we stayed and don't know if it's far from Vynohradne.

'Who was stationed there?' I ask, since Yulia is obviously waiting for me to ask.

'Well, the DPR,' she says.

She's silent for a bit, then continues.

'And a day later, the National Guard, our Ukrainians, came to our building. They asked:

**Is anyone here?**

*No.*

**You're alone?**

*Yes.*

*Well, **okay.***

'They were moving their rifle barrels, moving them in a threatening way. But we didn't give away our guys, we needed our guys because they chopped wood or at least protected us if everything got really fucked up.'

That's how I found out Yulia has a husband. And that he and three other men were with them in the basement. But I don't have a chance to say anything about that because she says:

'Later they kept coming back: National Guard, DPR, "Azov", the Kadyrovites, Russians, you know, there was barely time to change the flag on the building. But we didn't have any flag at all. We were just sitting and waiting for all of them to get out. Every day I was learning how to breathe: I breathed so I'd stop being afraid. You know how, you count to ten, inhaling, then exhale on ten. At first my head spun. But then it got easier.

'There was a day when it helped. The "liberators" came: shut your mouths, everybody on your knees, document check. And they're prodding with their machine guns, like, hurry up, why're you dawdling?

'I looked at them and breathed.

*one*

*two*

*three*

*four*

*five*

*six*

*seven*

*eight nine ten*

'Not out of fear. It was to stop my rage. If not for Platon, I would have chased that "liberator" out with a rolling pin to the neck, can you believe that? He would have caught his little slippers on the fence, though. But I was breathing.

'The only thing is, I couldn't hold back at one point and, at risk to myself and the little one, I say, "And you want people to accept you here after this? How are you going to sleep at night, with a machine gun in your arms?"

'He didn't answer. He just pulled the gun aside. For some reason I remember his eyes. There was nothing in them. Not hostility, not pity. He could have killed us but didn't. He was probably too lazy.

'But everything ended a week later. It got quiet. How were we supposed to understand that? We could hear the birds now. And I realised it was time to get out. Well, not get out, but evacuate. And so then the little one and I walked through the city for humanitarian aid. By then it was April.'

It's getting dark. She finishes off yet another cigarette. We go back inside the former sports centre. Supper's soon. People are making their way to the cafeteria. The former gymnastics room is nearby; they handle paperwork in there. There's a first-aid station in the former wrestling room.

At the locker room, there's a paper tacked up that says BOUTIQUE. People can take items gathered there. The majority of refugees end up here with one bag. Yulia's very proud that she was able to bring everything she thought she and her child would need.

She lists what she took. There are even nice shoes so she can go on interviews when she looks for work. And there's an immersion heater, too.

She counts on her fingers:

*Sturdy shoes.*

*Sandals.*

*Pyjamas for Platon.*

*Dress.*

*Snowsuit.*

*Blender.*

She stops when recalling what else. And I use that pause to finally ask, 'Yulia, why did you go to Russia?'

'Where else would I go?'

'Russia attacked Ukraine.'

'I'm aware of that.'

'Why did you go to Russia?'

And she repeats, 'Where was I going to go?'

I ask differently. 'Why didn't you go to Europe?'

And she answers, 'Who needs us there? They have enough needy people even without us. These days, if you're from Mariupol, that immediately means you're a passion bearer. But our city was big. There's not enough Europe for everybody.

'Plus I need to raise the little one. And I don't know A from B there, I don't know any languages. You can just stand there and blush or go pale, worrying you said the wrong thing. Russian's my language. I speak it, I think in it. We need to live, there's no time for me to think if I'm like this or like that, if I have to take off my shoes when I go inside. Help me, save me, yoohoo! We're refugees from Mariupol. So no, I'd never humiliate myself that way.

'So, basically, I'll live here. Mama stayed in Mariupol, we need to be nearby so she can come visit and it's not obvious how everything would be with Europe, that clear?'

I ask her about her husband. She nods towards the depths of the basketball court and calls to him: 'Vitali, wave to the woman, she's a correspondent.' A hoarse 'I'm here' carries from the last fold-up bed in a middle row. A sleepy man raises himself up a little on his elbow, waves to me, lies back down on his side and covers his head with a pillow. Yulia doesn't look at either him or me. She's focused on searching for something in the pockets of her jacket. And doesn't find it.

They bring supper. Sautéed meat and potatoes. She says she doesn't want to eat. She asks a volunteer in a red jersey that says GOOD to stay with Platon for a bit.

We go outside. She lights a cigarette and says, 'Yes, we'll make it, we've got nothing to lose. We're looking for housing now, so we can stay here. I'll hold on, I know how to breathe, remember? Why are you looking at me like that? Think about it: I'll find work faster here, get on my feet, I'll earn as much money as we need before Platon starts school. I can't think about myself now. I survived for his sake. And now we're going to live. The city here looks like Mariupol. It's the same sea. And people speak the same way, we don't stand out much. And the tulips look like ours, too. I really love tulips. You know, they planted lots of tulips *there*, in the park near our house, before the war. When we left, I turned my head and saw tulips. Well, sure, of course my heart sank.'

'They actually bloomed?'

'What, you think they'd stop growing because of a war or something? No. They grew, bloomed. There's a shell crater, there's somebody's grave, but here's tulips blooming all over. The wind started blowing, too, and their heads started swaying, like they were saying goodbye to me. I started crying then. But I told myself to go ahead and cry, but this is the last time, little Yulia. That's it. Long story short, I'm gone. I stayed there, in the basement. But Platon has to live so everything will be different for him. So nobody comes to stick an assault rifle in his face. That's the main thing. I don't give a shit who's right, who's to blame, or what basically happened there.'

I tell Yulia I don't believe her.

She gets angry.

'What truth? What will happen if I tell it? You and I will stop the war? We'll punish all the bad people and the good ones will go home if they're alive?

'Nobody needs your truth. We need to live. That's it. None of the rest matters. I hear how everybody around me says, well, what lots of parents say, that my child will grow up and I'll tell them the whole truth. And I say to them: "What's your truth?" Well, they're like this, they're like that. And I say to go see your neighbour, they'll tell you the opposite. And a third neighbour will say that, well, it wasn't like that at all. And the fourth will say a fourth thing. And the war will devour us all while we're finding out what that truth is and which of us was right. We're not the ones that started the war but it came to us and took everything. And there's nothing to sort out here. And there's no truth here. The war came and untied every-one's hands. And everyone came to the war with their hands untied.

'Yes, Russia started the war, it's you that attacked. But after that, everybody behaved badly on their own. Or not? There's nobody good in war. And nobody will tell you that truth. Nobody talks about it. Because at war the truth is filtered on both sides. Believe this, that doesn't apply to you, we'll sort things out ourselves. The main thing is to soak this up, but you don't need the rest. Long story short, there won't be anything for me to tell my son about who behaved themselves well. Everybody showed who they are, let's put it that way. That's why it's war.

'But I'll say one thing for sure. I'll tell him he was born on Ukrain-ian territory. That Ukraine is his native country, his land. He'll have a Russian passport but I have no illusions: everything is what it is, but I won't hide our family's truth. He should know. And hold that in his heart: I'm a Ukrainian. The rest is details we might not reach in our lifetime. Maybe later, at some point. But, personally, I don't believe it.

'Do you want to touch it?' Yulia asks, abruptly changing topics, and raising the hair on the nape of her neck.

I don't especially want to but I nod.

Yulia holds her hair and I first see, then touch, the small metal shard that sticks a couple of centimetres out of her head. It's cool, colder than Yulia's skin. Yulia takes a black magnet out of the pocket of her sweat jacket and attaches it to the shard in her head.

She says, 'Like so.'

She takes the magnet off and puts it back in her pocket.

I don't know what to say. I keep quiet.

As Yulia and I were talking, a uniformed security employee and another person, in civilian clothes, stood behind us the whole time. People at the refugee facility whispered to me that he's from the special services. But nobody knew which services.

They didn't step away from Yulia and me for a second. And when we spoke quieter, they approached closer, trying to hear every word.

I ask, 'You aren't at all afraid of them, Yulia?'

She shrugs. 'I'm over being afraid. I can't be afraid anymore. It's like that emotion's gone, it's finished. I don't know who or what could make me worse off than I am. See? You don't see . . . It's good you don't. It means you've never had this.'

I give her my phone number. I say to call me at any time, for any reason. I enter her number. I call her to confirm I entered it right.

We say goodbye. I write her a couple of insignificant notes from the road, she answers.

We write back and forth for another couple weeks. For no real reason, not about anything: I'm alive, are you? And then silence sets in.

Yulia hasn't been in any messaging system I know since 19 May 2022, and she hasn't been in contact. At the Taganrog temporary refugee site where we met, they have no information about the whereabouts of Yulia and her son. I don't know how else to search for them.

Yulia, if you read this, please make contact. You have my number.

# 3.

# The Belly

'I don't know if I love my daughter or not. Can you imagine how awful that is? I couldn't look at her after she was born, couldn't take her in my arms. I had no milk. But I also didn't want to feed her, I simply couldn't have.

'I didn't even know how to name her. I named her Lyuda. That's the name of the young volunteer woman who brought us here. Now I have a daughter Lyuda. But I feel nothing for her. I don't know why I gave birth to her. I don't know why she'll live. I was named Raya*: Mama said that was so life would be heavenly. But my life resembles hell. People only end up in hell for some sort of bad things they did. But we ended up in hell for no reason. Because the neighbouring country decided to take possession of us, because soldiers came to us. They shot, they peed and crapped in our homes, in the homes where we lived, where we loved each other. They defiled them.

'They attacked us on 24 February 2022. I was in the 20th week of pregnancy, so almost in my sixth month.

'I physically felt the war sucking the life out of me, even though it was still far away. But the world immediately turned black for me: I didn't want the child, I didn't want anything. I just wanted it to stop being scary. We lived in fear, in unending terror, for 16 weeks. And then we decided to escape. Because Petya, my husband, said I had to give birth somewhere in a big city. And so we escaped. Do you know what a wrinkle in time is? It's when time splits, and it's like you're falling into an abyss where there's no time, nothing.

* The name Рая, Raya, pronounced, RYE-ah, is similar to the Ukrainian and Russian words 'рай', which can be transliterated as 'ray' or 'rai' but are pronounced RYE, which means 'paradise' or 'heaven'. [*translator*]

*Timelessness*
*I fell into it*

'The last thing I remember well is Petya and me drinking coffee. We had a jar of instant coffee on the shelf in our kitchen. So I was pregnant and not drinking coffee, but Petya and I had coffee that morning.

'They were already shooting very close and everything was rumbling.

'It had actually already been rumbling for several days, it was the equipment arriving. But here it was, starting to rumble really close. The earth was shaking. I'm not exaggerating. It wasn't shaking hard, it was light, but that made it eerie. My husband and I sat down before leaving.* He put his hand on my belly. I looked at his arm, at the black hairs on his hand. And since the earth was shaking, the hairs on his hand were shaking hard, too. My husband's name is Petya. Did I tell you?

'We woke up Ilana – that's my daughter, she's six – and left the house. See, if it weren't for my belly, I would have picked her up, I would have carried her, I would have covered her with myself. I swear to you, I would have kept her safe. But it was hard for me. Even when my husband said I needed to sit down or lean over, I couldn't because my belly got in the way. And so I led Ilana by the hand.

'We either ran or hid. Soldiers were shooting each other very close by. But it seemed like they didn't notice us.

'I remember that it also occurred to me – this was a very quick thought, you know, like some sort of fantasy – that if we could be covered by the invisibility cloak in *Harry Potter* we would have run, run all the way out of the city. After all, there wasn't far left for us to run to get to a safe place.

'Now, though, I think no cloak would have saved us. Because it flew in from above. First it whistled, then it got very hot and there was a resounding crash. I instinctively grasped my belly with my hands and Petya, Pyotr, my husband, grabbed Ilana. That's what I think because they were lying together. But they were lying there,

---

* This is a custom in some countries: before travelling, one may sit for a minute or two in silence with (or even on) one's luggage. [*translator*]

black. It was already flesh. The burned flesh of the people closest to me, do you see what I'm saying?

'I don't know if they were in pain, if they felt something. I now ask everybody all the time what they might have felt.

'And then I fell into a *gap in time*. I switched off. People told me later that I was lying unconscious and holding Ilana's hand. Well, that or what was left of her. Soldiers found me, they were looking for their own.'

I ask, 'Which soldiers?'

'Yours. Your soldiers,' Raya answers. She continues.

'Russian soldiers entered Rubizhne that day. People told me later that there was very heavy combat.'

Raya's tears are flowing calmly, evenly and ceaselessly: they're like water from a tap, like breathing, like a forest brook. She doesn't wipe them. Tears run down her face, dripping from her chin to her chest and there are two huge damp spots on her bust. The thought suddenly occurs to me that it could be milk: sometimes nursing women's tops get soaked when the milk comes in. But Raya's not breastfeeding. She continues speaking, looking beyond me, out the window.

'Do you understand that my younger daughter survived because she was in my belly? But the older one died because my belly, where the younger one was, kept me from protecting her? I don't know how she and I are going to go on living, remembering what happened. Why should we live? I don't even know why I'm telling you all this. To be honest, I just didn't have the energy to refuse you.'

Raya's hands are folded on her knees. They're white, bloodless. The Berlin apartment that one group of volunteers settled her into and another group of volunteers pays for is empty but for a table in the kitchen, two chairs, a crib and the fold-out bed where Raya sleeps. She has no clothes beyond what she's wearing. And a coat in the entryway. The volunteers brought it for her.

Lyuda, a month-old little girl, has a pile of onesies, undershirts, overalls, nappies and rattles, plus a trendy pram. Strangers donated all that for her.

In July 2022, volunteers managed to take Raya, pregnant with Lyuda, out of Ukraine to Russia, bring her through Russia to Estonia and from there to Germany. That's the usual route for a refugee who's made the decision to go to Europe. But Raya made no decisions.

She doesn't remember anything.

'They asked me if I had any relatives in your country. But we had nobody. They also asked where I wanted to have the baby. I hadn't thought about that. I'd wanted to die, so I wouldn't exist, so there wouldn't be this belly, so I could go back to where we drank coffee the morning before leaving the house. And so I could have told them: Don't go, there's death!

'See, they weren't shooting at us, do you see what I'm saying? It was by chance. Anyone at all could have been there. Tell me, what kind of war is it when it could be anybody at all, why is this happening to us? Why did you do all this to us?'

Raya's no longer crying. She's speaking softly, not raising her voice. Lyuda's woken up in the crib. A volunteer comes to feed her. I don't know her name and Raya doesn't seem to either; the young women vary. I don't know if this volunteer speaks Ukrainian or Russian. She sings a lullaby in English over the baby's head.

Raya suddenly looks me in the eye.

'Did I tell you? I'm a Russian literature teacher by training. And you know, there's one work that I could never understand: *Anna Karenina*. I happened to be rereading it when the war started. And I got to the most incomprehensible part for me, when Anna gives birth to the daughter she doesn't love. That was always the hardest part for me, explaining to the kids that a mother could not love her own child, not feel anything for the child.

'And now I'm in that position.

'It's just that I no longer have anybody I could love. There's no love in me, not a drop. There's not even any hatred, that's what's really surprising. Just colossal tiredness. I even envy that Anna in a way. Throwing yourself in front of a train, that's so simple.'

# 4.

# Roots

Tanya smiles.

She shows the photos on her phone of her house in Vyshehrad.

'We had a really beautiful home, we built it with love. This whole story was basically about love: three little children, three dogs, chinchillas, a canary and love.

'Bohdan and I didn't initially realise what good fortune it was that we decided to live in the country and that we had our own house now. I gradually came to have a bond with that home, with that place: you wake up when everybody's still asleep, walk out on the front steps, stand barefoot and feel dew on your little toe, look up at the sun and squint. It seemed like I was flying at those moments. I even whispered to myself, so quietly: "Tanya, this is what it is, good fortune. You're fortunate, Tanya."'

Tanya and Bohdan finished building a large house in Vyshehrad in the summer of 2021.

And Tanya, who'd previously managed the Kyiv branch of a stylish French clothing brand, started living in the country with her children and dogs. I ask her, 'Was it easy for you to quit your job?'

She answers, 'Everything's easy when you're fortunate. And I was fortunate. We brought my mother to our house. And gradually, gradually, a sense of home began to grow. It's like the little pig says in the story: my home is my castle.'

Tanya laughs.

On 24 February 2022, Tanya, her husband Bohdan, their three youngest children and her elderly mother were at their home in Vyshehrad. Tanya's eldest daughter, Daryna, was in Kyiv.

On 25 February 2022, 25 people gathered in Tanya and Bohdan's home: Daryna and her friends and acquaintances, and Tanya and Bohdan's coworkers and relatives.

On 26 February 2022, dacha residents Pavel, Lyuda and their daughter came from Kyiv to the house next door. Pavel stopped by to tell his neighbours that he was a doctor and was always ready to come and help. They drank tea.

Tanya says:

'I'd pray quietly after everybody went to sleep in the evenings. I'd repeat a few words to myself, over and over: "I want them, my children, to live, just live. Just live, that's all." I don't know who I was saying that to: God, myself, the space around me or the Russian soldiers who kept getting closer and closer to our home. That rumbling was more and more audible. It made me nauseous.

'The children fell asleep but I couldn't. Night-time was scariest of all. Morning was easier. We made assignments: somebody cooked, somebody served, somebody heated water, somebody washed their hair.

'Hostomel's near us. There was constant shelling there. Fighter planes flew over us; sometimes they started bombing. Then we'd all hide together in the utility room, where there weren't any windows.

'We didn't cry, didn't shake; we were reserved and calm. A person is constructed in an interesting way: there aren't any panic attacks when you're most scared. If someone's deathly scared, you can't scare them more. It was easier for me: I gave my youngest, David, my breast; the middle child, Daiana, she's four, got a phone; and ten-year-old Danila was interested in everything: airplanes, explosions and trenches. It was like he was in a computer game. And I tried not to scare him: if it's a game, it's a game.

'We kept playing when the electricity went out and day turned into night. We drew by candlelight, acted out charades and played the ring game* or a word game.

---

* The 'ring game' mentioned here similar to the game 'button, button, who's got the button'. There are variations but players usually sit and then the person who's 'it' takes a small object, such as a ring or button, into their hands and then goes to each player, stopping to either drop or imitate dropping the object into each

'But then soldiers entered the village. I was paralysed when I saw the first tank out the window.

*Tank!*

*Tank!! Tank!!! Tank!!!*

*There's a tank driving down my street!!!*

'The tank was turning its turret – it looked alive. It was searching for a target, it could destroy everything, it could easily handle everything living. A tank has no heart.'

Tanya shows me a video on her phone: several tanks are driving one after the other along a grey Vyshehrad street in the grey mist of a March morning. One turns so its barrel is looking into the camera's lens. The recording cuts out.

Tanya says:

'Bohdan told me to pack a small, light suitcase with documents. There's a nature reserve behind the house, on the other side of a concrete fence. Bohdan said he'd lead us out of the house when the opportunity came. And that we'd need to run very fast towards the nature reserve. We'd be safe there and could hide for a little while.

'Bohdan and the other men were standing by an improvised checkpoint on the road out of the village. Bohdan called a few times and said, "That's it. Get dressed fast. Leave."

'But it's an adult who can get ready quickly and leave. And I had three small children to prepare: I'd dress them, we'd go outside and he'd call to say, "Cancel, everybody in the house, they're about to start shooting again." We'd run inside, lie on the floor and wait for the shelling to stop. That happened several times.

'That evening, he called again after I'd just put everyone to bed and exhaled. His voice was tense, "Tanya! Quick, quick, run."

'And I tell him, "I'm not going, Bohdan. I can't do this anymore, well, let it be what it will be, I don't have it in me." I felt like he'd get mad and didn't have it in him either. But he didn't yell, he just calmly said, "Tanya, I'm begging you, all of you leave the house right now."

---

player's hands. These two games diverge at the end: in the button version, the players guess who has the button, but in the ring version, the player who receives the ring is supposed to run to the leader ('it') without being caught. [*translator*]

'I dressed Daiana in a T-shirt and leggings under a ski suit, Danila got dressed himself, I pulled pants and a fall jacket on David, and I wore Uggs and a jacket. We forgot the suitcase. It's good I brought the phone.

'We left the house and I saw us – so lost, sleepy, awkward – from somewhere a little overhead and off to the side. This is how people leave the dearest place in the world, their stronghold. Maybe leaving it for ever.

'The question "why?" pounded in my temples.

'But I drove it off. Bohdan told us where we had to run and we ran. And behind us stood the house, where my dogs were barking, barking, barking.'

Tanya breathes in through her nose. She briefly sighs a few times. Takes out her phone. Shows me photos. Two German shepherds with shiny fur are licking both Tanya's cheeks. A happy-faced beagle is obeying the 'sit pretty' command.

Tanya says: 'They shot my dogs. They were shot a few hours after we escaped. I sometimes wonder if they would have shot us, too. They said they were shooting the dogs because of their barking. Would they have shot the children because they were yelling?'

I'm silent. I squeeze my eyes shut. But Tanya's not looking at me, she's continuing.

'Bohdan was telling us when to sit and hide from bullets, pressing our heads between our knees. But I had David in my arms. How can you drop to the ground and cover your head with your arms when you have an infant in your arms? I crouched and looked to the sides, as my children lay down and my old mother – she's 78 – was half-squatting while her older sister held her by the arm so she wouldn't fall. At some point, I lost sight of Daiana and Danila then my gaze found them again. The sky darkened again later, the shooting started, and we fell into a daze. You know, it was as if none of that happened to us: I didn't feel either fear or agitation. I didn't know how this would end for us and I wasn't thinking about that. Bohdan yelled "lie down" and I stooped, then he shouted "forward" and we ran. We were like rabbits. Russian military vehicles were moving towards us, from the nature reserve where we'd counted on taking cover, so we ran in the other direction. There was shooting from the road, too, so we turned towards another road. Then, suddenly, completely randomly, a car, a white Zhiguli, appeared on the road out of nowhere. A man I was seeing for the first time in my life leaned out of the car and shouted: "Women and children, in the car, quick."

'We approached the car stealthily, crawling, and climbed in: Mama, my mother's sister, the children and I. And the driver peeled out. I turned around and saw my husband and oldest daughter left in a gully; they're being shot at and I'm leaving. It was the scariest thing in my life.'

Tanya scrolls through her phone. There are photos of her husband, Bohdan, and her eldest daughter in the phone. They're standing together: Bohdan's a handsome. blue-eyed, greying man. And Daryna is slender and black-haired, resembling Tanya. Father and daughter are smiling in the photo, it's some sort of family holiday.

'That's my birthday,' says Tanya, 'in 2021.'

A pause.

'Hard to believe, isn't it?' Tanya says, rescuing our conversation.

'Yes.'

'The man in the Zhiguli brought us to his house and rushed back off to Vyshehrad. He was counting on being able to take someone else away, save them. You know, in those months, I saw many times how our Ukrainians suddenly showed unbelievable heroism and sacrificed themselves for others. Like our driver did. He saved us but they opened fire on his car on the way back and he died. There you go.

'But we . . . We survived. We spent the night in the house, where his wife and mother were. Everything was exploding around us, windows rattled, children cried. It was dangerous for the owners of the house. And the women told us: "You'll leave in the morning, we don't need you here."

'I knew somebody in the next village, a kindergarten director, so we went to her house. Daryna had made it there, too. She'd managed to start her car and leave the village. We didn't know where to drive, we just drove and drove. We were running away from the war.'

Tanya scrolls through her phone again. It contains identical photos of the road, alongside which are burned-out cars, charred trees, broken-down equipment and abandoned things that had been someone's life.

I ask her. 'Why did you take pictures of that?'

She says:

'It was a defence mechanism. Everything you take pictures of becomes the past. We rode for 18 hours, we were running away and the war was coming after us. I took pictures so everything we saw would quickly become the past.

'And then do you know what I realised? I realised the scariest thing in a war isn't the equipment, the bombs or the canister shot. The scariest thing is a person. We drove through a Russian check-point and a Russian soldier looked inside the car. He pointed his semi-automatic at us and asked us – women and children – questions about the disposition of troops, the location of our men and about our attitude towards the war. This was a living person but his eyes were dead.

'I was very afraid but later I didn't so much understand as sense that since his eyes were dead, that might mean he'd already died inside. That means there's no longer any faith or love in him. That means he'll never win.

'When he told us "go ahead", I was absolutely prepared for him to fire as we drove away, shoot at the car and that would be that. But it didn't happen. We drove and drove; the road seemed to stretch end-lessly. The children looked out the window and asked questions:

*"Mama, what's that, a foot?"*

*"Is that a dead foot?"*

*"Who had it?"*

*"And is that a tank?"*

*"And is that a kid? What is that, a dead kid?"*

*"How did he die?"*

*"Why?"*

'It got easier at the Ukrainian checkpoint. Our soldier leaned and stuck his head, instead of the barrel of a gun, in the car and he said, **"Hello. These kids are with you now? Which are boys and which are girls? How many are you total?"**

'And I was at a loss: three kids in the car, a girl and two boys, and my oldest daughter was in the boot, that was the only way we'd fit. And he laughs and pats my cheek. He reaches – he has some sort of boxes standing there – and sticks some chocolate and toys through the window to us. "Here," he says, "give these to your **children** in the car." And right then we all started crying, all together, can you imagine? This was the first time we'd started crying since the war started. And after that I cried all the time, until Germany. And in Germany, too. Because the world's turning upside down and there's nobody shooting at you anymore, there's no rumbling all around, you don't wake up in the night from the hum of airplanes or the clanging of tank treads. It's like you've been rescued. Both you and your children. You left, right out from under the bombs. But you're no longer you. You're no longer a person, you're a refugee. No, that's not it. Now you are the refugee.

'It's a big shock to walk up to a pile of somebody else's things that were collected and laid out by volunteers, and to ask for a package of disposable nappies. It's a shock when people ask you, "What kind of things do you need?" and you stand there and can't figure that out – it's apparently spring now and it'll be summer soon, so what do I need?

'They ask: "What don't you have?"

'And I automatically answer, "Oh, what do you mean, we have everything!"

'And I later remember that we don't have anything. We don't have anything at all now.

'I had everything in my life. We didn't want for a thing, so why am I standing here and digging around in a heap of other people's stuff, attempting to dress my children so we can continue our travel? So we can go even farther away from the home I loved so much?

'And every overnight stop, every calm night, has turned into torture because my children ask me questions before bed:

"*Is Papa alive?*"

"*What do you think, Mama?*"

"*Answer me, Mama?*"

"*Will we go back home?*"

"*How are the dogs?*"

"*Aren't they scared when there's shooting?*"

'And I always had different answers. When we were escaping, we already knew the neighbours had been shot. The chances our men survived were minimal.

'And you know what else is funny? My mother mixed up blini batter that day. And left it by the cooktop. And I just can't remember if we added oil to that batter or not. Because if we didn't, they'll stick when they're cooked, that's what blini do . . .'

A month later, a chance person who'd hidden from the war in Tanya and Bohdan's house called to tell her Bohdan was alive and he'd managed to survive, but the Russian soldiers killed the dogs. Their barking got on the soldiers' nerves.

Bohdan got in touch a week later – he'd made it to Kyiv. He told the story of the neighbours, Lyuda, Pavel and Sasha. And he said he'd asked the soldiers not to kill the dogs.

Tanya says: 'But what could he do?'

And she covers her mouth with her hand.

We're meeting during the third month of the war. By that point, Tanya and her children have lived in seven places. We make a videocall to Bohdan in Kyiv. He speaks slowly and matter-of-factly, so as not to get emotional.

'Hi, my dear. Everything's fine with me. I miss you. How are the little ones?'

Neither of them can bear a long conversation.

'These three months apart have to be told in person,' says Tanya.

'I miss you,' says Tanya.

'I want to go home,' says Tanya.

She touches my hand and asks, 'Do you have a home?' I shrug. First I left my city, then I left the city where my children were born, then I left my country. I live in a rental apartment in a foreign country that's not particularly glad to see me but I have nowhere else to go. I've been considering this rented apartment my home for eight years now. Ever since the point my country attacked Tanya's, which finally led to the big war that deprived Tanya of her home.

'I probably don't have a home,' I answer.

She says, 'Then you won't understand me.'

'Explain?'

'See, I was absolutely fortunate before the war. But I couldn't explain that to myself, couldn't formulate it. But now I've suddenly realised everything.

'*I'm doing pretty badly.*

'They take care of us here, the conditions are wonderful, people bought us clothes, the children enrolled in school, they found us psychologists, doctors, friends, everything! But I want to go home. I want to see Bohdan, to sense his smell, to wake up there, at home.

'I can't answer a simple question for myself here: What will happen later? Where are we? Who are we? When will I go out on *my* front steps again and look at *my* sky?

'It only seems like the sky's the same everywhere. I remember how it was over our house. I remember . . . Do you see what I mean?'

She shakes her head. She leans towards me. She says, 'It's like a plant. It can probably take root in any soil if you just pot it. But it has its own very best location, some kind of climactic zone where it grew, where it did well, where the soil and the air themselves nurtured it and made it stronger and nicer, where it had roots. You know what that is? It's a Motherland. And it's like that, upper case, my Motherland. My tiny patch of land that the Russian soldiers took away from me, that's my Motherland, they uprooted me from there and now I'm here. And I won't take root, I don't want to take root, Katya.'

She reaches for her phone again.

'Here, have a look.'

The telephone has videos Bohdan took in their home after the Russian soldiers left: bandages, someone's things, trash and mud on the floor, smashed windows, bullet holes in the walls, a mattress torn to pieces, the contents of a cabinet that was emptied out on the floor, and an antenna and mounting rack which are all that remains of the wall television. The washing machine's mangled but it's standing in its place because they couldn't carry it away.

'That's my home, that's our home,' says Tanya. She doesn't say more.

In October 2022, Tanya sent me another video. I watched it many times and know everything by heart. In the video, Tanya's children are running towards their house, touching its windows, doors and the front steps with their hands. Tanya herself is hugging the elderly neighbour ladies, then she abruptly bends and the camera focuses on two white plaques on the ground: her dogs' graves, their names indiscernible.

In the next sequence, a beagle runs up to Tanya – it turns out he managed to run away somewhere when the village was captured. The dog recognises Tanya; he jumps and licks the tears from her face.

Tanya goes into the house and says, 'There. I'm back.' The video ends.

A couple of weeks later they called me on video: Tanya, Bohdan, Lyuda, Sasha and the children are sitting at a table in a large house. New window glass had been installed, the trash was picked up and the house generally looks liveable even if there aren't yet lampshades over the light bulbs or curtains on the windows.

It's hard for me to talk with them because I'm afraid I'll start crying. But I thank them for calling me and for speaking Russian with me. I know it's hard now for many Ukrainians to speak with Russians and almost impossible to speak Russian, and they have a right to that. I tell Tanya that after we finish discussing the latest news.

She reflects and answers, 'I don't have any hatred. I wouldn't wish for anybody to go through what we did. Nobody needs that. And it won't teach anybody anything. Do you know what war taught me? That in a hopeless situation, in a situation when you don't control anything, it will be easier for you to survive if you have somebody to take care of. If it's a child, play with them; if it's an animal, pat them; if it's an elderly person, ask how they've lived, the elderly love when you ask about their youth, they smile right away; and if you have a garden, tend the trees. Hatred will only increase your pain. There you go.

'We, Katya, returned to our home and started reclaiming it. And I realised that what happened to us isn't simply a war, it's not country against country, not soldiers against soldiers. It's some sort of skirmish between light and dark, Good and Evil. Who were they fighting against in our village anyway? We didn't have one Ukrainian serviceman, nothing strategic, only people who lived in their homes and loved their children, their dogs, their land. They loved . . .

'And they came and started destroying that, shooting simply to shoot: at us, at our homes, at each other, they shot at each other, see? They basically didn't consider what they were doing, they'd simply stopped being people. And I'm very scared for them. Because it's easy to lose the person within. And then how do you find yourself later?'

I ask Tanya, 'Will you ever be able to forgive us?'

She answers after a silence: 'You know, Katya, anything can be forgiven, the issue is what we learn from this, and that we understand how we'll learn to live again. We can't change our neighbours. And that means this isn't about forgiving, it's about co-existing. That seems important to me. But I don't have an answer to that yet. And I don't know what to tell my daughter. On her birthday, she blew out a candle and said, "I want the dogs to come back and the war to end." '

On 23 November 2022, the day Russia launched more than a hundred missiles into Ukraine, I couldn't get through to Tanya, Bohdan and Lyuda for several hours.

It turns out Tanya was in Kyiv. Her oldest daughter had an operation on her knee just before that and on the day of the shelling, under massive missile strikes, Daryna and Tanya attempted for almost an hour to cross from one side of the street to the other on black ice, get in the car and leave for Vyshehrad.

Towards evening, Tanya would write: 'Don't you worry, every-thing's fine with us. There's electricity a couple of hours a day but we've somehow adapted. We store water and heat the fireplaces. And I hung strings of lights on the radiators for the kids, so they wait for it to get dark and then they're happy.'

I invite Tanya, Bohdan, Lyuda and everyone I know in Ukraine to come visit me, to wait out the hardest days. Each of them politely thanks me and says they'll stay at home as long as they can. Tanya will write, though: 'Can I ask you about something? Just answer me honestly, please.'

'Yes, of course, dear Tanya.'

*Tanya [26.11.2022 21.32]*

*Tell me, Katya, how are things in Russia? What do people say about the war?*

*Tanya [26.11.2022 21.35]*

*Do they even understand what's happening? Is it really true they're glad our children can't go to school, to kindergarten? Can they really be satisfied that people are freezing, that there's no water? Can they truly know that people are left in dark, cold apartments, including old people and little babies who were just, just born, and they can't be bathed or get warm, that people bring their children to petrol stations to plug in inhalers, and that hot food is now almost unobtainable for some people? Can they really know all that and want to continue bombing?*

*Tanya [26.11.2022 23.04]*

*But you know, as long as Ukraine wins, we're all generally prepared to endure. Everything's easier to bear if you know what you're suffering for. But I wonder how Russians explain their own sufferings to themselves. Why are they living so awfully, with so little freedom, twisting their con-sciences, have you asked them about that, Katya? What did they tell you?*

*We know what we're fighting for, but how about you?*

I'll try to be honest. I'll answer that no, of course, not everybody. But there are significantly more of those who think what's happen-ing is right. I'll write to Tanya that I don't know for sure if people who support the war understand how many problems and

misfortunes it actually brings. I'll write that I don't know if Russian
TV tells about people's sufferings in Ukraine: about the darkness,
cold and death that Russian missiles brought with them. And I'll ask
her to forgive me that there's nothing I can do to stop my own
country.

## 5.

# The Ring

She's in a hurry. Grey face, puffy eyes, and red hair coming out from under her hood.

Her hands are shaking. Gel nails, one with a rhinestone.

We're meeting at a train station in a small northern Russian village next to the city where she lives.

But she's still afraid people will recognise her.

She straightens her hood and looks around all the time.

'Please change my name for me. And don't write the city. Is it impossible for it to be totally without a name? Well, just a young woman, the widow of a member of the armed forces?'

'I can't,' I say. 'It's better with the name and the city. People who read need to understand who you are, what you're like and how this all happened to you.'

'Yes, it happened, it happened. What can we do with all this now? We definitely never dreamed of this. The opposite's what we . . .'

But she never finishes saying what's opposite.

She hands me a little card from a photobooth. People usually make these on a date: two young people smiling and pulling silly faces. The flash makes their eyes red and their faces glisten.

She says, 'That's us in Moscow, at the World Cup. We went there specially. We didn't go to the matches themselves – we didn't have the money – but we went everywhere, we people-watched.

'That was in 2018, remember? It was Lyosha's idea to go. Not for the football, he said, but to see Moscow and the people who'll come to Russia. And the whole world really had gathered here. It was so beautiful, they made quite a celebration for people! It seems like that's when we decided that when we got married we'd go abroad for our honeymoon. We wanted to go to Turkey, to Antalya. I saw on Instagram that they do beautiful photo sessions at the coast with newlyweds, you could go just for that. Well of course it's a memory for your whole life. We even bought rings. I can't look at those rings now, everything's because of them.

'Fine, let's leave Lyosha's name, you can't lie about the dead, it's bad luck. But change mine, okay?

'How about I'll be Gulnara, is that good? And please don't write our city. Our city's small, everybody'll figure everything out, I work at a school. Everybody there keeps tabs on each other.

'I never wanted to work at a school: I went temporarily, to start getting job experience. It's just that there's not much choice in our city. It's either a store or a school. Go to the school, Lyosha told me, I'll earn the money.

'Anyway, if you need it for readers, write Komi Republic so the region's more or less clear.

'It's all the same everywhere here.

'There's so much heartache for everybody now. Here, look at more pictures.'

She takes photos she printed from her phone out of her purse and hands them to me.

'This is us a year before the army, a bunch of us went fishing, it was at our friends' wedding. And this is when we saw Lyosha off. We sang songs. Nobody could have imagined anything like this.

'We were thinking he'll go into the army, earn decent money, we'll get married and we'll somehow find our footing later.' Lyosha wanted to go to college but we decided that would wait until after the service. He put in his paperwork and then put in for a contract immediately, in the first month. We were satisfied that everything was going according to plan and that's what he wrote to me: "Everything's going according to plan, babe: the motherland feeds, the motherland dresses and money's trickling in."

'Of course his mother was worried. Her father was in the military and they'd moved all around because of it. But we convinced her that it's all good, Lyosha just had to be patient for a while. Not that he was complaining about anything. Towards winter, his mother brought some warm things because he'd written that they were freezing. But they were still nearby then, close to home. Then they were sent to the Belgorod region.* We didn't go there. We just called for New Year's. He was asking, "How's the money, you're not spending it?"

'I had his card with me. And that's where the money went: 60,000 roubles a month. I paid the utilities for us and his mother, I hadn't touched the rest. Basically, anybody could be proud of a son or boyfriend like that. The rest just got drunk and hung out but Lyosha provided for me and his mother.

'On 21 February he wrote to me that there'd be trouble with communications. He didn't write anything more. And there was no connection with him at all.

'We later found it was the start of that . . . I can't tell you, by law I can't say what it's called. It's called a 'special military operation' here. But nobody calls it that, they say it somehow so it's obvious. And everybody understands.

'We found out Lyosha was taken prisoner near Mala Rohan on 26 February. We recognised him in a video.

'He says in the video that he didn't know where they were being sent, that he hadn't shot because he was taken prisoner in the first battle. I wrote comments there. First Ukrainians cursed me out, well, and later some person wrote on their behalf to his mother saying he'd help us get her son out of there but she had to fight for him.

'His mother and I decided that yes, we'd fight.

'That's when I wrote to you the first time, do you remember? You said you could do an interview, that being public might help us. And we'd almost decided to do it, well, his mother and I. But then the local military authorities came to us, at home. And they told us to shush up! We all had to keep quiet. Because there'd be an offensive soon and all our troops would be taken back. That's what the guy said. He also said that if we were going to talk a lot to all kinds of correspondents, things would get worse for us. Lyosha's mother would have problems at work and I'd be expelled from the institute. They gave us a food package: some bread, juice and canned meats. He also told us to hang

* Belgorod is a city in southwestern Russia, about 40 kilometres from the Ukrainian border. [translator]

in there, that Lyosha would be home soon, nobody was going to abandon him in captivity. But none of that happened. Other than that his salary stopped coming. His mother went to the recruitment office. "What salary?" they said. "What, is he fighting?"

'His mother didn't begin to argue; she was afraid to. She says it'll just be worse for him if we push for what's due to him, they might not even take him out of there. Well, fine, I think, we'll get through it. So long as he's alive.

'Lyosha called us three times from captivity. Me once and his mother twice. He didn't say anything in particular: everything's fine, he misses us and wants to come home, what can you say? He didn't call us himself. They brought him to a cell, hands behind his back, someone was standing in front of him, holding a camera that he spoke into. Lyosha didn't look so great but he seemed safe and unharmed. He said he loves me and asked me to wait for him.

'The recruitment office called us on 20 September. They told us to come in tomorrow to take Lyosha home. That they'd bring him.

'I didn't sleep that night. His mother and I cooked up a feast. I suddenly started crying when I was making the bed. Well, I'm thinking, thank God I waited for this. Do you know what I was thinking to myself? I was thinking it was good that he fought so little, that he hadn't done much bad. My father was in Afghanistan. I spent my whole childhood suffering his binges. He got brutal right away when he was drunk. And 'ghosts' haunted him everywhere. At night either he was killing or somebody was killing him.

'And so I thought that thank God it wouldn't be like that with Lyosha. What could he have seen there in three days of war?

'That's what I thought.

'They brought back four people, all from our part of town. I saw him right away on the bus. He was sitting with his cheek pressed against the glass. He wasn't looking at us. We greeted him with flowers. Brought him home. He was very thin. We wanted to feed him. His mother made the pies he loves, with egg and cabbage. I'd made pork with mayonnaise, with tomato on top, do you know that dish? He washed, changed his clothes and sat at the table. And I see something's not right, he's eating with his left hand.

'See, that wasn't immediately obvious. Maybe I'm so dumb I didn't immediately catch it, I really blame myself for that. But he was pulling his right hand away all the time. He wasn't showing it. And so I say, "Lyosha, why are you eating with your left hand?"

'His chin started quivering, he threw his fork down and went out to the balcony to smoke.

'"Why are you butting in," his mother says to me, "you have to know everything."

'He smoked, came back, and said, "Mother, pour! Let's have a drink, girls. And no more of those questions. What happened, happened."

'We drank. Sat for a little while. Somehow, the conversation didn't hold together. What can we tell him? That Zoika and Pasha, his classmates, have a new son? But we don't have one, no son was born. Or that Great-Aunt Lyuda died? Well, and what of it? Or should we have a talk about politics?

'And so we basically sat in silence. His mother quietly cried.

'Then we drank a little more and she left.

'I say, should we go in the bedroom? We go in and I, the fool, had laid our rings on the bed. In the little box, I'd got it ready. I thought this would be like our first married night after all that. I was all ready, shaved, washed. I'd stayed faithful to him. And I so wanted that when he came home we'd meet and be affectionate with each other, that's what I'd imagined so many times, how he'd put the ring on my finger. Yes, that was my dream, why hide it? But everything worked out differently. Lyosha went into the room, saw the little box with the rings on the bed, kissed me on the cheek, well, meaning, not really a kiss. And he says, "I'm sorry but I'm going to sleep on the sofa in the kitchen." And he went to the sofa.

'Well, yes, I'm a fool, a fool. But I didn't let on that I was upset. I hugged him, looked him in the eyes, and tell him, "Lyosha, you're my one and only, my beloved, I'll love you however you are. Everything will be good for us, just trust me."

'He moved me aside and went off to bed.

'In the morning, I came to make breakfast. I specially came out in just my nightgown. My prettiest one, kind of sheer. My hair was down. He came up behind me, kissed me in my hair very, you know, tenderly. And went outside.

'I thought he'd gone to smoke. I also thought that, there, now something will go right for us.

'But it turns out he went to the shed and hanged himself there, on a beam.

'When I washed Lyosha before the funeral, I saw everything as it was. All the fingers on his right hand had been chopped off. There were just purplish stumps sticking out.

'And that's it.'

# 6.

# The 'Lens'

In the middle of April 2022, Lyuda and I agreed to meet at Berlin's Ostbahnhof. She had asked if she could bring her daughter with her. I spotted them at the appointed time, standing by a yellow and blue cube that announced in several languages that Ukrainian refugees were welcome here.

Lyuda turned out to be petite.

This petite woman fought her way towards me through a vivid Berlin crowd. She waved her left hand, noticeably protecting her right shoulder. Or maybe only I noticed that. Sasha, her 15-year-old daughter, walked alongside her. To relieve the initial awkwardness of meeting for the first time, we started talking about Sasha's flat-footedness. We concurred it would go away with age.

And then Lyuda said, 'Good Lord, this is all such silliness. But I've suddenly realised it's important for me to talk about silly things. That's what I really want to talk about.'

And she added, 'Thank you.' Then she smiled. That was the first time I noticed that Lyuda usually smiles in difficult situations.

Lyuda and I were meeting to record an interview for a film I'm making about refugees. As it happened, the three studios I'd attempted to come to terms with refused. Nobody wanted to work with Russian journalists, particularly since Ukrainians were in charge of two of the three studios.

Unfortunately, that's all pretty understandable.

I tell Lyuda about this, to explain that we're going to film the interview at my friend's apartment – she's a successful Russian entrepreneur who left Russia in a hurry shortly after 24 February.

The apartment's under renovation. That reinforces a general

sense of unsettledness and transience. 'Ever since February, all I do is watch our world go downhill, bouncing like a little ball,' says Lyuda. I couldn't have put it better myself. Lyuda freezes up just before recording. She says she's scared because by deciding to tell me her story, she's voluntarily agreeing to relive it. I ask again if she's sure she's ready. Lyuda nods.

'I thought what we went through is what everybody goes through when they first fall into the meat grinder of the war and then, later, the trap of hatred that the war exposed. My story's surprising for my personal details. But it's basically not about me. It's about people. The war quickly turns some into beasts. I've seen people like that, who immediately lost everything human after being handed a weapon. They lost their conscience and compassion, too. I've seen that. It happens so quickly with people. But not with some. They don't break. They . . . If you can put it this way, they don't feel the "right" of power that they have behind them: the weapon in their hands doesn't immediately push them to destroy everybody and everything around them. Do you see what I'm talking about? It's some high degree of mercy, not for anyone in particular but simply . . . a caring attitude towards people, something that ought to be in all of us at birth because we're people. But some lose that very quickly. And they're dehumanised. I've seen that, Katya. It's scary. But I saw something else, too . . . I agreed to your interview to tell about that.'

I'm writing this chapter in late autumn of 2022. In April 2022, some Ukrainians who have been through the war call Russians orcs and want to annihilate them. And many Russians wanted to just disappear, too. Lyuda was the first Ukrainian woman I interviewed who, remarkably, uttered the word 'mercy' out loud, despite having truly suffered because of the Russians.

I was just as afraid of this interview as Lyuda. We took a long time pouring water into our glasses, settling in our seats and getting distracted by our phones. We went out to smoke. Drank coffee. Took out and put away sandwiches because it was impossible to eat. I waited until she was ready. And then she said, 'I'll never be ready. Can I just start telling from the very beginning?'

'I met Pavel a few years ago and that changed my life tremendously. Pavel was many years older than me and some people didn't understand our bond. I can't explain it to you, but I liked being with Pavel. Nothing scared me. Pavel took to both me and Sasha. And the three of us started living together. I admired Pavel, who was a paediatric ophthalmologist. You know, people talk about doctors with God-given talents. He didn't talk much about his work but when he'd start, I'd hold my breath, as we say.

'Did you know there are saintly people? Pavel was like that.

'I believed in him, trusted him. How can I put it? That's probably good fortune, right? When I heard Russian soldiers had come to liberate us, that was unbelievably surprising for me in, you know, the human sense. Who did you come to liberate us from? We just so happen to be free! We lived, loved, spoke the language we wanted to. I'd been speaking Russian my whole life, so what?

'Pavel, too.

'We hadn't prepared ourselves for any war in February. Just one time Pavel and I talked a little about how if anything happened, we'd go to the dacha, to Vyshehrad. It's beyond Kolonshchyna, about 40 kilometres from Kyiv. We had a small house with a bathhouse there that we built with our own hands, we put so much warmth, so much heart into it.

'And then the war started, at four in the morning, everybody doing their thing. It's just we didn't go to any dacha. Pavel went to work because it was his operation day, but Sasha and I stayed at home.

'The realisation gradually started to hit us that this was a full-fledged war. We were in it. They'd attacked us. They'd come to destroy us.

'Although I'm saying this to you now and the words themselves are horrifying, it's impossible to believe that had anything to do with us, that they'd come to destroy us. Nobody believes in their own death, right?

'On the third day of the war, we decided to go to the dacha. The human mind can't take in the scope of a catastrophe like a full-scale war, you take everything in piece by piece, in segments. That's why we decided to only stay at the dacha until Monday. Pavel had to go to work, to the hospital, on Monday.

'It turns out we were driving towards Russian troops. But we didn't know that. We got there, heated the house, ate supper. But the rumbling started later and gradually increased. That rumbling is the main sound of war. It increased along with the horror.

'But we hung on. We went to see our neighbours, Tanya and Bohdan, who lived year-round in our village. They have a big house, a lot of children, dogs and other animals. Some of their older daughter's friends came to their house from Kyiv, to save themselves from the war. There were lots of people, you might have even thought people had gathered for some family celebration.

'But that rumbling. It was increasing, it was nearing.

'There's the word "inevitability". That rumbling was inevitability.

'But we tried not to lose our composure. If the electricity's out, we'll chop wood; when there's no light, we'll sit by candlelight; when there's no running water, there's the well. Pavel and I went to the well. At first those were like our usual walks, the two of us. But Pavel went by himself after it got completely scary. Sasha and I stayed at home. All in all, it wasn't far to the well: you could make a round-trip in about ten minutes. But the rumbling was getting closer. Individual shots and explosions were getting audible. It was scary.

'A car came for Pavel a few times. People knew who he was and injured people in the nearby villages needed a doctor. They brought Pavel to [nearby] Nemishaieve, to Kolonshchyna and somewhere else. He operated, stitched up wounds. He didn't tell us the details. That's what he said, "You two don't need to know this, where I was and what I saw."

'That was 3 March. The night was restless. On the morning of the 4th, we moved into the sauna on the first floor. The house had cooled and was now impossible to heat.

'We ate breakfast. And Pavel said he had to go for water while it was light. We decided we'd drink tea together when he came back. I heated water in the house and brought the teakettle to the sauna. But Pavel hadn't come back. Soldiers came instead. They started banging at the door with their feet and rifle butts; they looked in the little sauna window. I managed to silently whisper to Sasha, "Press yourself against the wall." And I froze on the threshold with boiling water in one hand and mugs in the other.

'It surprised me that the soldiers were apparently speaking among themselves in Russian but it wasn't perfect Russian. They had some sort of accent. Sometimes they switched to some other language of theirs that I didn't understand, where Russian words cropped up. I saw through a crack that they were short, darker-skinned and had angular eyes. They were beating at the windows and doors with their rifle butts, swearing.

'I was most afraid they'd break down the door into the house. That would have been the end of us. When Pavel went out, I'd only locked it with the latch, not with the key. Well, I'd slammed it shut. Pavel should be back any minute.

'They couldn't open the door. They came into the house through the second floor. They didn't know if there were people in the house: they'd shoot first, then open the door to the room with their feet and shoot again. They went through the second floor that way, then came downstairs. But they didn't make it to the sauna. They came back. They crawled in again through the second floor, where Sasha's room is. They came up to the front door and kicked it – they were angry it wasn't opening. They talked about something among themselves and started to leave.

'I very quietly set the hot water and mugs on the floor and walked up to the door to lock it; I only turned the key halfway. They turned around at that moment, faced the house and started chaotically shooting at it. One bullet came through the door and went through my chest.

'It surprises me more than anything now that I didn't start screaming. I wasn't in pain. It's just that you go into a stupor when there's so much hot and red blood pouring out of you. I wasn't even scared that everything looked bad for me. I was scared that Sasha was alongside me and now she'd see me die.

'I said, "Sasha, they got me with a bullet but don't be afraid." Sasha started shouting.

'I tell her, "Sashenka, sweetie, don't shout. They'll hear. They'll hear, come back and kill us. Just don't shout, honey. Just crawl over to me."

'Sasha helped me roll on my left side, dragged me away from the sauna door, laid me on a mattress, then lifted and laid my head on a pillow because the blood was rising in my throat. It was getting very cold so she covered me. And then she lay down beside me and pressed against me. She silently cried. And then calmed down.

'I don't know how much time we spent like that. But I was beginning to feel like life was leaving my body. It was starting to get dark outside.

'I don't know how I decided on this step but we had no other options because if we didn't do something, I'd either die in Sasha's arms or the soldiers would come back. And then none of us would survive.

'I told her, "Sashenka, Pavel's not here, I can't stand up. Sweetie, you're the only one who can do something . . . You run to the neighbours, tell them Mama's wounded, tell them that."

'When Sasha went to the door, it turned out one of the bullets was stuck in the lock so it was jammed. It was impossible to open the door.

'Sasha was very scared. I couldn't even imagine how scared she must have been.

'I could never have imagined that my little girl, my Sasha, had so much strength, to see me, her own mother, covered in blood, to lay me down, wrap me in a blanket . . . And then leave me. Do you understand what she had to do? Leave me there, alone, but pull herself together and step into that hell. And go through it on her own. The earth was rumbling and the shooting wasn't letting up for a minute. She understood it was a living hell outside the door of our home. And there wasn't one person on Earth to hug her, take her by the hand, lead her through that hell and promise that everything would end well.

'She had to go through all that alone and the last thing I saw was Sasha taking a backpack, putting on her white hat, kissing me and leaving the room. She went up to the second floor and crawled from the balcony into the old pear tree that grew by our house. And then she ran through the field to Tanya and Bohdan's house.

'And I lay there, thinking about just one thing. Why did she put on a hat? She had a white hat. In the dark, in the black field, with shooting all around, that hat was like a living target. Why? Why? . . . I didn't have the strength to shout to her, "Sasha, you don't need the hat." I just closed my eyes. I lay and prayed that my little girl would make it.

'She knocked at the neighbours', at Tanya and Bohdan's, and said, "Pavel didn't come back, Mama's in the house, help, please rescue us."

'And Bohdan, the owner of the house, came with his brother Volodya to help me out.

'They'd barely left when Russian soldiers entered their house. They didn't see that. They came to me and when they realised it wouldn't be very easy to take me out of the house, they went back for tools. Right then they saw their dogs were dead, they'd been shot and there were soldiers in the house. And they tell the soldiers there's a woman lying wounded next door, she needs help. The Russian soldiers' commander, whose call name was "Old Man", said he'd help.

'He and Bohdan came for me a second time, the two of them. They shot out the window grating, came into the house and Old Man contacted one of his men on the walkie-talkie right away. He said, "There's a 300* woman, a local, who needs to be brought to the medical unit."

'The doctor answered over the walkie-talkie that they wouldn't go anywhere so late at night for the sake of someone like me. Old Man shouted at him.

'And I quietly asked Bohdan if he'd seen Pavel. Bohdan said, "You, Lyuda, don't think about that now, you need to survive. For Sasha's sake."

'I found out later that those same soldiers who'd done a job on our house shot my Pavel on the way back from the well, in our yard. Point blank. The doctor who treats children, right? I didn't see his

* The code '300' is for someone who's severely injured and needs to be transported. [translator]

body, I didn't bury him, I can't imagine how you can shoot a person who's carrying home two buckets of water for his wife and daughter. What kind of soldier are you after that?

'You brute, brute, brute, you beast, that kills everything living. I hate . . .

'I never saw Pavel again in my life. Only on that morning of 4 March. I want those soldiers to be damned. For ever, all . . .

'I'm sorry.

'I'll have a drink of water.

'Old Man, Bohdan and Volodya carried me on a blanket to Bohdan and Tanya's house. They brought medications from the soldiers' base. They gave me an injection and glued the wound, Old Man gave an order to the soldiers, they tied a mattress to a stepladder and me to the mattress, and carried me through a field and the forest to their base. Before leaving, I only managed to take off my cross and give it to Sasha. I kissed her. And I asked Bohdan to take care of my daughter if worst comes to worst. He nodded. And the soldiers carried me off.

'They walked for 20 or 30 minutes. I don't remember the way; I kept losing consciousness. There was rumbling all around. It was dark. The wound hurt; my arm was numb. But that Old Man walked alongside me the whole time. I apparently asked him about Sasha after I regained consciousness. Because I remember he told me at some point, "Lyuda, I promise you everything will be fine with your daughter. I give my word."

'They carried me the rest of the way to their camp, put me in a car and assigned a soldier to guard me.

'This was probably the scariest night in my life: the ground wasn't just rumbling, I was at the epicentre of that rumbling. That rumbling rattled the car I was lying in, me, and my wound.

'The soldier standing next to me kicked me all the time and would have killed me if he could. But he couldn't. Old Man had ordered him to watch over me. And he hated me, hated the order and yelled at me that my "Uke guts will fly all over the car if you make the slightest move, bitch. I have a loaded assault rifle, I control everything here, got that?"

'I was lying on my side, lying still. I tried not to shout when he beat me, so as not to stir him up. This was a brutal characteristic of his: the more he sees he's truly making you hurt, the more he rages.

'To be honest, I didn't believe for one second that I'd live until morning. But it started to get lighter. And some other soldiers came for me and carried me to another vehicle and brought me somewhere. I couldn't see where we were going. There was just a little of the sky, a little of the trees through a hole in the canvas. When somebody in the car shouted "air alert!" the car stopped and everyone inside ran into the forest, scattering. But I was left. I closed my eyes then and prayed that nothing would fly into the vehicle.

'The alert ended, the soldiers climbed back into the vehicle and we drove on. At some point we drove into a big place with a plastic roof. As the soldiers were dragging something out of the vehicle, a missile flew by, very low. And we all ended up covered in plastic debris.

'They took me out of the vehicle. A doctor came over. He injected an antibiotic and a painkiller. He wrote on my hand what he'd injected, at what time. He said that ideally I should be transported to a hospital by helicopter, the sooner the better, because almost two days had already passed and I could die from blood loss. But then he said there might not be a helicopter any time soon. There were battles going on and the helicopter was in use.

'"Our army," said the doctor, "is protecting you."

'I couldn't hold back and asked, "Who will they protect me from?"

'He kind of cringed and walked away from me.

'I don't remember how long I lay there. I lost consciousness again and came to after they carried me to a vehicle called a "Lens". It's a vehicle that looks like a tank. Without windows, without doors. It's for transporting the wounded. There were two wounded lying down, a few sitting and one concussed, who'd been blown up on a mine and was all torn to pieces, I don't know how he was hanging on. It seemed like he didn't fully understand where he was, like he was lost in both time and location, still in battle. He shrieked horribly, as if he weren't human, crying, his arms flailing. He was like a wounded animal. It was very, very scary.'

Lyuda's taking a break for a second, to have a sip of water and catch her breath, and then the doorbell rings. Everybody jumps. It cuts into the quiet as though it's not a simple doorbell in the quiet centre of a European capital but a burst of automatic rifle fire. A tall woman with black curly hair appears in the doorway. It's Tanya, who owns the house where Lyuda left her daughter, Sasha.

She came a bit early; I hadn't had a chance to warn Lyuda. I'd completely forgotten something more important: Lyuda and Tanya haven't seen each other since March 2022.

Petite Lyuda hangs on tall Tanya and they stand, embracing and crying.

I put my head on the table, I want to disappear, to dissolve and never again in my life see women who were united by war crying and laughing, as they embrace each other. But I can't be the third to embrace them because I'm actually a citizen of the country that turned their life into hell, something I remember every second of my life.

We take a break from filming. We go out on the terrace. Tanya hugs Sasha. Sasha laughs. Everybody discusses the news: Tanya's children started school, Bohdan's living in Kyiv. Restaurants have opened in Kyiv.

I say, 'Sasha, I'm sorry, we were talking about you being flat-footed. You're a hero, Sasha, you're so courageous!'

Sasha looks at her mother. Sasha says, 'It's better to talk about being flat-footed than about the war.'

But Lyuda and I need to finish talking about the war. We send Tanya and Sasha to the café around the corner. We each pour another glass of water. We wipe away tears. And Lyuda finishes her story.

'I recognised one of the soldiers in the Lens as the one who'd carried me out of Bohdan's house in the blanket with Old Man. That soldier and I spoke briefly, exchanging only a few words, as people who know each other. That soldier also brought me a thermos and stuck an IV tube in it so I could drink comfortably without raising my head. For the first time in two days I drank something hot. I was very grateful. I asked him, "Please, if you have a walkie-talkie, I beg you, contact Old Man. I just want to know my child's alive." He said he'd try. Then he went off duty. Under shelling, we continued riding in the Lens and picking up wounded; there was no clarity at all.

'Then I asked some other, new, soldier, what awaited me. A superior officer came and told me they'd prepare the wounded now and evacuate us to Belarus.

'I say, "Why take me to Belarus if Kyiv, my Kyiv, is here, 40 kilometres away? Am I really not allowed to just get home?"

'They answered that I can only get home if I get out of the Lens on my own two feet and walk to Kyiv along the Zhytomyr highway.

'I started crying.

'Nobody cared about what or how I wanted anything. If you want to survive, lie there and wait until they've prepared everybody and the helicopter arrives. Or maybe it wouldn't even arrive. Then you wouldn't survive. It's all simple. That was probably the point when I felt utter desperation. That was probably because a miracle always happens at the most desperate point. Anyway, the Lens opened up and my Sasha came in. It turned out that Old Man learned they were preparing the evacuation and decided to transport her to me.

'Two soldiers led Sasha through the forest at night. Nothing went wrong for her. Knowing about what has happened to girls who ran across Russian soldiers in other Ukrainian cities and villages, I realise that's a miracle.

'I understand it's madness to thank someone because I wasn't killed and my daughter wasn't raped. But I'm thankful. They gave Sasha a chocolate bar and a blanket. A couple of hours after she showed up, they shouted to us, "Get ready, the helicopter will be here soon."

'The Lens manoeuvred around a field for a long time so it could stop as close to the helicopter as possible. There was shelling.

'As soon as they opened the door, they shouted, "Whoever can run, move it!"

'Everybody ran, including Sasha. Soldiers carried me on a stretcher. Then we flew for about 45 minutes and wound up at a military hospital. It was at some military training site, not in a city.

'They put in drainage tubes and said it was unbelievable I'd survived. They gave Sasha hot tea and gave me a package of antibiotics to take with me. After that they brought us to a hospital in Mazyr, it's near Gomel. The doctors were all surprised and threw up their hands: one of my lungs was mutilated and pneumonia had set in.

'They settled Sasha and me into a private room and didn't let anyone in but nurses and the attending physician. The nurses came in two shifts and it was obvious how divided their community was. There were some who came and retold all the stifling propaganda: you should be grateful, they liberated you. But there were others who read the news on the Internet and understood what happened, who attacked whom. They understood perfectly well why I had an injury like that. But they couldn't express their support loudly. They were afraid of losing their jobs.

'As soon as I'd regained some strength, local human rights advocates came to my room and offered refugee status. In Belarus. Can you imagine?

'I said, "No. Never. I know missiles have flown and are flying into my country, including from Belarusian territory. Never. I want to go home."

'Then they told me that as gratitude for restoring my health and how I was treated here, I should grant an interview to state television. They also told me that an interview was my only chance of getting out. An exit fee, as it were.

'There were no other options. A journalist came and her task was to do a story about how Russian soldiers saved a simple Ukrainian woman from her own country's looters.

'And she did that story. Sure, I talked about how there were some soldiers and then there were others. That seems important to me.

'But it's also important that both kinds of soldiers came to our land, though nobody invited them. And they brought only grief, unhappiness and death.

'But the story they ran was about how Russian soldiers saved a Ukrainian woman from her countrymen, looters. They released us from the hospital after that.

'Then there was the bus, a filtration checkpoint, another bus, to Poland, then a train and Germany.

'We were greeted well here, I'm going through rehab, my arm has almost recovered and it aches a little sometimes. A psychologist is working with Sasha. We're trying to live, we're trying very, very hard to live. So that's my whole story.'

After she finishes speaking, Lyuda's silent for a minute but then she cries anyway. Like a child, like a little girl. She cries and simultaneously smiles – it's awkward for her to cry in front of strangers. She cries briefly, immediately wiping the flowing tears away with the back of her hand.

Sasha and Tanya come in. The crew's packing up their equipment, everybody says goodbye and they leave. Lyuda's distracted by the bustling and stops crying.

We drink tea. I ask her to show me pictures of Pavel. It's important for me to see them. Lyuda says, 'I don't have any. I don't have any pictures, Katya. I gave my phone to Sasha when they took me from Bohdan and Tanya's house. She had my phone and hers. They took both phones away from her when they sent her to me, to the Lens. The soldiers shot through her phone in front of her. But they took mine, it was an iPhone. They deleted all the pictures I had in the cloud. But they're using the phone. I sometimes see my number online in Telegram.'*

I ask Lyuda how she and Sasha are planning to go on with their lives.

She answers simply, 'I don't know. You know, everything's somehow simplified now: life, death, black, white. Russia brought us trouble. All our hopes and dreams fell apart. You can't bring anything back. Russia came, took everything away. But Russia didn't get happier, see? Our life turned out to be a Christmas tree ornament that somebody wanted to take away but couldn't because the toy fell and shattered. And only grief remained. Grief, Katya. And that's what we have to live with.'

*

* Telegram is a popular cloud-based, encrypted messaging service founded in 2013 by brothers Nikolai and Pavel Durov. Capabilities include messaging, file sharing and calls. [translator]

A few months after our first meeting, Lyuda wrote to me saying our conversation helped bring her closure on what happened. She'd watched the film with that conversation several times.

'I calmed down,' Lyuda wrote to me. 'I realised I'll live on. And I also realised I can only live on at home.'

Another month later, Lyuda made a videocall to me. She and Sasha had returned to Kyiv. And they'd gone to visit Bohdan along with some friends I didn't know. But those unfamiliar people looked into the camera and sent their greetings.

I asked Lyuda how Kyiv is, what it's like now. She thought for a minute.

'You know how it is when you have a child who's been very sick for a long time? You know they'll survive, the doctors already told you it's a serious disease but not fatal, but you see how bad the child feels and your heart's breaking.

'Kyiv emptied out but didn't surrender. There aren't many people: a lot went away and some died, like my Pavel. Those empty spots, voids left by those you can't bring back, are noticeable. They're perceptible. But I hope that wound will heal. We're learning to live all over again. We know so much about ourselves now. We know how little we need to be fortunate. There you go, Katya.'

I thanked her. 'For what?' she asked.

For the meeting, for the letter, for the call and that neither she nor Tanya nor Bohdan nor the people at the party that I don't know see me as an enemy.

Lyuda answered, 'There's enough grief to go around, Katya. Why add more?'

# 7

# The Hat

In Warsaw, Irina grew to love going to the market. It's now an almost daily ritual for her. She wakes up early, dresses nicely, puts on eye makeup and powders her face. And goes to the market.

Sometimes she doesn't buy anything. She just walks around and looks at groceries. Irina says all the groceries look beautiful at the Warsaw market.

Sometimes she does buy groceries. Brings them home. Lays them out. Wash. Cut. Cook.

She says it's very important after cooking to set the table and serve the food beautifully.

Irina often has guests in her small rented Warsaw apartment: her Ukrainian girlfriends have escaped to various spots around the world via Warsaw.

'One was recently passing through on her way to Japan,' says Irina.

That doesn't surprise her. And she says so.

'That doesn't surprise me. Basically, nothing at all surprises me anymore. I'm just occasionally surprised at how beautiful the groceries are. The tomatoes are so red they're actually jolly. The meat's very fresh, cut with such love, processed and then displayed so you can't take your eyes off it. There are many kinds of greens. You eat, eat.'

In front of me stands a plate of rolls and croissants that Irina baked before my arrival. She sits down in front of me, folds her hands and waits for me to start eating. Irina's dog Cora, a corgi, sits next to her. She's watching, too. It gets quiet. The apartment smells giddily of rolls.

I don't feel like eating.

I know Irina's from Bucha but when I was preparing for this conversation, I hadn't come up with a good way to start.

Ask: *How did you get through that?*

Ask: *How did you manage to take your dog out of the country?*

Ask: *Have many people close to you stayed in Bucha?*

Ask: *What would need to happen for you to return there?*

Ask: *Will you ever go back?*

Ask: *Maybe none of this even happened?*

Because in my peaceful life it's impossible to believe that people could do such things to people.

I can't actually use any of these questions to start this conversation. And so I tell her, 'You're very beautiful.'

And she smiles. We sit there. Cora the dog is tired of waiting for me to start eating so she lies down on the floor.

I ask Irina if she used to be an actress.

She laughs.

She's over 60 but women like her are equally beautiful and unattainable at 25 and at 45, and so on. She has a low, beautiful laugh. When she laughs, she throws her head back, like the most wonderful heroines did in old movies about love.

'No.'

Then she lowers her head and looks at her hands, at the rolls. And only later at me. Her gaze changes. Her voice is raspy as she says, '*I don't know who I am.*'

It's obvious she's very close to tears. But she's not crying. She rubs her palms together. Her hands are dry and I can hear the whispery sound of her skin. She continues, effortlessly, but it's as if she's speaking about a stranger. Not about herself.

'I don't know how to explain it but I don't sense myself. I don't know who I am now. Where I am, why I'm here instead of somewhere else. Yes, it's beautiful and calm here. And I need calm. But no way. Nothing matters to me. And I have no peace of mind. To be honest, if I were lying on white sand in Bali right now, I wouldn't be calm. I'd think about what's there, at home. And what will happen now to all of us. And how long this will all go on.

'My grandmother used to say everything that has a beginning has its end. That means the war will end someday, either in defeat or in victory. If I were asked a year or two years ago how the war would end, I wouldn't have known how to answer. In Ukraine people always said, "I'm staying out of it." We always lived kind of each to their own. But nothing's like that now. We're different. Do you believe that common grief can rally and unite people? I didn't believe it either. It seemed to me like there weren't many of us but Russia was such a big country. And then everything turned out not to be like that. We're different. And we'll win.

'I think about that all the time now.

'*We'll win.*

'Sometimes the thoughts and inner turmoil, and the fear about what awaits us, makes me nauseous. Literally. Then I go for a walk. Most often to the market. The market lulls me. I forget myself there, I go with the flow and float off somewhere, stop thinking about the war, maybe that's the right way to put it?

'I walk, look at the beautiful groceries, admire them and think only about them. Sometimes I go to the market with Cora.

'Cora and I took lots of walks in Bucha. We took a lot of walks in the park, it's one of our most beautiful parks, the one where there's a statue of Bulgakov.

'Did you know the Bulgakovs had a dacha in Bucha? They took summer vacations there.'

I didn't know. Sitting in the tiny kitchen of Irina's rented apartment in Warsaw, I attempt to imagine the writer Mikhail Bulgakov – not as a monument but alive (born in Kyiv in 1891, his father was a Russian theologian, his Ukrainian mother a schoolteacher) – suddenly finding himself in Bucha in March 2022. And I can't.

I ask her, 'Is it true that you moved to Bucha from Donetsk?'

I know the answer: it's true. Why do I ask?

And she doesn't answer the question. She just clarifies that she moved before the war. No, she hadn't had a premonition, it just worked out that way. It was in 2012, two years before the beginning of *everything.*

Now she asks me, 'Did you know that before the war, Donetsk

was the second most beautiful industrial city in the world? After Chicago.'

I didn't know.

'It's all true, that we had a million roses. A big, beautiful stadium, fountains. A very wealthy city and very beautiful. It was. A proud city. Maybe people didn't like us for that pride. But we loved our city. I didn't really want to leave, but I was offered work in Kyiv. I was the director of a Russian company. That was in 2012, see?'

I see.

In 2012 I was at the Donbas Arena stadium in Donetsk. A bunch of us drove from Moscow. England and Ukraine were playing. I think England won. That wasn't especially important because it was fun: beautiful football, beautiful people and a very beautiful city. I remember how surprised my friends and I were then at how beautiful a mining city could be.

When Russia attacks Ukraine the first time, in 2014, television reporting will show the stadium. For a short while it will become a humanitarian aid distribution centre for the self-proclaimed Donetsk People's Republic.

I talk about that.

And she shakes her head in response.

'I thought the whole time that God led me away. I didn't see them destroy my native city. I was offered work in Kyiv in 2012 and I went.'

She pauses.

Looks.

Says, 'I worked as the director of a Russian company. Somehow that sounds oddly intolerable, doesn't it? It's basically impossible now. Imagine, Katya, we had a completely different life in 2012. It was normal that there was a Russian company in Kyiv. And it wasn't shameful to work there as the director. You can see how much can be destroyed in ten years.'

Irina takes a mobile phone out of her sweater pocket. She finds a video. Turns the screen towards me. There are several cheerful cream-coloured terraced houses settled in among pine trees. The camera moves from side to side. There are trees and a paved road where a child is racing along on a bicycle.

She says, 'This is Bucha. I fell in love as soon as I got there. It's so green, so easy to breathe, it was so nice. The apartment in Donetsk sold so successfully and I moved so easily that I was surprised the whole time – it was like someone was leading me by the hand. And I was even lucky in Bucha. My building was the only townhouse in Bucha then, close to the forest. I bought an apartment on the ground floor, I had my own little yard, with pines and arborvitaes. In the mornings, I'd go outside, close my eyes, and just breathe.

'And lots of our people from Donetsk moved to Bucha. They didn't like us at first: Donetsk people are wealthy, Donetsk people are proud. We turned up our noses, that's what people said. But later everybody somehow got used to it: the best hairdressers were from Donetsk, the best dentists were from Donetsk. People got to be friends with us, everything somehow got better. And Bucha grew every year, getting more beautiful, too. And we lived there . . .

'I think all the time about how good it is that Cora and I moved to Bucha.

'Maybe fate caught up to me? What do you think?'

She scrolls through her phone. A new video.

There's snow lying on the ground. The cheerful cream-coloured townhouse looks lost. There's no sound but it's as if you can hear a slamming door. A broken window; it was shot. A scarlet-coloured tulle curtain bursting out of a star-shaped opening. Darting. Flailing.

The camera shifts to the next yard. A battered mattress lies in the middle of the yard. Its stuffing has all been pulled out, it's unpleasantly dirty.

The camera goes outside, moves towards a building across the street.

Irina takes the phone. She says:

'That was the scariest day of my life. I know for sure there'd been nothing scarier and am sure there won't be anything scarier. It was 8 March. They bombed all night, bombed all morning. Our building was close to the Warsaw highway. There's a single-family home across the way.

'In those days, my door was always open because we'd been under siege for some time and I cooked food for everybody: the ground floor's convenient to take it out and serve it.

'And so I'm cooking, a really big pot. And a tank drives up. It stops about five metres from my window, by the house across the way. And the upper part of that tank – what's it called, a turret? – starts rotating. The tank driver looks out, watching. Watching me. I'm standing like I'm under a spell.

'See, my window faces out, I always liked that: you're cooking and you look outside. And now I was looking outside and there was a tank there with its turret spinning.

'It spun and spun, and it didn't choose me. You know that feeling when a tank doesn't choose you? I can't explain what I was feeling.

'But the turret had turned towards the house across the way. And the tank fired. The fence toppled over. The dogs started howling and went quiet for the last time. The tank fired again. And then it turned around and drove away.

'The owners weren't there at the time. Their elderly mother was at the house but I can't say if she was alive or not.

'The owners came about 20 minutes after the tank. They saw the fence and the dead dogs, they had such beautiful German shepherds.

'And they went in the house. I never saw them again.

'Because the soldiers came back. They were all kind of short, I remember that they shrieked when they were shooting. First they shot at that house, then they burned it.

'And I'm standing at the sink with my hands lowered into a pot of water and I'm rubbing my fingers, on autopilot, they're stiff from the cold and from fear, and I see the house across the way burning. And my only emotion at all is devastation. I'm watching this like it's a movie. Only it's close.

'Then the soldiers come back again, about 15 minutes later. The flame's still high, the house is still burning. But the soldiers go into the garage next to the house. And carry out some kind of bags, bundles that were in my neighbours' garage. And they load them into their military vehicle. But there are pine trees in front of our building, I told you that already, right?

'Anyway, I'm watching the soldiers through our pine trees while they're bustling around by the neighbours' garage and suddenly I notice there's a young woman standing absolutely straight by a pine tree. Our eyes meet. And my eyes say, "Run, run over here."

'She darted over like a shadow, rushed inside and sat with her back to the sink. And I'm right next to her. And she starts crying, "My husband and his friend are there, they'd run there, where the soldiers are now. Where are they? Is this the end? Is this it? They won't get away from them alive."

'I looked out the window. They're still loading someone else's belongings, they're not stopping.

'I sat back down. And she suddenly says, "Happy holiday."

'To be honest, at first I thought she'd lost her mind from fear.

'But she smiles, "Did you forget? Today's 8 March."*

'I crawled over to the shelf, took a bottle of wine and opened it. She and I had a drink. Just as the soldiers finished loading. And then she ran.

'I stood by the sink to wash the glasses. And suddenly there's a crash. A young man, about 40, runs through the door, breathing heavily, eyes huge and crazed. Right at the door he exhales. "They're shooting there . . . Can I come in? They're shooting out of assault rifles."

'"Come in, sit on the floor, so what happened?" I say to him. His teeth are actually chattering, he's ashen. And crying. And you know . . . Well, how can you say this . . . But I'll tell you, so you see what happened to us. No, that's not it, it's about what those . . . subhumans . . . did to us. That young guy, he'd soiled his pants. Can you imagine that? A grown person, a man, was that scared.

'And those little soldiers with assault rifles were already running past the window. Firing in bursts. At whom? Why? For what? I ask myself this question all the time: Why so much hatred? Why so

---

* 8 March is International Women's Day, a national holiday in Ukraine. [translator]

much brutality? Where did they lose the human within, how did they get like that anyway? I never thought I'd see something like this with my own eyes. And now, all the time, I can't forget it.'

I feel nauseous from the smell of the rolls. Or not from that. I suggest we go smoke.

Irina has skinny cigarettes. We silently smoke by the window. She suddenly turns to me.

'Now I'll make you laugh. At our intersection, a Russian soldier suddenly starts walking up to people. With a cigarette, all business-like. First he was crouching at a distance, then he went up to people, asking where Kochubei Street was. Maybe he was looking for a woman, I didn't understand, but he was looking for somebody. People answered him that this is Shevchenko Street, you walk along it for three streets and you'll get to Kochubei. He gaped. "How's that," he says, "Shevchenko Street? I'm Shevchenko. So it turns out my ancestors were *natsiki*\*?"

'He scratched his head and left.

'So he's walking and people are talking about him behind his back, saying why didn't we twist his arms?

'And then they answered themselves. He had an assault rifle, what were we going to do with him and his gun later? And he kept walking, walking on. And you could tell from his back that he was seriously puzzled about his surname. Funny, isn't it?'

I don't think it's funny. But she's smiling. It's as if that story can displace the other one, the previous one. It's as if it's actually funny.

I ask, 'How did you get out?'

She answers, 'Almost by chance. I didn't want to go. And I didn't think I'd leave Bucha to go anywhere. Cora and I hid in the bathroom when the battles were going on: electricity, heat, water and Internet gradually disappeared from our life. Even the concept of something normal was going away. Eroding. Evaporating. Think up a verb yourself, I don't have the words now.

* Нацик (*natsik*) is, to translate Russian Wiktionary's very concise definition (accessed on 27 September 2023), a word denoting a member of an extremist, nationalist group. [*translator*]

'So you're an ordinary person, you walk in the park with your dog but then you're sleeping in your coat and hugging that dog on the bathroom floor. Then you're wearing ragged mitts as you cook something from other people's freezers over a campfire. Some concoction. I can still remember that smell. Kind of sweet. Disgusting. It seems like you'll be doing this for ever. You're not washing, you don't look at yourself in the mirror: you're not you. It was probably at that point that I stopped sensing who I was.'

She's close to tears again. And again she doesn't cry.

I know I'm preventing her from telling more but I can't hold back so ask, 'Irina, do you cry a lot?'

She looks up at me. She looks me in the eye for a long time and then, abruptly switching to familiar pronouns, asks, 'And what do you think?'

And I regret asking.

Someone's car alarm goes off outside. And then goes quiet. A bird lands on the outside of the windowsill. Looks at us. I recall how my grandmother told me when I was little that birds are someone's souls. I look at the bird, the bird looks at me. Irina's sitting with her back to the window and doesn't see it. She says:

'I didn't think I'd leave. I thought my death was already coming to me, that this was the end, it's over, there was nowhere lower to fall, just death.

'But a point came when the occupiers allowed moving around the city. And then out of the city, too. They took the elderly, disabled and children away on buses. The ones that survived. The lucky ones.

'I watched them and realised nobody needed anyone like me, I didn't fit the criteria for who they had to save, who they had to pity: I'm a middle-aged single woman with a dog. Who cares about me?

'But my neighbours took me. The ones who lived upstairs. We rode in a car, me and three other women. And Cora. It was very hard to leave, like you're tearing out your whole heart, all your guts, everything. It's like you're not allowed to leave but it's also impossible not to leave. See?

'There was a very strong, cold, penetrating wind. We were supposed to go on the Zhytomyr highway to Bilohorodka and from there to Kyiv. In peacetime, it was no more than an hour, even with traffic jams.

'After leaving Bucha, there were people walking along the right side of the road. Crowds of people. Little children, old people, all with some kind of backpacks, rarely with handheld bags. I noticed that a few were carrying animals in their arms.

'They were walking, wearing whatever, dressed all differently. A lot of them weren't wearing their own clothes. Their faces were black because we'd been cooking over campfires for so many days that the soot sank in. Nobody was looking at anybody then, though, I'm recalling all the details now so I can tell you.

'People just walked and walked then because they didn't have rides. I was lucky the neighbours took Cora and me into their car. It was very good fortune. I held her in my arms. Although you could say I was holding on to her.

'We drove slowly, at a walking speed. And there were checkpoints every two or three kilometres. We had to open the window so the soldiers could see who's in the car, that the passengers there don't have assault rifles. It was like that.

'And then there's one checkpoint, the inspector's this grown man, military.

'"Open the window."

'I open it, I was sitting by the window. He looks at me.

'"Good afternoon."

'And he looks right into my eyes. I got a chill on my spine. I recall how the pastor at home in Bucha who got us ready for evacuation warned us, "I beg of you, don't look them in the eyes. Look down or look the other way but don't look into their eyes, you won't hide your attitude, he'll see everything, won't hold back and he'll shoot."

'And so the guy says, "Good afternoon."

'And I'm starting to feel terrified.

'"Hi," I say, but this isn't me, it's as if it just popped out on its own.

'And then he suddenly says, "Put on a hat, you'll catch cold."

'At first I didn't believe my ears and I looked at him, I violated the ban. He wasn't looking at me. He was looking past me. He had a smooth white face and very blue eyes that expressed nothing but saw everything. He'd lost interest in me; they'd gone to look in the boot. "Open it. Take out the things. What are you carrying? Any weapons?" But I'd blanked out and hardly heard them because there were two corpses lying where they'd been standing, right behind them, I mean. Very little children, one in a swaddle blanket, basically a baby, the other a little older. Both dead. There's a blown-up car a step away from them. And a little further there's a boy on a bicycle, he's about 15, he was riding in a white sheet, apparently so they wouldn't kill him. But they killed him. And he was lying there like that on his side and there was a white sheet behind him, like a cloak. The soldier who'd advised me to put on a hat so I wouldn't catch cold was standing so his back hid that, do you see? What was he feeling? Can he even feel?

'We were leaving Bucha where there were corpses lying on the streets, there were cars with dead drivers behind the wheel, homeowners lying, shot, in front of the entrances to their homes. I saw all that but I didn't cry.

'I cried for the first time after seeing those little kids that his back had been hiding from me. Did he kill them? But he hadn't even covered them, he hadn't turned to them. He calmly told me about the hat, knowing there were dead children lying behind his back and that his country, maybe not him, had killed them. But how will he live with that?

'I don't know if those soldiers' mothers read them stories, sang them lullabies before bed, held them in their arms, pressing them to themselves when they cried at night from a stomach ache or just from fear.

'What got into them, what broke in them that they so hate ordinary people? I don't know what kind of people they are or why they're like that.

'You know, on 3 March 2022, my good friend's daughter, a medical student, was killed in our Bucha. She was 18. They killed her in front of her mother. She still can't tell the whole story. She simply doesn't have the words to speak about it.

'I haven't asked, of course, but maybe before they killed her they also asked her to put on a hat and button up warmer? How does that find a place in them?

'You know, I don't want for him, for them, the ones that did this to us, to experience what we experienced. No, all the same, I don't want for them to encounter that. But I want them to understand what they caused. And to acknowledge it. And that will be their punishment.'

The video from Bucha is still running on the phone that she placed with the screen facing up: shot-up fences and buildings, mattresses torn apart, stilled tanks with their necks twisted to the side, the post of an out-of-order traffic light bent in half. And someone's smashed window where someone's scarlet-coloured tulle curtain has burst out into the freezing weather. The wind flutters it, shakes it from side to side. It doesn't give up, doesn't tear and doesn't go limp, it's as if it likes being outside rather than inside, to call attention to itself.

Irina catches my gaze. She turns the phone so the screen is down. 'You should eat the rolls, they're fresh.'

## 8.

# The Refrigerator

There's this saying: *to cry your eyes out.*

I never understood how that could be. But looking at Galina Lvovna now, I see what it means.

Galina Lvovna's sitting on a chair in the yard of a house that's not her own. We're in the Taganrog area of Russia's Rostov Oblast, where her family is being 'temporarily' accommodated. She's sitting on a small folding chair. And she's a large, solid woman.

She's wearing a close-fitting sweater that's also not her own. Under the sweater is a flowered dress; she has socks and rubber flip-flops on her feet.

She's placed her hands on her knees and is looking straight ahead with eyes that have been cried out to an inconceivable blueness.

A warm southern wind tousles her hair. I can't figure out if her hair is grey or light blonde.

Galina Lvovna looks much older than her years. It's because of her eyes. She has the eyes of a very old woman.

I feel physically pained when she looks at me.

But she's not looking at me. She's looking straight ahead.

She says, 'Why did you come? I don't understand why you came. You're different. I see that you're completely different, you have different views, you don't believe *us*, you only believe *them*. Who raised you like that, who taught you like that, why is our pain not your pain, why are we not people? Why have they been killing us for eight years yet you don't believe us?'

The wind ruffles her hair again and lifts her dress a little. I see that her knees are black with bruises. My younger daughter has bruises on her knees, too: she takes figure-skating lessons and falls on the ice several times per session. But that's not the case here – Galina Lvovna is concerned about things other than figure skating.

I ask, 'Why do you have bruises on your knees?'

She looks at me as if I've harshly called her out and distracted her from something important that she'd been focusing on. It's as if it took that question for her to grasp that there's someone else sitting across from her here, on the same kind of folding chair, in the yard of some person's home.

She pulls the dress over her knees.

'Don't mind that. I had knee pads at home. I forgot to take them when we evacuated, I left them behind. And I'm on my knees all the time with my son: turning him over, washing, dressing, lifting him up. So there's bruises.'

A sparrow, plump for summer, lands on a rainwater pipe of the house whose yard Galina Lvovna and I are meeting in. It chirps loudly and persistently.

She's watching the bird. And she's forgetting about me again. Who's she speaking to? But she says, 'You see what kind of life we have, right? Do you see that or not? A young man, full of energy, almost two metres tall he was, my Seryozha. He could have lived normally, see? He has kids. And a wife.'

She cries.

There's an open window behind Galina Lvovna. I can look over her shoulder and see a room. There are bags, bundles and a chair. There's a bed by the window. There's a large man lying on it. That's her son, Seryozha. There's a television on the wall in front of him. It's on.

She says, 'We lived well. Don't believe anybody that tells you we lived badly – we lived very, very well! Everything was good for us. I was so fortunate. If I find it, I'll send you a picture, I didn't used to be the way I am now. Everything was completely different.'

She's crying. To try and help her stop crying, I ask her about her previous and distant life. Completely distant.

'What kind of work did you do?'

'Me? I was basically a kindergarten teacher but that was in the Soviet Union. I was born in Donetsk and grew up there. We had a very beautiful city, don't you be thinking like that. We have a park with metalwork figures, there were zodiac signs and other figures, some about love, some patriotic. More recently, sure, there were lots of figures made from artillery shells. But you yourself understand, it's that kind of time.

'*But we were living well, we lived well.*

'I had roses at home, definitely. I don't know now, of course, maybe those roses aren't there anymore, I don't know. They evacuated us in the winter. But the whole city was filled with roses in 2014. And later, when those military operations started calming down a little, people started planting roses again. So the whole city was flowery again in the summer of 2021. Well, how else could it be? Roses, they're our calling card.

'*Roses. Roses.*

'Why did you start talking about those roses? I started seeing everything right in front of my eyes. How we lived, how well we lived! I got married in Donetsk. I remember my wedding. I remember raising our children with my husband, it was hard. The nineties, you yourself understand. But we somehow lived, lived, even though there was no money, whoever would have told me then that being without money isn't the scariest thing, that I'd be a lot more scared.

'My husband's a military man and we travelled a lot. Around the Soviet Union when there was the Soviet Union, and around Ukraine after Ukraine seceded. So my daughter was born in Cherkasy and my son in Donetsk. Which is where we settled. And had already started getting established. That was such good fortune after a nomadic life: you'd buy curtains, a placemat, a ladle. And you carry all that into the home, knowing it's already yours, you're going to live with that, you won't have to bring it somewhere else, not put it in any boxes, there's no more bundles to tie. It really eased my soul when I realised we weren't going anywhere else.

'*Good lord, we lived so very well.*

'We went to the sea for vacation every year, to Mariupol. Can you imagine how that sounds now? But we were so fortunate, everything was so good for us. Who knew that wouldn't all last long?'

Galina Lvovna's tears are pouring down. She blots them with a hankie hidden in her sweater sleeve.

I ask, 'How did your good life end and your scary life begin?'

Now she's looking me in the eye. She leans forward a little and answers with a question.

'And you don't know? What, do you think this doesn't concern you? What, do you think that we, Donetsk, Luhansk, that we aren't people? Our problems don't concern you? Do you think the war came just now, in February? And how did we – who were without water and electricity under bombing – live all those eight years, what about us, who were dying? What about our kids who grew up in basements? Why don't you hear our voices? What about us?'

She covers her mouth with her hand. Somebody's calling to her from the building, through an open window. Galina Lvovna goes in. She closes the window from inside. And comes out a short time later, accompanied by two little boys of primary school age. One's a bit older, the other's a bit younger. They call her Mama and say they'll be back in an hour. She kisses them and then makes the sign of the cross to their backs.

She returns as if she'll be tortured. She sits down on her uncomfortable folding chair. Looks at me. I look away. I don't know how to lead this conversation. But she speaks.

'I struggled with this for a long time, for them to call me Mama. I'd tell them, you have one mama, I'm your grandmother. Well – this is what I told the older one – if you want, you can call me Mama-Babushka. But a child needs a mother. And what do you expect from the younger, he was a year and two months when everything happened, he doesn't remember his mother at all. But the older boy . . . The older remembered for a long time. But I recently came home and he's sitting, crying. "What's the matter?" I ask. He says, "Gramma, I don't remember Mama." I say, well, let's go have a look at the stars, you'll remember. That's what I said to them from the very start. I'd show them the sky and say, "Your Mama's the brightest star in the sky, she's watching you and smiling at you." They were still little children then, they'd argue about which star was Mama.

'How long will he believe that? How much time will pass until they forget what they went through, what happened to their mother, *what they did to all of us.*'

I want to ask her who 'they' are. But I don't have a chance. She's talking again. Talking without pausing, not taking the hankie away from her face. The hankie's wet.

She says, 'You know, they had a good family, my son did. I was very fortunate as a mother. You feel at peace when you see every-thing's worked out well for your son. And we'd done everything for them. We did everything: we built them a house next to ours. And so Seryozha, our son, went to their house to get Olya and the little one, to bring them to our house. Because there was already some shooting and we'd stocked everything in our basement: first-aid kit, dry food rations, candles, shovel, axe, bedding, everything. You get used to that fast. We got used to it, we thought we just had to sit it out, well, a few days, maybe a week. And they'd liberate us. That's what they told us. And we were prepared to wait. We thought we were lucky because we had a basement like that. And so we usually gathered at our house towards evening, ate supper and went to the basement. That's why Seryozha went to their house to get them. And the older boy was with us. Except right after he went outside the gate, first there was a whistle, then an explosion. And then another. And that was it.

'*And our life ended.*'

I ask if Galina Lvovna knows whose missile it was. She looks at me, not so much in surprise as in horror. She inhales abruptly, apparently so as not to say something rude to me. The question I asked is unacceptable and unthinkable, and she hasn't asked it of herself because the answer to questions like that is *always known*.

She looks me in the eye and says, 'Of course I know.

'*Theirs. Ukrainian. Fascist.*

'My husband and I ran to their house and our son was the first one lying there. He's big, a solid guy, we couldn't lift him and at first we thought he was dead. But he was unconscious. An ambulance came immediately and my husband and Seryozha rode away. And I went farther into the house, making my way through dust, through all the debris, through the smoke.

'My daughter-in-law Olya was sitting in the corner of the kit-chen. She was pressing the little one to herself. He was drenched in her blood, she had a severed artery. At first I thought he was dead, too. But I pried her arms apart and started pulling him towards me. He was clinging to her so hard it was impossible to tear him away. But he was alive, he was breathing. It turns out she covered him with herself and a shard went through her, his head had only been grazed **a little bit**. I pulled him away, pressed him to me, I'm rocking him and singing something to him. And right then, imagine this mystical thing: the refrigerator door opens right in front of me, and there's Olya's pans, bowls, everything . . . And everything's covered in holes. Can you imagine, there's a pan and there's red borshch pouring out of the pan, through the holes, onto our Olya, who's covered in blood. I'll never forget that picture until the day I die, it will always be in front of my eyes. I was beside myself after that. I howled, I scared the little one, I left the house, where people grabbed us and put us in an ambulance, too, off to the hospital.

'The neighbours told me later that our older one was running around outside until evening. He was asking to go home and called for his mother. The neighbours later took him in for the night. And so I want to ask you, maybe not you, but someone else who will answer us. *What's the reason* that all happened to us?'

Galina Lvovna is no longer crying. She's just automatically dabbing her face with a hankie. Then she lowers her hands and smooths her swollen knees. A car is parking somewhere outside the fence; rubber screeches, a door slams, there's loud pop music, people laughing. This is all happening very close by – there's a thin slate fence separating us – but it seems like it's on another planet.

Galina Lvovna and I are sitting together, on the same planet, even facing one another, but the distance between us is so great that I can't look her in the eye.

And she says, 'I understand that, well, they wanted power, money, is that not enough or what? But you can't do that. It's all human lives, it's fates. I'd like for them to dream every night of my children crying, how they call for Mama, how my son mumbles in his wheelchair from grief. Let that come to them in their nightmares. Fascists.'

I ask, 'When did people in Donetsk start calling western Ukrainians fascists?'

She says, 'I don't remember. But they were already calling them that in 2014.'

And then she says, 'You have to understand, our family was always outside of politics. And our Donbas somehow always managed on its own. And we spoke Russian, nobody interfered in our life. But all that confrontation started later, it was very strong. That was somewhere in 2013. And that confrontation was political in the beginning and then it poured out onto the streets. And we understood that Russia would defend us but Ukraine wouldn't – no, they didn't need us. And we waited for Russia, we were patient, we buried our children in the hope that the Russian World would come, Russian spring would arrive. We were so waiting for that, so hoped, but they kept bombing us, bombing and they were the death of us. And then in February 2022, when Vladimir Vladimirovich Putin recognised* us, we were evacuated, we were at a temporary housing site. And they had fireworks there. We drank champagne, hugged and cried. We were so glad. I'm looking at you and I realise you don't believe me. But you don't understand, you're different, I saw that right away.'

She checks the time. She needs to go feed her son. She leaves me sitting in the yard, looking at the sparrow. In the corner of the yard of the house where the volunteers settled Galina Lvovna along with her husband, her disabled son and her adolescent grandsons, there's a tiny – one square metre – little garden with two rose bushes sticking out of the ground. A white rose and a red rose. They're both blooming but each has only one blossom to offer. The wind rocks them slightly so red and white rose petals touch.

Galina Lvovna returns.

---

* On 21 February 2022, Vladimir Putin announced Russia's recognition of the Donetsk People's Republic and Luhansk People's Republic as Russian territory. [*author*] As noted here, these are Russia's terms for these two regions, both of which were occupied and annexed by Russia, and are internationally unrecognised. Often referred to by the international community as 'self-proclaimed' as Ukrainian territory that Russia has illegally claimed. Donetsk is the capital of the so-called DPR; Luhansk is the capital of the so-called LPR. [*translator*]

I finally ask, 'How do you envision "Russian spring"? How did they promise that you'd live?'

She's surprised. It's a strange question.

'Like before, everybody together, in peace.'

'In peace with whom?'

'With Russia.'

'What about Ukraine?'

'I don't even want to hear about them now.'

I tell her, 'Galina Lvovna, I have a recording of your voice right here. You said you used to live well, even happily. That was before 2014, before the campaign for the "Russian spring".'

'Yes.'

'Roses bloomed and there was a stadium and you built a house for your son and his family.'

'Yes.'

'And that was Ukraine.'

'Yes.'

'And what happened later? Who started the shooting?'

She's looking at me, almost afraid.

'Why is it you want to put me on the spot? You don't know any-thing about how we lived.'

We're silent. The sparrow takes advantage of the pause and calls out loudly. I gather my courage to ask the next question. I know I'm going to anger her again but I have to ask. So I do.

'Galina Lvovna, when did Russian soldiers first show up in Donetsk?'

She's looking at me, warily. But she answers.

'They came to defend us, what is it you don't understand? Nobody cared about us so they came to defend us from nationalists.'

'But in 2014 what Putin said in Zerkalny, about the first Russian soldiers, was that "they'd lost their way".'

She leans towards me, takes me by the arm and looks me in the eyes, without giving me an opportunity to turn away.

'What are you putting me on the spot for? Why are you doing this? You listen all the way to the end and you'll see. I'll use my family as an example to tell you. Before the shells started flying towards us, we didn't meddle, but the little one later had an operation and they released him from the hospital; it turned out nothing serious was hit. And my son was put first in neurosurgery but then everything was shelled and all the hospital departments became one department. They brought everybody to one building. There wasn't any water.

'In peacetime, there was a big pool with a fountain in front of the hospital. The firemen brought water there and poured it out. They'd bring it and we'd all run with buckets and jars, everybody got some with whatever they could. Seryozha and the ward had to be washed. And everybody was in that situation.

'But they don't stop for anything, they hit us all the harder. And there's already nobody left at the hospital. They took out my son's stitches and the doctor said, "You take him somewhere they can treat him: *we can't help anymore.*"

'We wanted to bring him to doctors in Russia but he was in such a psychological state that he refused. He said, "I'll only go where my children are." And his children were in Kyiv, with my daughter, their aunt. Where else was I going to put them? And so we went.

'We loaded my Seryozha into the car, we have a Zhiguli, a "tenner", do you know that model? And so we drove off. I fell asleep in the car. And I dreamed there was a black bus driving around the city. And everybody was running away from it, hiding, and it seems like I had to go to the market and I'm thinking, but what if this is some new route and I'll get there faster?

'And so I'm standing by myself and the bus is getting closer and I don't just hear the scary, deep, make-you-crazy sound as sense it in my gut. I see somebody trying to run away from the bus but they get sucked into it. And disappear. So the bus has these soft walls. And I'm standing, I'm not running anywhere. And it's like it's surprised at me, too, but it's driving right at me, not slowing down and not speeding up. And just then a word pops up in my head: INEVITABILITY. It's even pulsating, though nobody said it out loud. I'm starting to feel scared, I already want to walk away. I'm thinking there's a reason all the others were running away. But the bus is driving right at me, I can't even move my leg. I just hear an announcement inside myself: "Next stop: inevitability".

'I see there's nobody in the driver's seat of the bus. It's driving all by itself and its gaping emptiness is watching me. It's beckoning to me and scaring me, all at once. I start silently praying to God. Then I realise that won't help. Then I just tell the bus everything I love, listing things: that we live well, that we don't need anything, that my daughter and son have families, that my son's kids are already walking, that we built a house, that I'm a good grandmother, I can't die right now. I beg the bus not to pick me up because I have grandkids. And I hold my hand out to it, well, to the bus, and say, "Do you hear me, I have grandkids!"

'But of course the bus doesn't hear a damn thing, this was a dream. It's driving at me and I understand I won't be able to handle it, it'll take me away. I put my arms down and close my eyes, it's pulling at me, it's like I'm dying and that's it. I'm becoming part of that bus. I'll become part of the horror. I woke up in a sweat. The car's driving through Kyiv at night, we're already riding up to the hospital. Thank God we found someone at admissions who helped carry Seryozha upstairs. Naturally right to the emergency room. He was in bad shape.

'The doctor came in the morning and he says, "We're releasing him."

'"Why?"

'"Because. Because you're from Donetsk. We don't treat traitors." He turned and walked away.

'And he said to my son, "What, you're lying in the hospital, coward? He came here. You should have shot back."

'Do you see? That's what they said to us! That's what they told a person who lost his wife, who lost everything, who's bedridden and will never get up.

'We left there, found a regional hospital and they took care of Seryozha for us there. And they told us there that his spinal cord was damaged and he'll never stand, he'll never walk again. That's it, see?

'And we can't do an MRI because he still has metal shards in his spine.

'We came back. And our other life started.'

'Why didn't you leave Donetsk?' I ask.

'Where were we going to go?'

'To Russia, for example.'

'Do you know the word "motherland"? Our motherland is in Donetsk. That's our land. And we didn't want to go away anywhere. We wanted Russia to come to us, we were waiting for Russia.'

'But you're saying they were shooting.'

'They were shooting. And bombing. And when you get in a shuttle van you never know if you'll make it, if you'll come back. But we got used to that. You hear whistling, then an explosion – that's flying towards us. You hear an explosion then a whistle – that's away. The Grad shoots one at a time, mortars are different.

'Death settled in right next to us. We didn't shy from it. Why are you looking like that? A person gets used to everything. Want some water?'

Clear, ice-cold water flows out of a pump in the yard. I put my hands under it, drink and wash. The grandkids, for whom Galina Lvovna is taking the place of their mother, return from their walk, ask to watch TV and she approves. She says, 'Sit with your father. All the more fun for him. I'll be in soon.'

I ask her to show me a picture of Olya, who's her daughter-in-law, Seryozha's wife and the boys' mother. She says, 'They're in Donetsk.'

'You didn't take them?'

'How can you take them? When they told us to evacuate on 18 February, they gave us 20 minutes to pack. I had to get the kids ready, son ready, what photos?'

I say, 'And on the phone?'

She takes a mobile phone with buttons out of the pocket of her close-fitting sweater. She says, 'In Donetsk we didn't buy phones like you do, with little pictures. They're expensive, not secure. We got by with these. But don't you worry, I'm taking the bus to Donetsk next week, the volunteers are arranging it for us. I'll get some things there and was planning to get photographs, too. I'll send some to you to have a look.'

I ask if it's actually safe to go to Donetsk now. It's the war's inferno.

She sweeps a lock of hair from her forehead.

'You know, Katya, dying would have been too big a relief for me. But I think God apparently has other plans for me. You go, go, I need to run.'

A couple of weeks later, Galina Lvovna sends me photos, via the volunteers. A tall man with a bald spot is holding a bundle with a baby; you can't see the baby but the bundle's tied with a blue ribbon. Alongside him is a woman in a red sweater and a blue skirt; she has light hair and dark eyes, and her cheeks are all flushed. There's a child between them. He's holding the pocket of Mama's skirt.

The date is below: 13 June 2013.

# 9.

# The Iron

In May of 2022, Inga came to love an iron.

The iron moves left, transforming something wrinkled and shapeless into something warm and even.

'If only life could be like this,' says Inga. And she looks at the iron.

The iron calms her. Inga irons.

Surprisingly, she even irons jeans.

'I iron everything, even jeans,' she repeats, like an echo, 'but you can't iron out life.'

And so the conversation has very quickly come full circle. And we go silent.

The iron breathes steam, moving as it smooths someone's wrinkled things.

Inga says, 'Of course I'm lucky: I have a job, a place to live, nobody pries, I don't owe anybody anything. I'm like a character in a spy movie: it's as if somebody brought me here, gave me a cover so here I am, ending up with a clean slate instead of my past life, and in a place where nobody knows a thing about me. And I can say anything at all about myself to anybody at all. And now I can tell you, too . . .'

The iron moves from left to right, breathes steam and stops. Inga's looking at me.

I look at Inga's hands, which are holding the iron: they have bulging blue veins and a musician's long fingers and there's a wedding band on her ring finger. Inga has dark blue eyes in the middle of a pale, elongated face framed by wavy platinum hair with greyed roots.

Inga's 42. I could have said that Inga's very pretty but to say that, she would have needed to smile, at least at the corners of her lips. Inga's not smiling; she's looking at me. The iron's exhaling steam. And Inga finishes her sentence: 'But I don't want to tell anything. When you tell, you live it all over again. It's like ripping a bandage off an open wound, taking the flesh. It's very painful.'

The iron's moving from right to left. I say I'll probably go and it's too bad we planned to do this, I'm sorry. Inga looks up and sets the iron on end.

'No, sit for a while. I did promise. I'll tell you. And then I won't talk about it ever again. Not with anybody. I'll start my life all over again later. That's what I've decided. But right now I'll finish ironing.'

I sit back down.

'I'd dreamed all this before,' says Inga. 'Nightmares about war have tormented me since I was a child. I thought it was because of our childhood, remember how inspiring the movies about war were, and the heroes in books and textbooks – we were all just wild about military heroism. For some reason I remember really well about a lieutenant with a very tender surname, Romashkin,* hurling himself and a grenade under a German tank and dying. Remember that movie?'

I nod, though my memories are vague. I remember that it was a TV miniseries and not a film: my grandmother watched it in the evenings in the same room where I did my homework. I also remember that on one of those evenings Lieutenant Romashkin threw himself under a fascist tank along with a grenade. I squeezed my eyes shut. I don't remember Romashkin's face.

Inga and I are about the same age. We were born in the same country, the USSR, which no longer exists, and now everything's different for us. But the books and movies from our childhood were more or less the same.

She says, 'I dreamed about Stalingrad a lot when I was a kid. In details I didn't know when I was awake: streets, their names,

---

* The word 'ромашка' (*romashka*) is at the root of the surname Romashkin. 'Romashka' means chamomile in both Russian and Ukrainian. [*translator*]

destroyed houses. I dreamed that I was supposed to run, carrying a child, to the corner of two streets whose names I remembered well. In my dream I knew that I had to run on the uneven side of the street and that there'd be a command centre in the basement of a bread store and they'd save us.

'But in that recurring dream I never made it all the way to the command centre. I'd miss by literally a few steps: I'd make a wrong turn, mistake the building. An explosion would boom and I'd lose the child.

'I've probably woken up a thousand times in my life in a cold sweat because it turned out there was no child in my arms since we hadn't been able to run the whole way together. And it was this horror I could never get over: I didn't save my child and I'm alive but the child isn't.

'And when that actually happened, I felt nothing. It was as if I knew that would happen. Do you see what I'm saying? Because nobody sees.

'I can't explain to anybody what I'm feeling. I feel nothing.'

Inga keeps looking at the iron. And she doesn't look at me. It's probably easier for her to tell all this to the iron. But that's difficult, too.

She takes a few steps, from one corner of the tiny utility room to another. She sits on the edge of a clothes hamper and asks if she should start over.

She's instinctively putting off the scariest moment for later, starting all over again, time after time. From when there wasn't yet a war.

'We lived in a residential area, it was my husband's house, I didn't like it very much there, I kept wanting to live, as I put it, in a normal building. But he loved it. He liked that it was his house, the whole house was his, it wasn't a "hive", as he said. He liked that we had our own land and were always planting something – we had a kitchen garden.

'The main thing that reconciled me with that house is that my husband did what I asked: he put the kitchen sink in front of a window. When I washed the dishes, I saw the yard and the street. I even imagined what was out there, beyond the houses and trees. The sea. I love the sea.

'Not everything's tied to the sea in Mariupol, so it's not like usual seaside cities. We have factories, businesses, another life.

'But it was like I didn't notice that. I'm not sure how to put it but I had something for the sea . . . An addiction? Yes, an addiction. It was important to me that we had the sea in our city and that in the evenings we could go to the beach as a family. I drew the sea all the time, too. I'm a graphic designer by occupation but I drew at home for my own enjoyment: sea, sea, sea. My husband says, won't you ever draw one of us? I always answered that I'll draw you after I've learned how to draw the sea well. That was our personal joke.

'I'm from near Kharkiv.* Ever since I moved to Mariupol, I've told myself every day, "Inga, your dreams came true, you're at the sea."

'There's a sea here, too. Have you been?'

No, I haven't. 'Here' is Costa del Sol, the most popular coastline in tourist-oriented Spain. It's May now and the water's still cool but there's already lots of tourists. They're having fun, getting tans and swimming a little. Inga hasn't seen that. She doesn't go to the sea. She hardly leaves the house at all.

The villa where we met is on the luxurious outskirts of the resort town of Fuengirola. Inga was hired for work and a woman she doesn't know took her in at her home; she doesn't seem to need a housekeeper much. Neither the woman nor her husband have been at the villa even once since Inga started living here.

The woman who owns the villa found Inga through social media, where people who wanted to take in refugees left their contact information. Volunteer coordinators matched them up. That's how Inga got a job and her own room: she cleans, launders and irons. Even jeans. And she tells stories. Not to me but to an iron. That's easier.

'On the 24th, you couldn't really hear the explosions where we lived. I found out about everything from social media. I couldn't believe it, How could it be a war? What war? The twenty-first century and war? We were obviously living on a powder keg but you get used to that. And there was the sense that what was sometimes

---

* Kharkiv, Ukraine's second-largest city, is located in the northeast.

blowing up was someplace else, that another war couldn't happen. And that no war could possibly touch us: we're peaceable people.

'Our house didn't have a basement, only a small cellar, but you couldn't even turn around in there. And so my son and I had to move in with my husband's relatives, that's what he told us to do. My husband's in the military. And I hadn't seen him since 17 February. He only called. He'd usually say, "Hi-bye, everything's fine, kiss on the nose, be there soon. Or not soon."

'But this time he called and said to go to his mother's. There's a basement there, you'll sit it out.

'Even though there was already constant booming, everybody was still sure it wouldn't be for long. Well, two days, well, three, well, a week, max. Then my husband asked me to give the phone to Petya, that's our son. I don't know what they talked about. Their relationship has always been their own thing. Then Petya gave the phone back to me. And my husband told me what we should bring with us: flashlight, warm things, pillow, canned food and water. Petya and I ended up with a bag and a backpack. My Petya's skinny, thin as a pin. He put on that backpack and I teared up and told him to give it to me, son, I'd take it. But he said no, I'm a man, father told me I'm in charge while he's not here.

'And then I wondered what that means, while he's not here, how long he won't be here, when this will all even end. And it was at that moment that I had a sort of déjà vu. I immediately realised every-thing in advance, that we wouldn't make it, that this is the end. And I recalled what my husband said at the end of our conversation, no, it was what he asked me, if I knew how much he loves me. He'd never been a fan of all that mushiness. I was surprised and said, "I know. And I love you, too, Olezha."

'But I said it in kind of a hurry. It seemed like feelings weren't my biggest concern at the time.

'We went outside. It was cold. The city was already wrecked all over, buildings were on fire, there was black smoke coming from them, it smelled like burning and you could hardly see the sky. There was booming in the distance but you could hear shooting closer. You couldn't tell who it was or where it was coming from, though. Everybody was just shooting from all over. I can't convey that feeling to you: I'm standing in the middle of that hell with my son and it's like I'm suddenly seeing us from a distance. There's a child who's ten years old, he's my musician, he played in a violin competition, he's a soloist in the chorus, he reads books instead of spending his time with a phone, like other kids do . . .

'I'm sorry, I didn't mean to talk about that. It's just that right then I felt like I couldn't protect him if something happened.'

She's holding on to the iron like it's a handrail on a bus. She's not ironing, she's just holding on.

Let's shut it off, I say, it's hot.

And she says not to. 'I'm going to iron, to calm myself.'

The iron calms her.

'We didn't go to the bomb shelter right away. My mother-in-law had a theory that it's safer to stay in a building and sleep in a hallway on that, you know, stair landing. And we slept. The flashlight really came in handy, and the pillows, too, and everything we brought with us. None of it was unnecessary, my husband's a smart guy.

'We lay on the stair landing; Petya and I were nestled up together. I had a song about breathing in my head, do you know it?*

*I am waking up covered in a cold sweat*
*I am waking up with nightmarish thoughts in my head*
*As if our house is flooded up to the sky*
*And here left alive only you and I*

*There are miles of water all the way above us*
*And whales are beating their tails above us*
*And there won't be enough oxygen for the both of us*
*I am lying in the dark.*

*Listening to our breathing*
*I am listening to our breathing*

---

* This song is called 'Дыхание' ('One Breath') and is performed by the Russian group Nautilus Pompilius. [*translator*]

*I never thought before that you and I*
*Share one breath between the both of us*
*One breath*

'Petya slept well, he even got used to it over time and didn't wake up from the racket. But I slept in fits and starts, for an hour, hour and a half. And I had my dream about Stalingrad all the time. But it came in bits and pieces, flashbacks, so when I woke up I was always confused about what was a dream and what was reality.

'That morning, I woke up because my son's looking at me: "Ma, you're beautiful."

'That was the fifth or sixth day of life on the stair landing. We hardly washed and didn't change our clothes at all. All the other people – I saw this – their faces looked like they were sprinkled with dirt, they were grey, and their eyes were desperate, like they were bulging. And here's "beautiful".

'I don't remember how I answered because suddenly it started booming all around. Fear paralyses you in moments like those, it completely possesses you. You don't control yourself, it controls you. I think heroes in war movies who cover someone with their chests or throw themselves at the enemy with a grenade are people who can shut off their fear. I'm not like that. I was afraid all the time of tripping and not being able to protect Petya when the time comes. I'm sorry, I'm saying the wrong thing again.'

The iron's moving from left to right. She takes a breath.

'So anyway, soldiers ran into the entryway that morning and started shouting that there's going to be a battle, everybody had to go down to the shelter. And they shot in the air. And only then did Petya and I go down to the basement.

'It turned out there were already lots of people there, many of them with children. My father-in-law was kind of in charge, leading food preparation, shifts for cleaning and shifts for water expeditions. Those water expeditions were the scariest and most dangerous.

'At that point, they'd already totally shut down the electricity in the city: power and all the heating. The water main was broken, there was no water.

'And so the guys, our men, went to the Ice Centre in small groups. The ice had started thawing there and they collected melted water in jerrycans and bottles. And brought it to us. We boiled the water and cooked kasha in it. Well, it wasn't really kasha: three spoons of rice in a pot, so there was a dab of something for the kids' dishes.

'At first the adults ate thin soup made out of canned meat. And later . . . And later, you don't need to know, we ate all kinds of things. I probably won't ever eat any more meat now.

'In those first days, once I'd finally gotten my head together, I thought I could basically eat nothing at all. Why should I eat if I don't want to live? Why, really, was I alive? What for, for whose sake? But nature did its thing. You can't not eat. You could not get up or not talk. But that doesn't work: there's people around and they somehow pull you out of that drowsy state. I realised then that life is instinct. You'll eat and drink when the moment comes.

'I couldn't kill myself with hunger. I ended up being pretty weak for killing myself. And God didn't take me. I wondered the whole time what was wrong with me. Why didn't He take me, why had He left me here to suffer? I'm sorry, I'm talking about the wrong thing again.'

I ask if she wants to go smoke. She shakes her head. Wipes her hands on the sides of her dress. Sighs. Looks around the room as if she's searching for something but not finding it. Takes the iron and irons someone's T-shirt that's already been ironed several times. You can't tell if it's a man's T-shirt or a woman's.

Then she says, 'There's only a little left, I'll tell all the rest fast.'

I don't answer. She's saying that to herself. I'm not here. It's just her, the iron and her recollections.

'A day or two later, the soldiers found out people had been going to the Ice Centre for water. They started shooting at them. Why? I don't know, don't ask me. Why had they come anyway? Why had all this started? If all those "whys" were combined, there'd be an answer to your "why". There's no reason why! It's because they can. Because if you have a weapon, then you shoot with it.'

I ask her, 'What soldiers were they?'

She doesn't understand the question.

'Meaning?'

'AFU, Azov, DPR, Russian, what kind of soldiers were they?'

Her answer was staggering.

'It doesn't matter to me. I don't know what kind of soldiers they were. I didn't see them. What does that change anyway? Some people said their helmets were wound in blue, meaning they were ours. Others said they had white armbands – that means DPR. I don't know, I didn't see them myself. You have to understand, it doesn't really matter who's shooting in that situation – everybody's shooting. And you're like a rabbit because no matter who's shooting, he's shooting at you.'

I would run into this more than once later, that civilians who've ended up in the hell of combat zones don't distinguish who's shooting at them. They call everybody who's shooting 'soldiers' without clarifying whose soldiers they were. I had to ask more questions every time.

Only the soldiers they came across on the way out of combat zones stuck in their minds. Everyone I spoke with described them in detail. Apparently any soldier presents a threat when a civilian feels acute fear and an inability to defend themself. By all appearances, that's how things were in Mariupol.

I attempt to discuss my hunch with Inga but she waves me off. 'I don't know. I haven't thought about that. It's just, see, if your soldiers hadn't come, then ours wouldn't have taken up arms. You're the ones that came. It's because of you that all this started. And the rest doesn't matter. We're really talking about the wrong thing.'

She keeps silent. She returns to what she'd been talking about, to what my clarifying questions distracted her from. She remembers and starts at the point where she'd stopped.

'I just wanted to say that one day my father-in-law didn't come back after he went with the guys for water. None of those three did. We still don't know where his body is or how and who buried him. In those days it was pretty much impossible to find a dead person, identify them and bury them. I can even say that wasn't a top priority.

'What was important? That there was no more water at all. Or heat and electricity. And now the wives of the other men wouldn't let them go to the rink anymore for water. We started draining water out of air conditioners and boilers. We went around the building in little groups, drained and, again, boiled that water.

'We hardly left the basement. Because an armoured personnel carrier was driving around the perimeter and keeping watch on where there was any kind of motion. And then the shelling would start again.

'Only our remaining men crept out into the city in very small groups to find out what was going on and who was now in power where, because things weren't the same in each part of town, every-thing was changing all the time. But finding out about humanitarian corridors was the most important thing for us. But no corridors were being opened. The men came back with nothing. They just whispered about how many corpses were on the street: some shot in cars, some in line for humanitarian aid and some with water, like my father-in-law.

'I remember how this one woman in the basement was wailing, "How many cartridges do they have, that they just shoot and shoot. And they'll never run out and we're going to sit here for ever and that's how we'll die, without ever seeing the world." And everybody started crying.

'It was really awful in the basement, cold and scary. People's strength ran out quickly. The children started getting sick from the dampness, everybody coughing. Petya, too. He's always been a little weak, my boy, frail.

'But he and I had a good spot in the basement, that's what I thought. We were settled right by the exit so fresh air came in there. I'd tuck the blanket in for him, with our pillow right close by, and I'd say, "Breathe, breathe, the fresh air will cure everything, my son." And he'd hug me: "Mamochka, just don't you worry."

'I wanted to rock him in my arms like he was little, that was my impulse. But he didn't let me. And I whispered in his ear all the time, talking about our happiest memories: rides at the amusement park, the time he fell off his bike and Papa and I both blew on his knee, how he sang "Ave Maria" in the school chorus but I was crying and forgot to record it on my phone, how we played Spot It! and his father tricked us and we caught him and made him cock-a-doodle-doo under the table . . . I'm sorry, that's probably not important.

'Anyway, on 19 March our men came back from the city and said some people are leaving basements and going down to the sea, there's allegedly some safe place there and there'll be an evacuation from there. A lot of us start getting ready to go. I say, "Petya, why don't we go, too, we can't sit in the basement anymore."

'He agreed. We thought we'd go with the first group and leave tomorrow. We started getting ready.

'It was a restless night. I hardly slept. I was checking our things the whole time and shielding Petya. And suddenly, at about five in the morning, there was quite a crash. A shell hit one of the apartments in the building and everything started burning. The man whose apartment it was ran upstairs with his buddy and started tossing all kinds of possessions out the window, probably trying to save things. Then the military came and asked why they were trying to save their stuff when they should save lives instead. But they were our military, they were speaking Ukrainian, that was obvious. And they helped put out the fire. They brought sand and used a fire extinguisher, too, they had one with them.

'The men came back to the basement. It got light out. Petya had already woken up by then. We had a bite to eat and somebody said it's time. They started gathering us at the exit. I remember how one woman made the sign of the cross over us and looked me straight in the eye. And then, suddenly, right at that moment, there was a very loud explosion. A bomb had fallen right on the front steps of the part of the building where our basement was. And everything caught fire. There was very caustic smoke because the plastic canopy over the front steps had started melting. Somebody shouted, "Wet a rag and hold it to your mouth so you don't suffocate!" But then there was another explosion outside and a terrible crash – our building had started to collapse. Can you imagine what it's like when a 12-storey building's collapsing? It's very loud, it's scary. People started forcing their way to the exit. It felt like there was heat from an oven coming in but they shoved the children out even so and crawled out themselves.

'And I remember Petya and me forcing our way out, too. And we make our way outside through all that burning and run, run behind everybody else, down to the sea. And the shelling just intensifies. The building's burning, it's hot and there's shooting from all over. If that's not hell, you tell me what hell looks like. Petya and I ran and reached the school, the one in our residential part of town. We stopped by a wall, by the entrance to the bread store. It flashed in my head that I'd already seen this, that this already happened to me. Right then, Petya says, "Ma, I left my backpack in the basement." And just then our 12-storey building collapsed.

'Something flew into the school, too. There was a horrible crash, it was like I'd been scalded. And I couldn't feel my arm from the shoulder down anymore. It was probably at that moment that my hand let Petya's hand go. Probably then. But I don't remember. You have to understand that I don't remember anything after that.

'It seemed like I was calling him but maybe I wasn't, maybe that was only in my delirium.

'Do you understand what that's like, you can't remember how you lost your own little son, the only one you have? All I remember is I'm very hot and there's pain in my abdomen, I can't breathe. I'm losing my child, I don't know where he is. What could I do? What had I not done? What had I done, what had we all done wrong, so you're like this to us?'

She's pressing her wrist against the hot iron. The iron sputters and I don't initially realise what's happening. It smells like burned flesh. She's burned but doesn't take her hand away from the iron. I tear it out of her hands.

And she keeps repeating, 'What did we do to you? Why are you like this to us? I hate, I hate you, I don't want to live anymore. I don't have anyone left.'

I stroke Inga's hair, embrace her. We bandage her. I notice signs of other iron burns on her wrists.

We go to the kitchen. Drink iced water.

And she tells me that someone picked her up, with a wound in her abdomen, and brought her to Berdiansk,* that doctors – a man and a woman – treated her in a regional hospital for a week and a half. That the guy was later shot but she doesn't know who did it or why. And she, still not walking, was sent to Warsaw via the humanitarian corridor and from there to Madrid, to a big, white, cool hospital.

Inga says, 'I asked everybody, where's my son, where's Petya? I described him. But nobody said anything to me. They kept nodding at me, saying he'd definitely turn up. And that I shouldn't worry, I had to gather my strength. It's just nobody said why.

'In Madrid an interpreter came to see me in my room. She said she worked in the hospital but not in this department. She said she's a volunteer and apologised for speaking Russian.

'You know, for some reason everything came pouring out of me, down on her. I started crying, I asked her to leave. I couldn't listen to anything more about either the war or volunteers. I just wanted to have a phone so I could call my husband to say Petya was gone and I was the one who hadn't kept him safe.

'That volunteer gave me a phone later. A brand-new iPhone, oh, how I would have dreamed of that before. But for some reason I just looked at the box for a few hours and couldn't touch it. I was sitting on the bed – I was able to get up by then – and realised now I'll put the phone on and it will tell me for real that Petya's gone.

'And that's what happened. I found one woman who was in our Mariupol group who saw Petya being carried to their bomb shelter. But she said he was already dead. She said he wasn't breathing. She also said he had a head wound, meaning he died fast. You know, I think all the time: Did I let go of his hand before he died or after? That's important to me. It's so scary to die alone if you're a little boy.'

Inga's sitting, rocking on the chair. There are photographs in her phone, downloaded from the Odnoklassniki† social network, they

---

* Berdiansk is a port city on the northern coast of the Sea of Azov.
† 'Odnoklassniki' (Russian) means 'Classmates'.

have the watermarks on them. The photographs show a boy in black trousers and a white shirt, standing in front of a school chorus with his mouth open.

In another is the same boy, a little younger, sitting on a pony and waving.

In a third he's on the shoulders of a light-eyed man with a short haircut; they're both laughing.

'Oleg died in the battles for Mariupol, that's what his unit told me. They should be sending me documents; his commander still has some of his personal things. There's also government money for me.

'I don't know where he died. I don't know where my father-in-law is, I can't find my mother-in-law, I'm searching all our public social media pages but so far there's no answer. My girlfriends, the ones I've been able to find, have told me they've seen that my mother-in-law apparently put up a photo of me and my son, that she's looking for us. But I can't find that post. The girls say, though, that my mother-in-law left for Russia and has been searching for us from there. I don't know if that's true, but I don't want it to be.

'I'm estranged from my parents, I can't expect any support from anywhere. They moved to Orenburg* back in 2008 and they've lapped up the propaganda. On the 24th, Mama wrote to me, "Take care of yourself and Petya, it'll be over soon!" And she put a smiley at the end, can you imagine?

'For some reason it's especially repulsive right now that I speak and think in Russian. But I don't know Ukrainian, can you imagine? I've lived this long and don't know it. I want to learn it now. I will learn it. I don't want to speak the language of the people who killed everyone I loved, the ones who destroyed everything we had.

'Did you know they're now inviting all Mariupol residents back to the city to live under the new authorities? How is it they imagine I'm going to walk down the streets where the body of my child, my husband and his father lie? Who do you have to be to agree to that?'

---

* Orenburg is a Russian city on the Ural River, about 1,450 kilometres southeast of Moscow. [*translator*]

She drinks water, taking big swigs for a long time. Chews her fingernail. Drinks again.

I ask her, 'What can I do for you?'

'I don't need anything,' she tells me. 'At all. You know, hatred is the only thing I can even somehow feel. And nothing more. It's like I don't exist. But I exist: I walk, I move, I iron. I just don't understand the reason for it. Can you explain that to me?'

I can't.

I ask if I should give her contact information for a psychotherapist.

She says that the woman from the hospital sometimes stops by; they talk, that's enough.

'Do you believe in fate?' she asks me.

I don't know how to answer. I do but don't believe in it.

'In all this time,' she tells me, 'I haven't had the dream about Stalingrad even once. And I don't dream of my husband. Or my son. There were just a couple times that I dreamed that a boy's singing, so, so delicately, mournfully, in a chorus, and I'm trying to discern his face and can't.'

We embrace when we part. She says, 'Thank you, I feel better for getting that out of my system.'

I'm thinking that won't last long but I don't say anything. There's a car waiting for me around the corner from the villa where she lives. It belongs to the same woman who owns the villa. She's my childhood friend. She and Inga have never met; they communicate through volunteers. The owner's Russian and she says she's ashamed to show her face to Inga.

# 10

# The Demon

I hadn't asked about this but Ruslan says:

'I don't usually have dreams. I'm a guy, I've been in the wrestling hall with guys my whole life. I think women dream more? No? They don't? Well, I don't know. I never had any dreams at all. Or maybe I just didn't remember them. But after the hard shelling had started it's like I'm sitting in a basement and there's a demon in front of me. He's just like he's supposed to be, with hooves and a tail and horns on his head, they're slimy, see what I'm saying?

'And in the dream, that demon's fidgeting around in front of me, rolling on the floor and roaring with laughter. And I'm sitting, I can't move my arms or legs. I'm just begging him, "Don't kill children, don't kill children, you hear?" It was night-time and the shelling in the morning started off many times harder than before.

'Same thing a day later. I fall asleep and he shows up. I'm not so afraid now, it's more like I'm mad at him. I ask him, "Are you the one that gave the order to shell children, answer me!" And he laughs again. And he bares his yellow teeth, it's not nice. And he has bad breath. I tell him, "You're quite something, that's enough, cut it out! Can't you see how much grief there is!" And he doesn't answer. He just grins, that's it.

'In the morning the shelling was hard and strong again. The next night we barely slept: it was impossible to close your eyes because of the rumbling. But we held on, we were still staying in our own apartment. Everything went quiet in the morning. I thought the battles had passed us by now and continued on, towards the factory.

'But the demon came again that night. He sat down and watched. His red eyes didn't blink. I say, "Why did you come? Go away! You just make everything worse, just grief and tears and death." And he laughed a little at first, then stood and left. But he didn't go the whole way. He turned around. He looked at me and smiled, so I woke up from the horror.

'My family and I sat down for tea. It's morning. Such a bright, sunny, chilly morning. I still remember that I was thinking it was like before, a usual morning with the family. Suddenly: incoming. And imagine, we're sitting, just like we'd been sitting at the table, but the side wall was cut off along with the rest of the building. Like a knife cut it! The whole next part of the building had completely collapsed. We jumped up and ran down the collapsed slabs of our prefab building. It was 10 March, I remember. It's strange to say it, but I would have recognised that demon if I'd seen him.'

To be honest, I was about to leave before he started telling me his dream. Ruslan, his wife Irina, daughter Katalina and I were standing by the gate of what used to be the Aelita tourist resort complex, which had been turned into temporary accommodations for refugees. And right then Ruslan suddenly told me about the demon.

Katalina asked him, 'Why didn't you tell us before?'

'I don't know. I had other things on my mind.'

He hugs her. She sticks her head under his arm and quietly laughs into her father's armpit.

'What's up?'

'It suddenly just felt funny. When I'm feeling down, I tell myself I'm a wrestler's daughter. And now I was just thinking, what kind of wrestler are you, you're just a teacher. A phys ed teacher at a school. Like Nagiev on *Phys Ed Teacher*,* see?'

'Nagiev drove an SUV. And I take the shuttle van.'

'That's not the big thing.'

'Then what is?'

'The big thing, Pa, is that he's bald and you're not.'

'That can always be corrected.'

---

* A Russian TV comedy series where actor Dmitry Nagiev plays the main character, who originally came from criminal circles and gets a job as a PE teacher at a school.

'Oh no, Pa, you don't need to do that. It wouldn't look good on you.'

She pats his greying head and kisses him. They smile at each other. He says, 'Let's go inside.'

They walk towards the cafeteria, arms around each other.

I'm left with Irina, Ruslan's wife, just the two of us. Watching as they walk away, she says, 'Imagine, that's our daughter. But she's closer to her father than her mother. Always has been. But especially now. For them, I end up being like . . .'

'Like who?'

'It's hard to explain. All my kin are in Odesa. You see that Odesa isn't Mariupol.'

'And so?'

'In Odesa people know for sure that we aren't Russia, we're Ukraine. There aren't even conversations there about that "Russian World". And my family there doesn't think at all like my husband does.'

'And what do you think?'

'I think that I'm here with him and our daughter. But for them, I'm . . . Well, with me, they're . . . It's like walking around with an unexploded bomb in your bag. He' – she nods towards her husband, who's receding – 'knows what I think. But I saw everything he saw. Your own eyes don't lie, right? But now there's nowhere for us to go: on the one hand there's punishers, on the other, there's traitors. And nobody cares about you.'

She turns around and walks away.

Doesn't say goodbye. Doesn't say anything reassuring like 'see you'. Doesn't wish me a good trip. Doesn't say anything. A petite woman with a Greek surname and patronymic in her passport and a huge Ukrainian-Greek family in Odesa, a Ukrainian city that Russia's bombing again today.

Irina walks away without once turning around.

I'm left on my own. I'm thinking back to where I started.

Five hours ago I was standing in this exact same place: a few summer cabins, a heated building, cafeteria, laundry and boiler room; weeping willow and a half-dried artificial pond where boys are chasing a lone frog. Dazed by spring and the children's hot pawing hands, the frog madly rotates its eyes and hops halfwittedly, randomly, attempting to bolt. But it ends up inside the pond's wall, floating alongside it. It looks dead. But no, its feet come together, its head rises. The boys grab it by the thick neck. Everything starts all over again.

'They're from Mariupol,' Olga said right into my ear. She ended up in Rostov's Left Bank temporary housing facility before the war even started, in mid-February of 2022, as a result of compulsory evacuation from Donetsk. 'They arrived yesterday. They don't talk with anybody. They just sit, the three of them, at a table, look at the sun, they can't get enough of it. Poor people. They probably missed it, so much time in a basement.'

Ruslan, Irina and their daughter Katalina are about 20 metres away. But I still don't know their names yet. I need time and strength to gather up my courage and go introduce myself.

I inhale a full chest of air, as if I'm getting ready to dive, and walk over to them. 'Hello, my name's Katya, I'm a journalist, please talk with me.'

Ruslan moves aside, freeing up a spot at the rectangular table. He has an anchor and 'Zhdanov' tattooed on his arm. Mariupol was called Zhdanov in Soviet times, in honour of Andrei Zhdanov, a Soviet functionary who was a Communist Party leader and close associate of Stalin.

Ruslan catches my gaze. He says, 'I inked it in the army. That's how much I missed home. Now, though, I wanted to hide it at filtration when I left with the family. There's harsh frisking for ink. But they didn't ask.'

He extends the arm with the anchor to me and introduces himself. 'Ruslan. And my family: Irina, though she won't talk. And Katalina, my daughter.'

Katalina's eyes are two tones lighter than the southern, April sky. I ask Ruslan why his daughter has such an unusual name. He hugs her and smiles broadly.

'My wife and I were on vacation at the sea in Romania when she realised she was pregnant. And we were so happy lying on the beach, daydreaming about what our daughter would be like. There

was no doubt we'd have a daughter. And there was a little girl running along the shore: light, curly hair, a pure angel. And her mother
called after her: Katalina, Katalina. We exchanged glances and
decided. Katalina . . . At filtration, by the way, they also asked what
kind of name it is. But they were asking other things, too.'

There's a pause. That's how any conversation now comes up
against the war and its aftermath. Ruslan looks at me out from
under his brow. I help him by asking, 'Did you get through filtration
easily?'

'Easier than others, you could put it that way. I saw how they
were denazifying some people there, have you heard that word?'

I nod. He turns away and now speaks not to me but to his own
hands, and to the table they're resting on.

'That guy in the uniform asks me, "What did you see?" And I tell
him, a lot more than I'd've liked to. Both how yours were killing and
how yours were getting killed. I looked death in the eyes, like I'm
looking at you. I saw grown men walking down the street, loudly
sobbing, one's wife was killed and they wouldn't allow burial, the
people not allowing it were his own, the neighbours. Because there's
a garden here, somebody's yard there. And everybody was still
hoping to live a little. We were still hoping to live a little . . .'

*PAUSE*

'Hope is like that in a person, tough. You go outside the house
and somebody's lying there without a head, without legs, just a
stump. But your mind's still hoping, what if they're alive, they're
just turned, uncomfortably contorted. "Isn't that right, comrade
officer?" I ask the guy.

'And he asks me again, as if he hasn't heard enough, "You saw
corpses?" Ludicrous, of course. I was living among those corpses. I
walked through them in the morning and evening. I learned not to
react. We all got like that there. You see corpses, it's like you're
seeing trees. And that's all there is to it, officer, I told him.'

*PAUSE*

'And he says to me, "Right, right, I understand all that but you'd
better not talk about that more with anybody." And then he asks,
"Are you going to undress?" Not a question, of course, I'll undress if

I have to. But I didn't have to undress. So he didn't notice the ink. Or pretended not to. Anyway, they photographed us, took fingerprints and let us through.

'And you know what? So we were riding, riding for a long time, we spent several days on the road before we made it here, but it was like I was having a conversation with that officer the whole time. I want to tell him how we lived, how we waited, how we believed in you, officers like you. And what we got. Corpses, mud, ruin and hatred, that's what your "Russian World" brought us.'

*PAUSE*

'The "Russian World" we were waiting for. We believed in it, believed in you, Putin. That you'd come to us and we'd start living differently. We were waiting for that.'

Katalina takes her head off his shoulder. Irina says she needs to step away, an urgent call. Katalina also remembers some pressing matter. The two of them stand and quietly walk off, one after the other.

He cracks his knuckles, then his neck. Clears his throat. He says, 'I see you're different. And I don't think you'll understand me. You don't need the kind of truth I have. People don't need truth now. Only their own correctness, isn't that right?'

I ask him why – understanding which way things were going – they didn't leave Mariupol sooner, before the war, before all this happened to them.

He shrugs.

'It's hard to say. I love the city. Up to a certain point, it was actually believable that it was possible to stay and wait for Russia, can you imagine? But in 2014, the Russians only got as far as Novoazovska. Everything ended there. The DPR couldn't control Mariupol; our city's feisty. And there were lots of drunks among the DPR people, and all kinds of other things I don't want to talk about. So they were chucked out of the city fast and another course was set. Another national idea started sprouting up in people's minds.

'I work at a gym, I'm a wrestling coach. Any big man who wants to achieve anything in our city comes through our gym, through me. So you could say that "Azov" matured before my eyes. I knew a lot of the Azov guys personally. And I won't say they're all hard-wired, like *natsiki*. That's propaganda. I don't know why that was spread around. It's just the guys had ideas and they were given a platform, resources and opportunities. They turned out to be keeping busy. And those who weren't keeping busy – the DPR people, Russians and others – were quietly degrading. And the stronger ones bent them into shape. And the ones who didn't want to be bent wiped out the others.

'We lived pretty close to the Azov base. There were light poles around the unit. Each one had this written on it: "Azov Battalion, hotline number". There were banners around the city, too: "EXPOSE THE SEPARATIST". And that had a hotline number. Security service officers or the Azov guys came to see people they got complaints about. They'd bring the person to the aerodrome and torture them. All Mariupol knew that our aerodrome was where they tortured undesirables. Not to death but with educational goals. Then they'd release them and before you knew it, the person had calmed down a little. And from then on, mum's the word, breathe out of the two holes in your nose, don't stand in the light.'

'What about you?'

'What about me? I'm a coach. If I asked everybody I worked with about their political beliefs, we wouldn't be talking anymore. But you know, I lived in the belief that we'd end up in Russia sooner or later. And that if there's going to be a war, it'll last a week, maximum. That Putin and the people around him know what they're doing and know their work . . .'

Now he's looking me in the eye. His head's tilting forward a little, like professional wrestlers do. He's looking me in the eye, as if now I should answer the question of why nothing happened the way he believed it would or the way he was promised by someone I don't know about, someone I don't know, whose views I don't share.

'When did you realise everything would be completely different?'

'I still can't completely believe that. I can't, I keep turning it over in my head, over and over, and I can't. The city was in ruins when we were leaving. It's basically like that everywhere. My aunt's house near Mykolaiv was levelled, she's homeless now, and who the hell knows what's going on in my wife's Odesa. This is what "Russian World" turns out to be? We don't need something like that. And I ask myself what we do need. And I don't know the answer now. I no longer know anything. I'm tired.'

The boys hounding the frog make their way to our table. They're shouting so Ruslan and I can no longer hear each other. I want to ask them to be a little quieter. He stops me, unexpectedly speaking to me with the familiar form of 'you'.

'Hold on. Let them have the chance to be kids.'

The frog changes direction, luring the kids away.

As they leave, Ruslan says to me, 'They haven't had this life for a long time. When you're sitting in a basement, it's "be quiet"; if there's an explosion, it's "lie down"; if you want to eat, it's "tough it out". I don't know if they'll be forgiving about this childhood of theirs. And the big thing is, why are they getting this? You know,' he says, suddenly stopping short, and scrutinising me, as if he still doubts he can speak with me about topics like this.

Then he shakes his head, makes up his mind and continues: 'I have so much hatred, spite, inside me, a lot of dark stuff I can't ever either understand or forgive. Somewhere in the middle of March – we were already without either an apartment or a home or a car – it was a chilly evening and we were standing with people in the yard, cooking food. It was getting dark. It was around six, the shelling usually quieted at that time. And then the Azov guys suddenly come by, looking for a place to spend the night. Our guys and I went over to them, all calm, like adults, and we say, "You guys, when's all this going to stop? Do you have some kind of prediction? Our strength is running out, the women and children are all frozen, a lot are sick and wounded, when will it all end, what do you think?" And one of them grins and says, "When you start devouring each other, that's when it'll end." And they left.

'The next day they came back to our yard at that same time. They made themselves at home and launched a drone – they were look- ing for a target to fire on. We go over again, "What are you slimebags doing? You're going to start shooting from here now and the payback's going to fly in, are you out of your minds?" They say, "It's the same road for everybody." And I say, "Where to?" Do you know what they answered me? Do you know?'

'No.'

'They answered that it's the same road for everybody, to hell. And you know what? I absolutely try to tell that to people, the ones that left for Europe or the ones who stayed in Ukraine. They don't believe me. Two people unfriended me on Facebook. And these are my classmates. We were around each other our whole lives, we grew up together. And now they're in Germany and don't believe it. I call one, write to another, I say, why don't you believe me, I'm a witness to all this, I'm a live witness, why don't you believe it? And they just deleted me and that's it. Silently.'

For a while I don't know what to say. And then I decide to say what I feel. Lying's useless, pointless. I tell him, 'Ruslan, do you realise I've heard a lot of stories from Mariupol? And they vary. And it's not everywhere that only *one* side is to blame.'

He nods.

I ask him, 'Why is that?'

'I don't know. But I'm not lying to you.'

'I know. I believe you. And the others I talked with before you, I believe them, too. And where's the truth?'

He keeps silent. He's silent for a long time. Probably about three minutes. I have time to notice his daughter and wife coming out of the building and discussing something close by, looking at us from time to time. Then they walk in our direction, after apparently coming to some sort of agreement.

'There's no truth that can be shared with everybody, that's what I think. Everybody has their own. See, the issue here is about who was where and who saw what. The city was surrounded and it was impossible to know who was shooting from where. At first we were on the Left Bank but then we evacuated to my mother's, on the Right Bank, near the Zaporizhzhia highway. Without knowing it ourselves, we ended up in a strategic spot for the AFU. And we paid for that in full.

'If Azov was positioned on the Left Bank and the DPR went on the attack, then the Russian troops attacked from the Zaporizhzhia highway area and the Ukrainian military defended itself. There was a Ukrainian soldier, a grenade launcher, on the roof of our building. The Russians couldn't bring him down for a long time. They either overshot or undershot. When there was shelling, we'd usually leave the room and lie in hiding between two rooms so we wouldn't be wounded by shards. They butted heads for so long that "our" grenade launcher was the lucky one and everybody relaxed. We stopped hiding.

'But that day they suddenly started whacking "our" grenade launcher, off the schedule. It was morning, we were drinking tea. Incoming . . . and half the apartment's gone. They hit it along with a whole stairwell of apartments. The building collapsed like a children's book, I even had the chance to be surprised. We slid down over the slabs. Our car was still in one piece, we made it to my brother's; it wasn't far.

'My wife and daughter asked to go to the bomb shelter. I went in once and started having a panic attack. Allegedly men aren't supposed to talk about that but that's how it was. I knew I wouldn't survive in a bomb shelter. My wife went. But I kept trying to keep my daughter with me more. When there was incoming, she'd run to the basement and I'd just lie down and stay there. You know, for some reason time really drags in those moments. Everything happens slowly. But it's awful.

'One time was genuinely awful. I went to the area by the black cherry grove for water, there's a spring there. I'm walking with jugs, I look, and there's soldiers with blue armbands running around. Well, I think, they're ours, fine.'

'Ours meaning Ukrainians?'

'Well, who else, it was still Ukraine then.' Ruslan's annoyed that I interrupted him. He continues.

'I look further and there's a guy who's crouched, he's shooting an RPG launcher, then there's another guy. I look closer, they're pummelling a residential area: there's children running, people walking, there's no military there at all. And I just lost my freaking mind from what I saw and unintentionally went ahead to have a better look at what they were doing there. And there I see one of them turning in my direction and aiming at me, probably from a distance of 200 metres. I – thank God you can't escape an athletic past – jumped as hard as I could into a gully and started crawling. I heard an explosion behind me. But I'd already crawled off without looking back, running on all fours. I'd cleared out. I'd already tossed away the jugs, I didn't need any water, nothing. I caught my breath a while later. Well, I'm thinking, I'll go and calm down, walk around a little. I went closer to the centre of town where I could get a signal, right by the police school, there's a Wi-Fi repeater there. I wanted to read the news, to somehow recover. I approach and there's a whole crowd of people. They're handing out bread. The line was about 300 metres away, maybe this was actually the start of the ten-storey buildings and the residential area. But I didn't have a chance to orient myself before a soldier in camouflage runs out, hoists an RPG launcher on his shoulder, and fires right into that crowd of people. There's wounded, shouts, moaning, flesh. It's a real river of blood, it ran off everybody into one stream, flowing along the white snow. That's really etched into me. But I didn't see any armbands at all on him. Only that his helmet was wound in blue tape. Which one is it? You can't tell. I got so scared at that point. Not that they'd kill me. That they'd kill my loved ones and I couldn't do anything.'

Katalina noiselessly approaches us from behind, puts her hand on his shoulder and her mermaid-like eyes look into his, which are exactly the same but faded, and asks, 'But why didn't you tell Mama and me about that?'

Ruslan shrugs.

'I don't know, there probably wasn't any time.'

They – wife and daughter – sit down on either side of him.

He kind of softens, deflates. He suggests going to their room for tea. 'Just,' he says, 'don't pass harsh judgement, we haven't settled in yet, we've only been here two days. And everybody handles us quietly, carefully, in undertones, like we're critically wounded. Well, we still haven't recovered. We're just warming ourselves in the sun, like that woman told you.'

'You heard?' I ask.

'She has the kind of voice a deaf person will hear.' They laugh.

We go to drink tea. There are spice cookies with the tea.

As we drink the tea, I ask about their plans. He knits his brows.

'Russia has the second army in the world in terms of power. It'll win. That's inevitable.'

I clarify that no, no, this isn't about geopolitics, it's about you, about what will happen with you.

*PAUSE*

'They promised me there'll be a passport in a month. And then I'll go work in my speciality. Meaning as a coach. There's no other way for us. We're not going back. There won't be a second attempt.'

They come to see me off. And I ask, 'And why didn't you go to war?'

He shrugs.

'I'm a teacher. A phys ed teacher. It's a peaceful profession. You can go further if you want: I'm a wrestling trainer. But there's no automatic rifles in wrestling, see? And so I'm here. Is it humiliating? Well, yes. Do my wife and daughter look at me like a loser? Possibly. But I know where I'm headed. We have nowhere to return, see? You can't bring back what was, it's gone for ever. I had offers to go there, to guard the new leadership. But that won't happen. In the first place, they're not leadership for me, in the second, the people going there now don't know the city, their hearts don't feel it and they haven't seen how the heart was torn out with the flesh. Because it's one thing when you see it on TV and completely different when you see it all in real life. The people going to guard the brand-new mayor haven't seen people dying on the frozen asphalt, bloody hands lying around on the benches where you gave your girlfriend flowers, charred beams at the site of the movie theatre where my wife and I held hands or shell craters in the park where I carried Katalina around on my shoulders when she was little. And the big thing is, what was that all for? Who did they save, who did they make happy? No, no, we're not part of that anymore. That's it. That life is gone. There will be a new one.'

I ask him to call me from that new life and I shake his hand on the arm with the 'Zhdanov' tattoo. I hug Katalina and Irina. And then he tells me his dream about the demon.

And then I leave.

Katalina's the first to greet me when I come back to the Rostov temporary refugee housing site a few weeks later.

'Just don't ask Papa about jobs.'

'It's not working out?'

'Nothing's like he thought. It's hard. He's depressed.'

We sit and talk with Ruslan at the same table as in April. But the weeping willow's leaves are already as long as a person's finger, the artificial pond has definitively dried up, and the boys have been sent to the children's camp in Anapa,* freeing the frog from torture.

'But I'm still here,' says Ruslan.

'Are you tired?'

'It's seesawing from spite to powerlessness: there it was soldiers with assault rifles running after us and ruling our lives, but here? It's different here. Here we all owe everybody. They saved us, right? And you can't explain who saved us, how, or why. We left Mariupol towards the end of March. Everything around was black from fires and there were explosions, there's no place left unharmed. We wanted to leave a day earlier but didn't make it. What I mean is we didn't fit on the bus because they'd loaded a dead man, a relative of one of the passengers. They'd gone through evacuation and he was killed by a shard right in front of them. There was shouting: whoever had something, plastic sheets, bags – they wrapped him up and put him in the baggage compartment. And they pulled people's things out. They said whoever's things these are will go tomorrow. They were our things. We had to go on another bus. There was shelling as soon as the bus left, with incoming in front, incoming to the side. I just closed my eyes and I'm thinking, whatever happens – happens. I'm no longer in charge of my life.

'And so that feeling increases every day. I don't know why I'm

---

\* Anapa, Russia, is on the Black Sea's northern coast, about 400 kilometres from Rostov-on-Don. [*translator*]

living, who for, what for. I no longer need anything. I don't want anything. You think I, a grown man, feel good living here, with room and board, trudging around with nothing to do? Well, fine, we were in withdrawal for a week, two, okay. My girls stopped crying. But a month and a half? And there's no end in sight to it. They locked us in this cage and we don't have the right to leave here and start running our own life. Little soldiers over here, little bureaucrats over there, that's how it is.'

He cracks his neck in both directions. And walks away. Katalina and I are left. She's scrolling through photos on her phone that her classmates send from Mariupol.

'Just imagine, there's nothing. Nothing that we loved is still there. We'd go walk around at Veselka, the park, after school, it was so pretty there. But now it's gone. There's nothing, nothing. Only the sea. But where would the sea go? Do you want some tea?'

We go to the common lobby to make tea. There are now lots of people from Mariupol who've gathered together at the temporary housing site and are watching the news on one of the central Russian channels. The news tells of how the electrical and water supplies were restored; the next subject is the heavy fighting in the Svatove–Kreminna area.

Ruslan was promised work papers for Russia in May, then in June, July, August, September, October and November. In December, the temporary housing site on the Left Bank of Rostov-on-Don closed. Refugees from there were divided up and sent to other temporary housing sites, one of which is the Vizit Hotel, a three-storey prefab building on the outskirts of Rostov, where people formerly from Mariupol, Donetsk, Berdiansk, Kherson and other places now live.

They tell Ruslan his paperwork will be ready soon and he'll be able to start a job in 2023. He doesn't believe it. But he keeps silent. He no longer has the energy to argue, stand up for his rights, fight or simply somehow express his opinion. Ruslan has aged and lost weight. Katalina has shot up in height and matured.

She wants a cat for her birthday but cats aren't allowed at the hotel. Katalina also dreams that her father will find a job by next

May, when she'll have her birthday, so they'll be able to rent housing and get a cat.

Katalina says, 'That's a normal and very realistic wish, right? I don't believe the war will end because there's so many people that need the war, I don't believe we'll go back home, and even though I really missed it in the beginning, now I look at pictures my classmates send and I realise that I feel nothing for that place now. I don't believe Mama will smile again, how can you smile when your whole family's being bombed? I don't believe in anything anymore. I want a cat. I'll pat her and play with her, too. We had a cat, we even had two. One got scared by an explosion and ran away. I don't know what happened to her. And the other one died. I want a cat.'

I hug Katalina.

It's sleeting. And there's no feeling that the New Year, 2023, will start on this earth in a week.

On TV they're showing Russian earthmovers demolishing the drama theatre in Mariupol. The job's almost done: the theatre's portico is falling under the pressure of a backhoe's bucket. And all the bricks, all the bas-reliefs, all the premieres, triumphs and flops are turning into a heap of stones.

A young correspondent from a Russian government channel is speaking about the demolition of the Mariupol theatre. The site behind him is surrounded by a plastic banner with portraits of classic Russian writers. A gust of wind changes the classics' facial expressions and it looks for a minute as if Dostoevsky is laughing.

One of those watching TV in the Vizit Hotel's lobby says, 'Well, that's that. Now it's definitely starting from scratch.'

The others keep silent. Ruslan clears his throat and goes outside. He stands, he breathes; his hands are shoved in his pockets. Rostov's steppe wind, as biting as if it has sand, blows in his face.

Things are lively by the hotel's fence, where people are smoking and discussing news from home.

'And my grandma called from Mariupol, she's praising Putin, says he's so good he sent a space heater as a New Year's gift. And a Christmas tree . . .'

'Zelia* should've sent her one.'

'No, she curses Zelia. Says he promised there wouldn't be a war but it came, that means he's a liar, she says, your Zelia stole our peaceful life, she says. But Putin sent a space heater and a Christmas tree so he's her very own father.'

'There's power and water again in Mariupol, it's liveable, there's something to say thank you for. But in our Donetsk, my daughter-in-law says there's no water, no power. Dogs, she says, howl really loud at night, they just want to eat all the time or maybe they're bored. My daughter-in-law saw one running, its belly's cut, it's got GPS on its neck, guts hanging out and the GPS is blinking. It's fucked up, son of a bitch, Apocalypse.'

'War.'

'The fuck's it for.'

One of the smokers shows a phone with a picture sent by relatives who stayed behind in the city: Christmas trees for sale on a damaged square, not far from a multi-storey building with burned-out windows.

The man showing it comments, 'Life's coming back, anyway.'

'It hadn't been planning to go anywhere last year,' they tell him.

People quickly find Internet videos of Mariupol's Christmas tree in December 2021. It's standing, lights twinkling, across from *that very same* drama theatre.

'And remember, seems like it fell in the wind, it was from the rustling wind back then! One of our grandmas lives in those parts, said that's a bad omen.'

'Oh, damn,' says the raspy female voice of someone invisible in the darkness. The smokers put out their cigarettes and disperse.

* 'Zelia' (Зеля) is a nickname for Ukrainian President Volodymyr Zelenskyy. [*translator*]

# II

# Eyes

Irma's sitting, facing a window, with her head tilted a little to one side. It seems like she's been carefully following along as summer changes to autumn and autumn ends. While I'm standing behind her and telling her who I am and why I came, a big, ruddy elm leaf breaks off and floats past her window, slowly spinning.

But Irma's blind so she doesn't see that. In the middle of the leaf's motion, something a sighted person definitely wouldn't miss, she finally turns her wheelchair towards the sound of my voice.

A pink scar stretches diagonally across Irma's forehead, from her hair to her brow.

Irma touches the scar with her fingers as she thinks. Her fingers are slender, almost translucent. *Cold*, I think. But I don't actually know.

Irma says, 'Just don't move suddenly and don't touch me with your hands. I'm a *new* blind person. I'm not used to it.'

Fine, I say. I want to say something else but she gestures to stop me. She says, 'What are you going to do? Will you sit down or will you stand, what do you want to know, how much time do we have?'

I answer and then I ask, as I've asked all the interviewees, if I need to change her name in the book. She smiles.

'Life's so strange. When I was little, my mother and I dreamed I'd be a famous violinist and my name would be on concert posters all over the world. It's strange that in the end, I'll stay in people's memory as the woman in your book from Berdiansk who went blind trying to catch her cat. It's funny.'

I say I don't find anything funny about that.

She shrugs.

'There's something funny in anything if you're looking. Well, in our case, it's a diabolical irony. While I was waiting for you, I was thinking of speaking Ukrainian. I wanted it to be difficult, unpleasant, for you. I wanted to do something so you'd feel my pain.

'Although at first I didn't even want to see you . . . Meaning to talk with you. But they told me you're different, you're not like . . .'

She stops, as if she's searching for a word. Then she finds it.

'You're not like all Russians. Although in essence, what do we know about all Russians beyond that they're ever so calmly keeping silent and going about their business while their government sends us missiles? It seems that's enough of a definition for not wanting to know more about you.

'But later I thought that if I speak Ukrainian you might not understand something. You won't understand something about me, about us and about how you ruined our life. I'll speak Russian so later you can't say you didn't completely understand something.'

I nod. Then I suddenly remember what I'm doing. I say, 'Yes, of course. I'll sit next to you, by the table, is that good?'

Now she nods. She can't see me but I can see her.

I ask what her cat's name was.

'The cat's name was Mouse. She was grey. Small, smaller than the usual cat. We called her Mouse. We thought that was funny.'

She smiles, truly smiles, maybe at the memory. She asks me, 'Did you know that blind people have dreams? I do. And I *see* in my dreams, can you imagine? In my dreams there's no war and no peace, it's something in the middle. And I'm not surprised at what I see: husband, son, cat. It's an ordinary life. But then I wake up, open my eyes and there's darkness. So it's like it's the opposite because where there's a dream, everything's like being awake but when I'm awake, it's a black, impenetrable night.

'In the first days, I asked to have a flashlight shined in my face. I didn't believe it, I felt it, to see if it was hot. I couldn't believe that now there'll be darkness for ever. I don't know how to explain that to you. It seems like the darkness that came in my particular case isn't just my personal darkness, it's an existential darkness. We're all in the dark. There's no other explanation for all this.'

She touches the scar with her fingers.

On 12 March 2022, Irma ran out of the basement of her building in Kherson* during mortar shelling when Mouse, the cat, who already seemed to be used to the war, was suddenly scared by the din and dashed outside. And Irma dashed after her.

'The last thing I saw was Mouse scampering in the bushes. Or maybe I just imagined that?' says Irma.

Then she frowns, bites her lip and asks me, 'Can you help me light a cigarette?'

I help her: I just support her hand that holds the lighter. She furrows her brow. This is unpleasant for her. She says so.

'It's very difficult to learn to ask. Especially for something elementary.'

We open the window. Irma smokes. She tells about how she lay on the ice-cold ground for an hour or even longer because the battle was going on and nobody dared come out of the basement for her.

'You couldn't figure out if I was alive or dead.'

Irma's injury resulted in optic-nerve damage. But that was initially unclear.

'I was in the hospital, in total darkness, and I understood from the conversations that my life was over, that it was ruined, like our city.'

She requests that I not ask about medical details. And she says, 'I was lucky. I ended up on an export ferry from Berdiansk. It brought me to Istanbul. Then Israel. They operated on me there. And then they brought me here, through volunteer channels. Quite the excursion. Irony again, do you feel it? I'd dreamed my whole life of travelling and went through half the world in a couple months of *this* spring. But I didn't see those cities. I only remember how they smell and how they sound.'

Irma's now in Germany, in a small, clean room of a social housing building: bedroom, toilet, shower, common kitchen and living room, plus a social worker on the floor round-the-clock. She has a German residence permit stuck in her Ukrainian passport. Leaves are slowly but decisively falling from the huge elm under the window.

---

* Kherson is a port city on the Dnipro River, near the Black Sea.

She says, 'They tell me my vision could be restored but I don't believe it. I don't know why I don't believe it but I don't believe in anything good anymore, only the AFU. So I believe in our guys. They're our only hope. The fate of the whole world is in their hands, see what I'm saying.'

I don't answer but she doesn't need me to. She grasps at the scar on her forehead with her hand, tilts her head forward a little and says, rocking in the wheelchair:

'I think about them, about our soldiers, every day from morning until night. I pray for them. You know we were taken quickly: Berdiansk, Kherson. It was different in Mariupol. But for us it seems like all the most terrifying part lasted a week. But that depends on how you look at it. The human factor started later, when they went around to buildings searching for traitors, pulling them out, sitting them in a basement; some disappeared.

'When the shelling started, they chased everybody into basements. Other basements, see what I'm saying? You sit there, look at the people alongside you and wonder who's really for whom. And when will your friends from yesterday inform on you to the Russians for your views? Which of them will break first, who'll write a denunciation? Who'll put up a flag? Who'll betray their country for what benefits?

'I wasn't afraid. I'm a military daughter, military wife and military mother. Only now, *my* people are killing each other. But maybe not. Maybe they at least spared us in that part of hell.'

Silence sets in. Irma's hand finds a glass on the table. She lifts it and brings it to her lips. Attempts to take a drink. I want to tell her the glass is empty, there might only be a drop in the bottom. But I can't think of how to tell her about that. Irma lifts the glass to her lips, attempts to take a drink and realises there's no water.

Annoyed, she asks, 'Get me some water from the cooler in the living room, to the right of the entrance. I'm going to need to take a drink. My throat gets dry all the time.'

I get some water. Come back. She's calmer now. She says, 'I was born three years before perestroika in Tashkent, where my father served in the military. I was born during the last happy years of my family's life when my father was a young colonel and he and my mother dreamed of moving to Moscow. But we moved to Kherson. And lived there until 1991. The Soviet Union collapsed along with our life. My father was transferred to Liski, near Voronezh, and he and my mother received Russian citizenship. They'd been Soviets, then they became Russians, there you go.

'My mother's from Poltava, my father's from Kharkiv. Now they're those people from Russia who fight fascists. What do they do to you there, can you clue me in?

'When I was 15, my father's service buddy and his son came from Kherson to visit. They came to have a look at Moscow. That was Venya. Venya was supposed to go to Kyiv the next year, to the Suvorov [Military] School that's now named after Ivan Bohun.

'The evening before they left, Venya told me, "Don't look at anyone, you'll be my wife." I'm a military daughter so I obeyed. Lord, the way I went to visit him, that was quite a time, such love.

'I remember each day, each of our dates and I'll never forget.'

Irma suddenly stops. She hadn't been planning to tell me that. She rubs the scar. Takes her hand from her forehead, knocks her fingernails on the table. And finally says, 'What were you asking about? What interests you in particular?'

But I hadn't really asked her about anything yet. And I don't know how to ask her about where her son and husband are now, if she's in touch with them, if they know about her, what they say and when they last spoke. Instead of that, for some reason I ask her, 'So did you become a violinist?'

She shrugs.

'I moved to Venya's with a violin under my arm. I went to school in Kyiv. We got married. Somehow everything was complicated after Fedya was born. Motherhood was difficult for me: I had no milk and Fedya was sickly. And we went to Kherson to my mother-in-law's. When I was sitting in the basement, I kept attempting to recall why we hadn't moved to Crimea. All the doctors said it would be better in Crimea. But we went to Kherson.

'At the time I thought that's how in every stretch of our life we make some kind of choice that determines our life. That's what I thought even before I ran after Mouse.

'After all, if we'd moved to Crimea, then of course we would have left immediately after the occupation. And then I would have gotten my way immediately – we would have gone to Kyiv. And there wouldn't have been any Kherson or any basement, Mouse wouldn't have run away. Well, and all the rest, too.

'But that did happen. It all turned out the way it turned out. We moved to Kherson in 2003. Fedya was three years old.

'Now I understand what a fortunate time that was. Have you ever been to Kherson? No. Well, it's too late. That Kherson's gone.

'We had a private house, it was Venya's parents'. I remember how all the relatives came for Fedya's birthday. We set out a big table, sang songs, hugged and kissed, and got drunk. My father said a toast about the Soviet Union collapsing but all of us are its children and it's this big motherland of ours, it's held together by people, by human . . .

'And that's all blather. They're bombing us on the 24th and he and my mother call and say, "You," they say, "you tell the troops when they come in that your father's a Russian officer, his whole chest's covered in medals, they won't touch you." That's beyond me. Help me light this, please.'

She lights it and continues. 'We didn't manage to leave. The person who promised to take us away, along with Grandma and Grandpa – that's Venya's parents – ended up being an informer, a collaborator. There's a lot of them now. There were others, too. But we didn't make it.

'Our neighbour, a medic, brought people out to unoccupied land during the night, taking the risk every second of running across your soldiers. But I know for sure he took about 50 people. I don't know what happened to them. It's hard in my position to keep in touch now. I need to accept that, too. But I don't want to. I don't want to even think about the fact that I'm blind now. And that this is my life, for ever.'

I ask her for a cigarette. We smoke together by the open window. Irma either asks or confirms: 'They say the outdoors is beautiful here.'

'The usual,' I say, 'but the elm in front of your window really is beautiful.'

She says:

'Mouse and I didn't want to go to the basement at all. A military man came, started yelling to everybody to go downstairs, everybody had to leave their apartments, air alert. I stuffed her into a bag, I was hurrying and couldn't find her carrier. I think that's what predetermined everything.

'When I told Venya about that, he told me not to even think about coming up with any of my theories. That's what he said: my theories.

'But what are my theories? I'm just attempting to understand what I did wrong. Don't we all think about what we did wrong, what made us come to the places we came to?

'I basically thought my son would work in IT but he's at the front, he rushed off to help his father. And . . . And how can I hold him back? I didn't want to anyway.

'See, ever since 2014, from the point your soldiers started killing us, it became obvious that this is a fight to the death, that nothing will be left of our dealings but pain. Nothing but pain and hatred.

'We tried to the very end to somehow not be part of it. But one of Venya's classmates died. And Fedya's volleyball teammate, too. He was called up and died in the first month, he was 19.

'Our country's small so all our dead, all our wounded, are visible, in full view. You can't hide them. We've been swimming in our children's blood these eight years that your propagandists are now telling us about.

'I grew up and was raised in Russian, we always spoke Russian, but now I hate the language, it's the language of war. And don't tell me about Pushkin. Maybe later, in hundreds of years, we'll recall your Pushkin. For now we're burying children, we're burying our cities and our life.

'Venya calls me every three days, his commander somehow arranges a videoconference. A woman from downstairs comes and holds the camera. And so? I'll never see him again.

'They called me from the command, they said our son Fedya was wounded. And Venya confirmed that, too, said it's nothing awful, shoulder, shards went through. The radial nerve was slightly hit but it'll recover. And Venya said he saw him, that everything is truly fine.

'The way he said that, I didn't believe him. I started yelling, asking for Fedya to call. He called two days later. Also by video. "Ma, it's me," he says. And I'm going crazy, it seems like it's not his voice. I asked him where we'd travelled the time he started drowning and a random herder saved him. I asked which shoulder blade has a mole. I asked who Papa and I were "in the story I told you every night".'

Irma's not crying but it's as if she's howling: she's inhaling with a harsh, raspy sound but it's hard for her to exhale. I touch her shoulder. She shakes my hand off.

She says, 'They said he'll get better and they'll let him come visit me. I told them I need to touch him, I need to smell him and only then will I believe it's him. But I said that even as I'm wondering. And what if I'm wrong, if I don't recognise him? If they bring me another one. If they tell that one, the other one, everything about Fedya, teach him something of ours, and make him do those tricks, like a dog. How will I understand that nothing's right, that it's not my son?'

That fear seems absurd to me. I pat her arm. I say what will destroy her trust in me. But I do so unwittingly.

I say, 'What do you mean, you're his mother. You'll recognise him. You'd recognise your own out of a thousand and one.'

'What do you understand about this? Have you ever had a son and a husband at war?'

I have not. I shake my head; she doesn't see that.

'Do you see that there are only three of us now: Fedya, Venya and I? We have nobody. We don't have our home, the bed where we slept, we don't have our grandma and grandpa, who're old and were forced to grovel for new masters. Have you heard the word "occupation"? Have you even heard anything about this war?

'I . . . I . . . I don't know why I let you come.'

Her hand fumbles around the table, she finds the glass and she drinks.

As she drinks, I look at her and realise everything between us is lost. And that's not because I touched her arm.

Irma speaks without exclamation points. She doesn't see me and she speaks not to my face but to a spot of sun on the table a little beyond me. But I shudder at every word. And she doesn't see. She simply speaks and I listen. Then I can't listen. I cover my face with my hands. I hold my breath. I know I can't cry because what will she do if I cry? So I don't cry. But Irma doesn't see that either. She says, 'You know what. You can kiss my ass with your pity, with that empathy of yours, with your questions.

'You can kiss my ass along with your attempts to understand us.

'Kiss my ass.

'You and your country, kiss my ass.

'May you all croak.'

I turn my back to her, to leave. She doesn't see that but she probably feels it. And she continues speaking to my back.

'*I'm telling you that in the name of the Ukrainian people, kiss my ass.*

'*Get out of here right now.*

'*Don't shut the door, let it air out.*'

I leave the door to the entryway open, too.

I walk down the street for as long as I can. Late autumn's wind and rain are irksome. People are bundled up in their raincoats, running for cover. After reaching the centre of Leipzig, I walk back. Evening is falling. I find her third-floor window and look at it. As long as I have strength, until I'm frozen to the bone. Only then do I leave.

I know she didn't see that I came back.

I can't explain why I did that. All explanations are worthless.

Exactly a month after Irma and I met, Kherson again became Ukrainian. I didn't dare call Irma to tell her about that.

I'm sure she found out without me anyway.

# 12

# Eight Hours

Tamara's tall and stately, and her skin is the type where her cheeks are rosy in any weather and any light. She's wearing a light blue sweater and a leather jacket. Her long, light-brown hair is down.

I'm waiting at Moscow's Novoyasenevskaya bus station for her bus from Luhansk. That's how we're finally meeting, though we've known each other for about five years now.

Tamara gives me a box of 'Evening Donetsk' chocolate. I drop it on the ground in surprise: I didn't think the chocolate factory in Donetsk was operating since it never occurred to me that you could manufacture chocolate where there's bombing. Tamara picks up the box. Gives it to me. Curious, she looks around. 'Is this Moscow already?'

'Yes,' I tell her, 'but it's not the very centre.'

We go down into the Metro. There's news – city and national – on screens in the subway cars. The crawl at the bottom tells of the war, there are statistics, Ministry of Defence reports and exchange rates for the dollar and the euro. But people aren't following that, they're looking more at their smartphone screens.

The announcer's voice calls on passengers to be 'polite to one another, offer seats to the elderly, the disabled and passengers with children'.

The train sets off.

'This is the life,' says Tamara. She says something else that I don't hear because of the subway noise. She waves it off, for later.

We come out of the subway and walk up to the oncology clinic.

Tamara asks, 'Will we definitely have enough time?'

'I promise,' I answer.

★

We have very little time: eight hours. And during that time we need to get to a consultation with an oncologist who'll take a biopsy from Tamara's breast, look at her paperwork and decide how to handle the malignant tumour. Put in simple terms, we need to figure out if Tamara's cancer can be treated in Luhansk, under wartime conditions. Tamara, however, isn't considering other options. I'm the one who insisted on her visit. She hadn't been planning to come to Moscow.

On the medical side, we have to do everything through connections because Tamara doesn't have a Russian passport. Only Ukrainian and LPR, and she won't receive treatment in Moscow with those documents.

We've set aside two 'medical' hours. Then I've promised to show Moscow to Tamara. She'd requested, 'Show me so there's something to remember later. I doubt I'll come here again.' According to our plan, after the assessment, a walk and buying gifts at a shopping centre, Tamara will get on a shuttle that will take her back to Luhansk. A ticket costs 2,699 roubles [about £25].

'You just pay,' Tamara says, as we're walking away from the subway, 'and there's no war! It's all so fucking badass. And people are all so satisfied, so fed and clean. You've got the life here, it's like we're fighting there and you have nothing to do with it. You Russians really do totally fucking amaze me.'

It's 1,000 kilometres from Luhansk to Moscow. When Tamara and I talk on the phone there's often audible sounds of explosions and sometimes the connection cuts out. Sometimes Tamara herself drops out, too, then returns and writes that she had to sit for a few days in a basement that the local authorities call a bomb shelter. Or maybe an incoming hit a transmission tower and it took a long time to restore. Or she doesn't explain anything, she just writes, 'Hi, I'm alive.'

In Moscow – this surprises Tamara a lot – there's not much that alludes to the war beyond occasional banners on buildings with images of striped St George's ribbons shaped as the letters Z and V, photos of soldiers on billboards fitted out with QR codes that lead to error pages, plus words written on private cars driven by patriotic-ally inclined city dwellers.

'The way you live, holy fucking shit.' Tamara's unendingly surprised. 'So has it been like this all these eight years?'

'Yes.'

'Fucking wow. It's like, damn, I came to the moon. Let me have a smoke.'

She smokes and I ask, 'So who did you end up leaving the kids with?'

'My sister. I said to sit in the basement and keep out of trouble. I'm more afraid than anything that *the* incoming will happen when I'm not right there. You get me?'

I nod.

Tamara goes on: 'It's not scary when you're together. But people suffer a lot later if you're apart. You won't understand that, just believe it.'

She puts out the cigarette on the sole of her shoe. We're approaching the clinic. I ask, 'How are you feeling?'

'I'm fine, don't piss your pants,' she says, 'we'll make it.'

And she winks.

Right then I tell her I'd like to set aside some time to record a conversation, too, during these eight hours we have. Tamara makes a face.

'Well, damn, you are pushy. What, so we won't walk around your malls? We'll talk about my fate? Fine. Just change my name. People at home will recognise me.'

We go inside the clinic. There's a coat check, shoe covers, registration.

Tamara wilts noticeably.

They take the biopsy material from her breast behind closed doors. I sit in the hallway and listen to the noises in the office: metal objects clanging; Tamara, the nurse and the doctor talking. I can't make out a single word but I can hear Tamara laughing.

I recall how she and I started corresponding over social media, on VKontakte, five years ago: I was planning to make a documentary film about the 'line of contact', which is what, first in military jargon, and then more broadly, people have called the theoretical border between Ukraine and the self-proclaimed LPR and DPR that has been controlled by the Russian military since 2014. At the time, I wanted to make a documentary film about people who live in the populated and constantly shelled areas adjacent to the 'line of contact'.

A journalist I know suggested Tamara to me and put us in touch. With daily shelling in the background, this mother of two children, who's a native of the village Triokhizbenka in the Shchastia region of the Luhansk Oblast, earned money using her webcam, showing intimate parts of her body or having virtual sex with foreign clients for money sent via PayPal. ('Shchastia' means 'Happiness' and it will later become clear how horribly incongruous that name is.)

'No, I don't accept your people or ours, what the hell do I need them for? Wankers. Only foreigners! The Yanks are my kind of people. They pay, they do the work and then they wish you a good day, no perversion at all,' Tamara told me over the phone during the summer of 2020.

I was planning at the time to go to the Luhansk area with a film crew; Tamara was going to finish using the webcam and get a job as a sales clerk at a mall.

'Everything seems to be calming down here, thank God. So that means there's no more *force majeure* and it's time for me to get on an honest track, otherwise my blessed husband will come back before I know it and I'll be here turning my pussy for the camera,' says Tamara.

Tamara's husband went off as an LPR self-defence volunteer in autumn of 2014 after his younger brother, a 14-year-old, was severely injured by shards from Ukrainian mortar shelling and went into a coma.

'Well, he said, that's it, this is fucked-up shit, it's the last straw, he won't let it go and he's heading off to defend us. I told him, "For fuck's sake, Roma, how are you going to defend us, who the hell knows where, in some brigade or other? Are they like you there, fools who left their homes and kids behind? We're right here: pink and warm. Sit at home, guard us here with a rifle so no son of a bitch shows up out of nowhere and grabs your woman by her ass or slaughters the kids." No, he went. There were lots of them then. They liked fighting. What, you get in plenty of shooting, drink vodka, too, no responsibility at all. While your old lady and the kids are running to the basements from the incoming. But of course you're a fighter! You're defending the motherland, my fucking word. Who is that motherland? Where is it? Somehow, I'm already confused,' Tamara told me in 2020.

During six years of military operations in Donbas, she saw her husband once, pretty much by chance when they ran into each other on the street in Luhansk, where Tamara and the children had evacuated during heavy fighting for Shchastia, where she then stayed in the hope of a better and calmer life.

Although, as Tamara told me, the real reason for the move was faster, higher-quality Internet that would enable Tamara to work uninterrupted in the webcam field. Tamara had always perceived that field as temporary, speaking happily and shamelessly about clients.

'Shelling's always at the wrong time. I had a client, an elderly guy, from Oregon, I think it was. And he's already, well, what can you say, peaking, almost coming, and I, I'm all pretty with my tits in my hands, stroking myself, panting. And then – out of fucking nowhere! – there's shelling. Crash, screams. He asks me, "What happen, baby? Does that mean your kid's there making a racket?" "It's nothing," I say, "no happen there. The neighbour's cabinet fucking fell. You go on, honey, go on, don't get distracted." Anyway, all kinds of things happened, there'll be something to remember when we're dying. If we live that long.'

The office door opens. Tamara walks out. Pale, despite her rosiness.
'Did it hurt?'
'You know, I've always thought whoever uses something improperly in life will get cancer in *that spot*,' Tamara says philosophically.
After the biopsy we go together to a doctor I know, to talk about Tamara's cancer. The doctor speaks to her for a long time about her options. He stresses that Tamara's young and if it's not possible to keep her breast, then she could get nice implants that would be even

better than a natural breast since Tamara has two children and her shape's a little . . .

Tamara interrupts: 'Can I do that at home?'

'To keep the breast or do a quality mastectomy, no.'

'That's not what I'm asking. Can I do the most necessary treatment, no frills, but so it's at home? *That organ* isn't a must for me, I need to go home. It's just she,' Tamara nods at me, 'said nobody there would give me full treatment, that it's only in Moscow.'

The doctor looks at Tamara, then at the papers, then at Tamara again, then he says he needs to step out for a bit.

He steps out.

'You basically said we'll just do CT [scan] and not all this,' Tamara hisses at me.

'Basically, CT doesn't treat cancer,' I say.

Tamara didn't tell me for a long time that she had cancer and she only asked for help when it turned out that all but one CT device in Luhansk had been damaged by shelling. And the queue for the only remaining device was more than three months. Tamara didn't have that much time. She'd called then and asked for help. And she later agreed to come.

The doctor returns. He says, 'The surgeon who will operate on you in Luhansk is one of the best specialists in his field, the father of one of our remarkable Moscow doctors. Forgive me, I didn't know. That's how all of it . . . hm . . . turns out to be interconnected. So the only thing that's unavailable now in Luhansk because of . . . because of . . . because of certain, I hope, temporary difficulties, is the CT, computerised tomography . . .'

'Because there was an incoming there. Fuck all's working,' Tamara says, helping the doctor.

'And so,' the doctor chimes in, 'we'll do a CT for you right now and you'll go home, you can be operated on there and—'

'I don't need the tits.'

'And if that's how things stand, I absolutely trust your specialists.'

We leave. We go to another clinic building.

They do Tamara's CT scan there.

A doctor walks over while I'm in the corridor waiting for her.

Confused, he says, 'Listen, I thought there was no oncology there at all, that it's a total zombie apocalypse.'

I'm silent.

The doctor says, 'I asked his son why he didn't leave, what, you didn't tell him to leave? And you know what he answered?'

'What?'

'That somebody had to stay there. Because somebody needs to treat them. It's strange we don't think about that, but it's not just wounds there, there's other things, too, everything happens there. It's just *there's also* wounds. It's probably like that.'

Tamara's satisfied as she comes out of the CT scan. They announced that she even slept a little during the procedure. The Moscow doctor looks at the result, calls somewhere again and speaks quietly with someone. They write down my address to send the biopsy result: they need that to confirm if Tamara's cancer can be successfully eliminated with a simple operation or if she'll need chemotherapy and radiation.

We leave the oncology centre.

She says, 'Shall we smoke?'

We smoke.

A wedding party drives past. A champagne cork shoots into the Moscow sky from the window of a black limousine. Monetochka's song 'I'll Survive' is playing. Young people are singing along, laughing.

Tamara's gaze follows the limousine. She says, 'You and your acquaintances were surprised that guy stayed and is operating. Is it hard to understand or what, that people live everywhere? And they somehow adapt everywhere. And if they adapt, then there can be cancer. Or is cancer only where you live, like a bonus for a good life? But people like us, let them die from bullets? But we're alive, too. And we have kids, too, and they also get sick, by the way, with, for example, tonsillitis. Fancy that?'

We get on the subway again and she scrutinises the passengers again, curious, but now there's a certain defiance, too. We ride to Red Square and walk around. We go to a shopping centre and get ice cream.

She slowly pokes the ice cream with her spoon, hardly eats and then tosses the spoon aside, with a clink, then she hits the table with the edge of her hand and says, 'Fuck it, I can't.'

She glances around at the people in the café, looks at me and tugs at a napkin on the table.

She repeats, 'Katya, I can't. I can't, fuck it, understand how everything worked out this way. They told us, Here you go, you're living so miserably because your Ukraine doesn't need you, come join us, we'll protect you, we won't let anybody hurt you. They told us Russia's so strong, so big, so rich, but Ukraine's going to crumble any day now because all its rulers are idiots, Jews and addicts who hate their people. But how did things turn out, Katya? Can you just explain to me how it turned out? We believed you but you didn't need all that after all? You were just bullshitting us? You're living here, just like before, but we don't have a damn thing left? And some people aren't alive now. Those people, what did they die for? For the Russian World? For an idea? For what fucking idea? For the ideas of your Putin, for his grandeur? Fuck off with your ideas, fuck off with your Putin. You're just ruining everything. Why did you come to us anyway, why did you open your mouths at all if this war has nothing at all to do with you? Your children go to school and even eat cheese pancakes while ours sit in basements. Do you know what they learn? They learn how to tie off a wounded person's detached leg with a tourniquet so they don't die of blood loss. But you have primers here, right? Educational systems? You study English, don't you? What kind of Russian World is it when you sacrifice some people so others have only the best and keep getting richer? That's all, fuck it, let's go, I can't take more. I feel sick to my stomach. Where's that train station?'

We rode silently to the station. Tamara was no longer examining either the passengers or the subway, and she wasn't asking about anything.

Before the shuttle leaves, I ask her, 'Tamara, you can go in any direction from here, to Ukraine if you want, to Europe if you want, there's no problem with that either. You can even come to Russia. You do speak Russian. Please, do it, Tamara, you have children. They can't grow up under shelling.'

She's silent. She's twisting the tab on the zipper of her leather jacket. Her fingers are long and pink, her nails are polished in cherry varnish. She's running the zipper tab up and down. Up and down. Up. And down. And she says:

'When they evacuated us the first time, they took us away on buses. It was crowded, everybody was sitting side by side, lying. Some were in the aisle. One family – I don't know where they were from, I only saw them during evacuation – had a corpse riding in the baggage compartment. They'd been planning to evacuate together but the man, that woman's husband, was killed. And they brought him with them anyway, it's just now he was in a bag. The driver was such a good guy, he agreed to put it there. But someone's things could have fit there!

'They rode and the mother cried the whole time, the children either cried or asked these questions so you burst into tears if you want to or not: "When will Papa get up? Is Papa going to come with us? Where are we going? Will Papa be there with us?"

'Basically, rough.

'They had the grandmother and grandfather with them, too, it was like the grandmother was already out of her mind, she sang the whole time. Singing, just singing some songs. Kind of folk songs. And one of them – or maybe it just seemed that way to me – was the song my grandmother sang to me at bedtime. About cats that sleep, do you know that one?

*Tired cats are sleeping,*
*Uncles sleep and so do aunts,*
*Everybody all around*
*Has to sleep, very sound,*
*But not while on the job.*

'When I was a kid and listened to that song, I always imagined aunties and uncles who slept at work. That really amused me. I'd fall asleep with a smile. And so she started singing that song (or was I just imagining it?) and I fell asleep. That was a first during this whole time, I fell asleep so calmly, quietly. Even though I was lying on bags in the aisle of a bus. And so I dream that everybody in the city's asleep. They'd either died or were sleeping but nobody can be woken up. There's this piercing quiet: cars are standing still and birds are sleeping on branches. And people are frozen in the poses they were in: standing, sitting, on a pedestrian crossing, in a store. And only I'm alive. I walk up to them, touch them, but nothing. Everything's still. I look up and see what looks like a hole in the sky, you know, it draws apart, and I can see the nose of a missile there. It's suspended too, frozen, fallen asleep, I don't know how to say it. But I understand that as long as everybody's sleeping, that missile will be in limbo too, it won't fall. But as soon as the world wakes up, it will also start to fall. And so I have this choice in my dream. Either I wake everybody up and the missile falls. Or everybody sleeps and I live alone, with that death sticking out of the sky.

'The bus braked suddenly and I woke up. For some reason I sometimes recall that dream and can't decide if I did the right thing. What would you have done?'

Tamara's looking me right in the eyes. I'm lost. I answer, 'I don't know, Tamara. I don't have an answer.'

She slaps me on the shoulder. 'Who gets which fate, girlfriend. That's my answer. Just now, I had a look here in your Moscow and realised that some people's life is a mother, but for others it's a step-mother. We didn't choose. It just worked out that way. Well, fine, bye.'

Tamara hasn't written to me again and I haven't called.

I found out from the Luhansk surgeon, the father of the colleague of the doctor I know, that Tamara's operation went well but she did refuse the mastectomy.

# 13

# The Bottle

The name of the Czech theatre *Husa na provázku* translates to 'Goose on a String'. The theatre is in Brno and it's always in the thick of things: controversial shows, high-profile performances and scandalous projects.

True, I hadn't known anything about any of that before visiting Brno.

I came to Brno to meet with Larisa.

But Larisa was stuck in Kharkiv. Russian missile strikes had overwhelmed the city, the infrastructure was knocked out and residential and non-residential buildings had no electricity. It was dark and cold in Kharkiv. Larisa was with her mother in one of those dark, cold Kharkiv apartments.

But I'm waiting for her in Brno.

I walk back and forth in front of the lighted façade at the Goose on a String Theatre and marvel at its funny name.

Larisa sends me a message proposing we have a videocall towards midnight, when the load on the electrical grid will drop and the Internet will be a little better, too. She sends me the address of the apartment in Brno where we could have met in the evening . . . but won't.

I can walk to her building and have a look at it from the outside.

'Imagine everything inside for yourself, you're a creative person, you have an imagination,' writes Larisa.

I'm grateful to her for the trust. I'll definitely go and have a look. But later.

For now, I'm looking at the showbill for the Goose on a String Theatre, in the hope of finding something there to help me pass the time. I stumble across a reference to debates concerning the war in Ukraine 'with the participation of opposition cultural and public figures from Russia and Belarus'. That's what was written; I translated with Google Translate.

It also said – I translated this, too – that Czech moderators would lead the debates.

I went. The auditorium was full. Sitting on the stage on the Belarusian side were Andrey Stryzhak, head of the Belarusian Solidarity Foundation (BYSOL); poet Andrei Khadanovich; and journalist Iryna Khalip, who did time in a Belarus prison for taking part in demonstrations against the President of Belarus, Lukashenka.

From Russia were writer Anna Starobinets, IT manager Lev Gershenzon and political scientist Alexander Morozov. Representatives of Ukraine hadn't been invited on stage, apparently so proximity to representatives of the aggressor countries wouldn't cause annoyance. It worked out that six citizens of Russia and Belarus, as well as moderators, were sitting on stage, while Ukrainians and others sat in the hall and could ask questions.

The answers were interpreted for the audience. At times the hall hummed like a sea or forest.

No, nobody shouted. But passions ran high. Representatives of the aggressor countries were asked if they could look Ukrainians in the eye. Several said they could, though some said no. But then everyone chimed in and said they help Ukrainian refugees a lot. Try to help.

Then people from the audience asked if they understood that they're to blame, along with Putin, for Russia attacking Ukraine. Everybody responded differently. They referred to philosopher Karl Jaspers and discussed collective guilt and attitudes towards it.

It seemed strange to me that the writer, poet, IT guy and the political prisoner-journalist turned out to be the people who had to answer for Russia and Belarus. But the audience thought otherwise. They asked and asked.

It turned out that I personally knew half those sitting on the stage – they'd fled their countries. Some fled several years before the war started, some left in February 2022. Not one person sitting on stage at the Goose on a String Theatre ever had anything to do with either the political or economic governance of their countries yet they were on that stage as representatives of Russia and Belarus, meaning as accomplices to war. People asked them questions:

'*But doesn't it seem to you that the best outcome for Russia is to break up?*'

'*Do you actually wish for the defeat of the Russian army and victory for the Ukrainian army?*'

'*What do you have in mind when you talk about Ukrainian victory?*'

'*How do you speak Russian in countries that openly came out against Russian aggression in Ukraine?*'

'*Why are Ukrainian refugees being kept in Russia?*'

'*Why is the opposition silent, why are people not protesting?*'

'*What happened to the children who were unlawfully taken to Russian territories?*'

'*. . . Why . . .*'

'*. . . What . . .*'

'*. . . Why do you . . .*'

'*. . . Where do you . . . How?*'

'*. . . Is it your army? You say your?*'

'*. . . Aren't you ashamed?*'

*Aggression*

*Putin*

*You – that's Putin, Putin, Putin*

*Russian is the language of war*

*Smells of blood*

*Of blood*

*Russia smells of blood*

*You smell of blood*

*Why are you speaking Russian?*

*How can you look Ukrainians in the eye?*

*How do you regard?*

*How?*

*You? You! You! . . .*

I'm not feeling well. I leave the hall. It's clammy outside. During the time I was inside, someone used a black marker to write 'Glory to

Ukraine' on the event poster. There's a smell of mulled wine and something that's imperceptibly (inexorably?) Christmassy.

I walk down the street. I'm trying not to look at people. At some point, it occurs to me that if I look up, they'll recognise that I'm Russian and . . . And what? They'll chase me out of Brno? Put me on a plane and send me to Russia? Or the opposite: not let me on a plane. They'll put me on the stage of the Goose on a String Theatre and start asking me how I can still think in Russian? Enquire if I sense the smell of blood coming from myself? Do I understand that I'm an accomplice to Putin's war and I'll never rid myself of that label?

Larisa messages. She's ready to talk.

We call each other.

She's sitting with a phone in her hands. Light from the screen illuminates her face. She's wearing a sweater and a jacket.

'How are you?' I ask.

'Cold. It was scary when they bombed. Now it's just cold.'

Then she says, 'I'm tired.'

And then this: 'I keep ending up in extreme climatic traps because of Russians: in the summer I was dying from the heat, but now it's from the cold.'

How about that, I'm thinking, she thought up 'climatic traps'.

Then Larisa says, 'It's even funny.'

But she's not laughing.

I ask, 'Why did you go to Kharkiv? Wasn't everything good for you in Brno?'

'I needed to wrap up this one situation with my mother-in-law. In any case, everything that happened to me had to do with her,' says Larisa.

She adds, 'I wanted what was best.'

I ask, 'Has it been worked out now?'

'It's been worked out now. She's already in Kharkiv, in the hospital. Only now they're bombing and it's cold at the hospital. It's us, the healthy ones, who understand what needs to happen. But she's disabled. She's . . . How can I explain it to you . . . She lives in her own world. She's like a child, a big child, she doesn't control herself, doesn't sense things. Because of her illness, it's like she's always in a duskiness she can't get out of. And imagine you're wandering around in your own subconscious, living by groping around while there's explosions thundering outside, something's always happening, they grab you and move you from place to place. And now there's the cold, too. I'm afraid for her. We don't understand how she perceives what. Or what scares her more and what scares her less. Not much is known about people like her, about what actually happens to them. We can only guess.

'She was already feeling poorly when Kolya and I married but she still recognised people: she recognised him and sometimes me. But less and less later. It's so awful to observe: it's like forces are dragging the person off into another dimension. You want to hold them back, you attempt to hold on to their hand. But nothing works. Basically, Kolya's mother wound up in the hospital because it got dangerous for her to live on her own. We were visiting her twice a week. She no longer recognised anybody.

'I visited her after Kolya went into the army. And I've always considered her my responsibility as long as Kolya's serving. We've known each other for a long time. Kolya and I have known each other since I was 15. He's three years older. His mother was always good to me. She was always rooting for us . . .'

The connection breaks off.

I call but Larisa's unavailable. I call again; unavailable.

I open the news. Russia's shelling Ukraine again. There are air alerts in all oblasts. Including Kharkiv.

But it's warm at the hotel where I'm sitting in Brno. On the other side of the wall, a woman and a man are arguing in French. I can't figure out the words but I can tell from the intonation that they're arguing. He just answered her with something short and mean. And left, slamming the door.

Larisa calls back. 'It was Kolya calling, my husband! His call interrupted ours.'

'How is he?'

'Fine. Just really tired.'

'How long since you last saw him?'

'It works out to half a year. I came to Dnipro in the summer, from Czechia. They gave him time off. It was just the two of us for about a week. It was hard.

'It's like each of us turns out to have another life behind us. Meaning it's like this person is dear to you but he's already ten years older than the person he was.

'I scrutinised him the whole time, wanting to grasp what had changed in him. But I never did. He's just a different person. But I'm waiting for the war to end, I want to talk with him about how we'll live. Basically about everything.

'And I want to ask his forgiveness. For real this time.'

'For what?'

'For weakness. I could have behaved better when everything happened. But I couldn't.

'I thought I was strong, I'd cope, but everything happened totally unexpectedly. And I turned out to be weaker than I thought I was.'

Larisa's breathing rapidly. She asks to take a break. She places the telephone with the camera side down and I can't see or hear what she's doing. She comes back to me four and a half minutes later and says, 'I'm ready. Just don't interrupt me. I'll tell you everything but you ask later.' I nod.

She says:

'Kolya went off to serve in 2020. He went as a contractor. That was voluntary, deliberate. He and I discussed it together. They sent him to serve on the border with the DPR, where everything was more or less calm. I had no cause for anxiety.

'But then the war started.

'And it started a little earlier for me than for others because he sent me this text on 19 February . . . Well, he was basically saying goodbye. He'd apparently had a very rough night. I don't want to read it now, a lot of it's personal, my nerves wouldn't take it, there's no need. But the point there was for me to take care of myself and his mother. And to move away if I could.

'Of course I was shaken. And there was no communication with

Kolya. He showed up later and said everything was apparently fine, the threat was gone. And then everything started full-scale on 24 February: explosions, tanks in Kharkiv and panic. Kolya wasn't in contact and I didn't know what the right thing was to do. For two weeks we went around to basements and bomb shelters. Sometimes the shelling would catch us at home and his mother and I would lie between two walls, embracing and praying. You know, don't you, how to find two walls?*

'Whenever I go into any building now, I immediately look for two walls, it's automatic. I feel uncomfortable if I don't find them.

'But it seemed like I was starting to lose my mind under all the shelling. It was scary all the time, you're always waiting for incoming, you feel all the time like you can't protect either yourself or weaker people. My stepfather went into the Territorial Defence Forces, my mother and I got really blue, the both of us. And I then said, "Ma, let's go." We were lucky. We met a good volunteer at the border. He brought us to Brno. We found housing quickly and everything somehow started falling into place.

'But Kolya's mother was left in Kharkiv. And I decided to get her out as soon as I could catch my breath. See, the psychiatric clinic where she was had fallen under the occupation. There was no communication with them at all, I couldn't even figure out if she was alive or not. I now understand that was my big mistake. But I decided to go there myself and try to get her. Both Kolya and my mother told me not to sneak in but to wait until our side beats the occupiers. But I couldn't do that. Sure, I may not be the smartest person but what happened – happened. I'm going to send you a video now so you understand everything. It'll take a long time to load.'

She does send a video, there's around 20 minutes in it. A white line runs around the circumference of a dark blue circle as the video loads.

---

* What's often called the 'rule of two walls' says that, under bombing, the safest places inside a building are located at least two (windowless) walls away from the outside of the building. [translator]

Larisa says, 'At first I searched for volunteers but nobody agreed
to sneak in under the Russians and take somebody to Ukraine. Volunteers from the Ukrainian side didn't work with the occupied
territories at all and from the Russian side, well, you yourself understand who's a volunteer there and who's—'

The connection cuts off. There's more news about shelling.

The video has loaded.

I open it. It's a recorded videocall.

*Two men in camouflage and balaclavas are standing next to Larisa. The
top she's wearing is torn and Larisa herself is dishevelled and looks very
scared. One of the men says to the camera:*

*'She won't get out of here, this is it for her. But if you'll collaborate with
us, everything will be good for you, there'll be money and you'll have a
woman and you'll have it all. But if you won't collaborate with us, consider
yourself doing her in. We'll send her to the front, to the guys, she'll help
them, clean up, wash, and help the guys who've been sitting a few months
without women. Tell me where you are, where your division is, what you're
serving as, who you're with.'*

*Kolya answers that he's serving his motherland, Ukraine, he's at the
front.*

*Somebody in a balaclava goes into a rage from the lack of specifics in the
answers; he hits Larisa in the face. And now she's yelling into the camera,
'Talk, asshole, fuck!'*

*'Talk,' the person in the balaclava calmly repeats, 'if you want her to
stay in one piece.'*

*Larisa's crying. All the videocall participants are silent for a while. The
sense arises that the call 'froze'.*

*'You hear me?' the person in the balaclava asks Kolya.*

*'I hear you,' answers Kolya.*

*'Enough . . .' Larisa's shouting unintelligibly. 'Just talk!'*

*'How much money do you want, maybe, how much money do you want
to let her go?' Kolya's nervous, attempting to convince the kidnappers. 'I've
got two, three, I'll drop it for you over Trust Wallet! She's going to get my
mother.'*

*'Enough already! Talk!!!' Larisa shouts.*

*The men in balaclavas nod approvingly and egg Kolya on, 'Go on, talk, don't you hear?'*

*Kolya shouts over their voices, he's addressing her, shouting, 'I've got nothing to tell them! What am I going to tell them? That I'm a soldier? What am I going to I tell them? I don't know what they want!'*

*The military men in balaclavas ask another dose of clarifying questions:*

*'What division?'*

*'What responsibilities?'*

*'Who is the counterintelligence agent?'*

*'Who's monitoring the troops?'*

*Kolya doesn't understand about either monitors or agents. One fighter in a balaclava continues hitting Larisa; the other attempts to continue questioning but by now nobody hears anybody.*

*'Your rank, full name, your rank.'*

*A shout.*

*'I'm a soldier in weapons operations.'*

*'Hold on, I can't hear you. Don't yell, bitch, shit.' The man turns to Larisa and squashes her face. 'Don't yell. I'll strangle you, shit. Now, repeat.'*

*Kolya's responses don't please the person in the balaclava, who threatens to cut off Larisa's tongue. She's shouting, it's heart-rending, and Kolya loses his temper for the first time, then attempts to speak calmly.*

*'You're a sadist, am I understanding that right?' he asks the person in the balaclava.*

*'I'm re-establishing Soviet power on fascist-Nazi territory. I'm the biggest denazifier of nazi fuckfaces. You know how many people have gone through my hands and how many more will?'*

*'But you're trying for peace in the whole world. And freedom for people. So people live happily, like in the Soviet Union,' says Kolya.*

*'Yes, peace. Because you . . . Listen to me. Because you let a clown take power. A buffoon . . .'*

*'My wife's trying to rescue my disabled mother.'*

*'. . . and they made a war.'*

*'What do some kind of clowns have to do with it? She's just trying to rescue my disabled mother who's in a war zone!'*

*It suddenly gets quiet and for a moment it seems like the speakers are starting to understand each other. But Larisa's shout cuts through the quiet: 'That's enough! Now there's no place for your . . . !' She starts shouting unintelligibly. 'Just take me away! Don't be a dumbass!'*

*'Sweetie, I told you not to go. Because . . .'*

*'Listen, you're being asked specific, pointed questions,' the man in the balaclava says to Kolya.*

*'Do you understand that or what?' she shouts. 'Do something!'*

*She shouts again. The recording cuts out.*

I rewind the video back and forth. I stop it, attempting to examine the expressions in the eyes of the man wearing the balaclava, attempting to examine Larisa's wounds, attempting to believe that everything I've seen isn't a dream, a lie, a theatre performance. Larisa calls back. Missiles were hitting Kharkiv again. The connection had cut out.

Larisa asks, 'Did you watch?'

I say that I don't know how she endured it.

'I shouldn't have yelled at him, I shouldn't have let them get to me, I should have been strong, see?' she says.

I don't see. I ask how she even ended up in that room with those people.

Larisa says:

'I decided to go get Kolya's mother myself. Her psychiatric facility's in Strilecha, that's a village right on the border with Russia. It turned out you can't get there from Ukraine, there's military everywhere. So I decided to go through Russia. I entered Poland from Czechia on 16 August, then on to Belarus and from there to Russia.

'They took my phone away at the border, in Bryansk. They rooted around in it for a long time and then brought it and showed me photos I'd deleted before the trip, they're of Kolya during our vacation, sometimes he's in his uniform, sometimes not.

'"Yours?" they asked.

'"Mine," I answered.

'There was no point in denying it. I explained in detail that I'm going for my mother-in-law, like I said. They let me through. I didn't have any kind of premonitions or suspicions that something bad would happen to me.

'I went to Belgorod because that's where I found people over the Internet who were supposed to bring us to occupied territory in a microbus. We agreed to meet at the checkpoint in Belgorod. I stayed in an apartment until then and went to the checkpoint on the day the volunteers told me they were ready to leave. Four people in masks and military uniforms without identifying markings approached me at the checkpoint. They took me by the arms from both sides, one nudged at my back and they sat me in a car without saying a word, put a bag over my head and we drove off.

'I know this isn't important information but can I say something about the bag? It was very thick. And at first I thought I'd suffocate. I tried to lower my head so I could breathe out from under the bag but that didn't work. And so I swallowed air like a fish, I just couldn't get enough air.

'That was while we were driving. They beat me later. And when they beat me, they let me raise the bag so I could breathe. Nice guys.'

She's breathing as if the bag's on her head again. Then she calms. She continues.

'They didn't beat me with their hands. They beat me with a bottle. A plastic bottle of water, I'd never run into that before. But do you know what? Apparently a bottle with water doesn't leave marks. You can't find them on your body later. It turns out they're not superficial wounds but deep ones, internal.

'I couldn't look at a bottle of water for a long time after that. Everything inside me tightened up.

'But I'm over that now.

'Basically, they beat me and the one who didn't, he was smothering me a little the whole time, covering my mouth, covering my nose. He found a little camping knife in my makeup bag and kept drawing it along my throat. The other one constantly took out his pistol and poked it at my chest. We'll shoot you now, he'd say, and this whole story will basically end.

'At some point I really believed they'd shoot me. But they didn't shoot, they needed something from me, they asked about HIMARS the whole time, where they were, how many there were, all that. They didn't understand that my husband's just a contract service-man, not an officer at all, nothing specific.

'I told them. But they didn't believe me. And then they started calling my husband. They ripped my top before calling, tore my jeans to make an impression, the effect of intimidation.

'And I'm still ashamed, you know, that I didn't say to him, "Kolya, they can screw themselves, don't pay attention to them, I'm doing fine, you just keep calmly fighting."

'I'm ashamed, see, that I gave in to all that panic. And scared him.'

She wipes her eyes. I can't see tears in the dark. She says:

'After the call, it was like they'd already let off steam. Everything was now most likely automatic. But by now I basically didn't care. If they kill me, they kill me, if they don't, they don't. My stamina for fear was gone.

'Those guys in camouflage brought me to the Belgorod pre-trial detention facility then they put me on trial for a fabricated case that I was on drugs, then they put me in a local prison cell for ten days, solitary confinement. Nothing scarier than that has ever happened to me. It was scary for my husband and my mother because they'd started searching for me. They searched the whole border zone for five days. And they found me five days later, I won't say exactly how. They found me through Russian human-rights activists, people who're risking everything in the world by extracting people like me from what I won't call the great beyond, but they're the most desperate situations. They stand against the huge machine of the Russian military and security chiefs and sometimes win. It was like a movie in my case: a young woman comes, tells me she's a lawyer and says, "I have a letter for you from your uncle in Voronezh."

'I say, "What are you talking about, I don't have any uncle in Voronezh."

'And she says, "No, you do, you just don't remember."

'She held out a note from my mother, there were words from my husband jotted down. And it said there that I'll be greeted when I leave the cell after my term runs out, that I shouldn't worry.

'And that lawyer woman really did meet me and so did Roman Kiselyov, a Russian human-rights activist I'm indebted to for saving me. They helped me get out of Russia. That's basically all.'

She goes quiet for a short while. Then she says, 'To be more exact, that's not all. I haven't seen Kolya since then and you can't explain everything over the phone, you understand what I'm saying.'

I nod. The connection cuts off.

It's loud next door. My French neighbours are reconciling; there's moaning and the bed's shaking.

I go outside for air. I'm walking to the address where I was supposed to meet with Larisa. It's a building like any other, an ordinary four-storey building with wide windows. There are three dark windows on the second floor. I understand those are hers. I call her and show them.

'Yours?'

'Yes, they're ours. I don't understand how we'll go back now, when.'

'Why did you go to Kharkiv now?'

'I wanted to hug my mother-in-law. My heart ached. And when they were liberating the territories, they managed to evacuate the psychiatric hospital to Kharkiv. Sure there were losses, both among staff and patients. A few people. But that's inside information.'

'Are you planning to come back to Brno?'

'I don't know. My whole life's a mess now. My mother and I thought we were going to pack our things, our documents, and take anything valuable out of here for good. And the main thing was to tell my mother-in-law, face to face, that I'm leaving for ever. But I already went to see her twice: I hold her hands and still can't say it. And I feel guilty before Kolya. And if I'm here, there'll be a chance to see him sooner and there's a better chance to talk things through in person, see?'

'Will you show me the windows again?'

I turn the camera and go closer.

Larisa says, 'When I was there, when I'd read our news from there, it was like everything was in the fog, behind obscure glass: a three-year-old child died, leg ripped off, where was it? Who did it happen to? Not us . . . Life there went on, just like always, there's theatres, cafés, work. And that's probably the right thing, but I still just can't fall into that rhythm even though I've dreamed all my life about living in Europe. But probably not like that, not like that.

'They live their own life there but I just dream about that bottle at night, the one they used to keep beating me with. And I want to shout but I can't, I don't have the strength, there's no air in my lungs. And now I've come to Kharkiv. And it's like there's a nightmare around me, somebody dies from shelling every day, every day brings us suffering, but I'm at home, with my people, and Kolya's closer. And the bottle's going away, it's not in my dreams anymore. And I'm not afraid of it.

'I was even thinking of signing up for paramedic courses and going to the front. I'd probably be of more use there. And I could somehow explain to Kolya that I'm not the one who yelled at him out of fear, I'm someone else, I'm worthy. What do you think, what's the best way to proceed?'

## 14.

# Peppa Pig

Sasha was taught about hospitality at an early age. And so she greets us as one should. There's a tablecloth on the table, and on it are pastries, candies, a dish of mandarin oranges and three plates with various pretty sandwiches. We're journalists, a whole film crew. People usually greet us with something delicious. And Sasha wanted to do that, too.

But she didn't invite us to the table when she greeted us. She couldn't force herself to.

She speaks about that honestly, saying, 'I can't. It's somehow not what people do. You're killing us there but I'm drinking tea with you here.'

And then she looks down and says, 'Please forgive me.'

*Pause*

This wafts in from the next room:

*I'm Peppa Pig! This is my little brother George. This is Mummy Pig. And this is Daddy Pig. Oink!*

Anyone who has children flawlessly recognises those words. I have children and I do. It's *Peppa Pig*, the unending British series about a family of pigs who laugh, oink and never feel downhearted.

Sasha says, 'Katyusha watches Peppa all the time. She gets obsessed with her and calms down so much. She loved Peppa before the war, of course, but not like now. Now she clings to the tablet as if Peppa's everything. But there is something to that. Everything was good for Katyusha. We're a big, friendly family: Papa, Mama, Grandma, Grandpa, everything around her, everything was just for her. We jokingly promised to give birth to a little brother for her fifth birthday, to be her Georgie. Well, what kind of brother could there be now? Go ahead and ask questions quickly, she'll give us 20 minutes to talk, then come running. She's afraid a lot now, anything at all can scare her. Should I start telling you from the first day of the war?' Sasha gets down to business without pausing.

Sasha gets up and closes the door partway so her four-year-old daughter won't hear our conversation but so she can still see her. And go to help her if need be.

Sasha looks uncertain as she moves around the apartment, wringing her hands and shrugging her shoulders. It's noticeable that this is a stranger's apartment. I nod at the religious icon standing on the sideboard.

'Did you bring that with you?'

'What do you mean?' Sasha says, afraid. 'Everything's the landlady's. Katyusha and I were lucky with the apartment. The woman upstairs, the local woman, she's Polish, and her daughter's working in England or something, I didn't understand. And so she let us live here for now. Everything was a little neglected but I scrubbed, washed and ironed. But I'm trying to stay out of trouble by not touching much. Did you see their crystal in the cabinet over there? I told Katyusha, don't even go over there, heaven forbid. So go ahead and ask, what should I tell you about us?'

I ask Sasha about her line of work.

'*Shvachka*,' says Sasha.

That's a Ukrainian word. And I don't understand it. I ask, 'What?'

'Oh, well, a seamstress, yes. But I haven't worked in that profession since the war started. Our Katyusha was always very sick. I sat at home with her and later got a job at a daycare so I could be with her. We wanted her so much, we were very afraid of losing our Katyusha. She was weak from the very start. So I was always with her, always to hand. But my husband had already been telling me that when Katyusha goes into the young group, that's it, I'll leave the daycare and go to sew. I love sewing. I'd already found out about a shop so I knew where to go. I was planning on April.

'But what can I say about myself now? We've had a completely different life since February. You came to us and all our plans were ruined.'

The sound of Peppa Pig returns as Katyusha comes in with her tablet. She sits down at her mother's feet.

'Oh, Katyusha,' Sasha says, throwing up her hands, 'get up, there's a draught. Can she sit here? She won't bother you?'

I take a gift for Katyusha out of my bag. When I was arranging the interview with Sasha over the phone, I asked what her daughter likes. I have two boxes with Peppa Pig puzzles. Katyusha puts the tablet on the back of the sofa and starts putting together the puzzle without getting distracted from the cartoon for a second.

*'You can help with the shopping.'*
*'Oh, goody! Oink-oink.'*

'Oh, you brought so much,' Sasha says, suddenly upset. 'She already has a ton of toys here, how will we take all this?'

'Where?'

The question stumps her.

'Well, where will we go from here?'

Pause.

'Someday. What were you asking me?'

I hadn't asked anything.

On Katyusha's tablet, Daddy Pig has returned home from work tired. Mama, Peppa and George are waiting for him with a special supper. Daddy Pig sits down and everybody notices how fat his tummy is. Daddy's family roars with satisfied laughter. Oink-oink.

'Papa,' says Katyusha. 'Mama, Papa's there.'

'Papa, Papa,' says Sasha. 'Oh, how's our papa doing there? You know, after the war started, I kept him at home all the time. I went by myself, with just Katyusha, to the bomb shelter, the store and for water. I'd tell him, you stay at home, I need you, I love you, I'll look after you. I know you're not a coward, I say, there's no need to prove that to anyone. But I don't want to be a widow, I need a full-fledged family, I need to raise Katyusha, so stay at home for now, wait it out.

See, he hadn't served, hadn't gone to war, he doesn't have experience. And I looked after him. And now what?'

'What?'

'Nothing! He's there. We're here. But Ukraine doesn't have enough soldiers and his turn will come any day now. And he won't sit tight, he's proud. And he'll go, and he'll go . . . I'm afraid to think about it. You know, it always used to seem to me that things couldn't get worse since what could be worse than bombs flying at the city that's dearest to me? But it was worse when your tank turned down our street. Though yes, it spun and spun, then left. They chased it away.

'But then it got even worse when there was war all around and Katyusha started getting temperatures. My husband's sleeping in the hallway and Katyusha and I are sleeping in the bathroom, dressed, in a blanket. Katyusha's crying all the time, you know, so shrilly, like kids cry from pain, "Eeeeee! Eeeeee! Eeeeee!"

'And that was making me lose my mind. They're bombing outside and here's your child who doesn't feel good. What could be worse? But that happens, too. It turned out to be an ear infection. And I ran to the doctor with her during the bombing and then we went to pharmacies to gather up the antibiotics. But there was nothing, it was all for the wounded. But we found them, found them . . .'

*And so the noisy house has woken everyone up. That's Miss Rabbit in her rescue helicopter.*
*'Is everybody alright down there?'*
*'Yes, thank you.'*

'Katyusha,' says Sasha, 'turn that down a little, please, the nice lady and I can't hear each other. So what was I saying? They'd promised to bring us bread on 3 April. Of course I went. A huge queue had formed. I stood and stood for about 20 minutes and then I suddenly started feeling uneasy. I turned around and started walking towards home. I hear a whistling behind me and a sound as if a lot of people had suddenly gasped. I turn – the shell fell in my queue. There was bloody mush there. A few people were moving the stumps of limbs, it was awful, God forbid you see that. But I saw it. Everything inside me went cold, my head was spinning and I couldn't breathe. I thought about rushing over to help people but I didn't run – I ran in the other direction, home, because that's where Katyusha was. And another bomb fell while I was running but I didn't look back.'

'Do you understand who was bombing?'

'I understand, of course I understand.'

Pause.

She's looking at me in amazement and then she very slowly asks, 'Can I tell you everything, the way it is?'

'Yes, of course you can, Sasha, say it.'

'It was the Ruscists.'*

Pause.

'The Ruscists, well, the Russians, your people, understand? Do you hear me? Those were your bombs. They killed our people. And I don't know why, what did we do to you? Why are you like this to us? How did we bring that all upon ourselves? Our Kharkiv has always been a Russian-language city, I'm a Russian speaker but I know Kharkiv is Ukraine. And I speak Ukrainian if need be. I was born in what was still the Soviet Union, I don't remember it, I don't know what was good there and what was bad, but that time's gone and another has come. We lived quietly, we didn't want anything from you. What is there here? Why did you come?'

*'It's a wishing well. You throw a coin into it and make a wish.'*

'Here's a little coin,' Katyusha repeats after the voice coming from the tablet.

Sasha touches my arm and says, 'Please forgive me about the Ruscists, I just get emotional. You know, my husband and I were in Saint Petersburg, in Russia, before Katyusha was born. It's very beautiful there, we liked it. And we have relatives in Russia, yes,

* 'Ruscist' is a portmanteau word that combines 'Russian' and 'fascist'. [*translator*]

they're distant, we haven't talked with them in a long time, and there are acquaintances, normal people, pleasant ones we met on a tour and went with to a café. We thought we were being friendly with Russians but then what happened? You probably have acquaintances, too . . . well, from Ukraine. They never did anything to you. So why are you like this to us? I don't know what to think about all this, I don't understand what you need from us, I don't understand how to treat you. Basically . . . Forgive me . . .'

Sasha bites her lip. I understand how I need to answer. I take her by the hand and say, 'There's no reason to ask my forgiveness, it's all deserved. It's not you that bombed my country, my country's bombing yours. And I don't know the words I can use to ask your forgiveness.'

I seem to be crying. I never cry at interviews. But now I don't have the strength to hold back. The doorbell saves me. The Polish neighbour who gave Sasha the opportunity to live in the apartment is going to the store so came to find out if everything is okay and ask if Sasha needs anything.

They speak a blend of Ukrainian and Polish. The neighbour asks about our film crew. She asks, 'From Russia?'

'Yes,' nods Sasha.

The neighbour looks me in the eye and says to me, in English, *murderers*. And says to Sasha in Polish, *do widzenia*. She turns around and leaves. Sasha locks the door. And suddenly takes a very deep breath.

She says, 'What have you done? You've so ruined everything all around you for years to come, wrecked so many lives. But we won't have another life. And neither will you. You can no longer fix it, do you see that? It's for ever.'

'What's for ever?'

'The curse is for ever.'

Katyusha has put a puzzle together. She looks up from the tablet and says, 'And I go to Polish daycare now. They all give me presents. They give me Peppa Pig, too. Want me to show you?'

I do.

Katyusha heads off in search of the Pig. Sasha says, 'When we were crossing the border, she dropped her Pig in the fuss. There was so much shrieking. And our volunteers immediately called here so they'd find a Pig for her here. So all Przemyśl* knows Katyusha's a Peppa fan.'

Katyusha brings a large Peppa Pig and two smaller ones. One of them seems to be George.

I ask, 'Do your pigs speak Polish or Ukrainian?'

'They speak my language. And what language do I speak?' Katyusha asks Sasha.

Sasha and I exchange glances.

Peppa Pig's neighbours chatter in the background, in her porcine world. In my world, Sasha from Kharkiv tells me:

'I regret that I agreed to talk with you. There's too much of everything, too much that's painful. I talk but it doesn't get easier. But I started so now I'll finish telling my story. I started losing my mind from fear. It was very dangerous in the city. My husband and I decided we needed to leave. We packed our things and went to the train station with Katyusha. There were lots of people. It was hard to breathe on the platform. We jostled and jostled but, stupidly, didn't squeeze into the train. Everybody was going. With children, without children, men, women, with baby carriages, with dogs, I saw one woman with a goat. And someone had chickens shrieking in a crate. Everybody was trying to escape the city, I don't know where they were going. We didn't know either, we were jostling through like everybody, working with our elbows and wanting to squeeze onto that train. But we didn't. There was automatic-weapon fire on the platform, it was the men from the territorial defence attempting to disperse the crowd, they were shooting upwards when the train set off so people would back off and not grab on. But right after it set off, the city was bombed. And everybody was already running wherever they could. Those who'd sized things up went into the subway. It was very scary again. And I was no longer comparing if it was more or less scary. I'd turned into a wild animal, into some sort of cat. When there was booming, I just

---

* Przemyśl is a small city on the San River in southeastern Poland with a population of around 59,000. [translator]

covered Katyusha with myself. I now think I shouldn't have done that because she started being more scared of my fear.

'Anyway, another train left that evening. This time we worked more diligently with our elbows, pushing some away, wedging in somewhere . . . A person changes quickly in those conditions. We'd all become like wild animals, we'd started fighting for survival. Nobody was looking now at how polite or well raised you were. You saved yourself and your children. Just instincts. Nothing more.

'People were sitting everywhere in the train carriage: in the aisles, in the vestibule, on the floor. Some had two children, others four, or animals. You know what struck me? It was quiet. We rode for a long time but the children weren't crying, the dogs weren't barking. The children were mostly sleeping. And mums were crying. I looked at the faces around me and I started feeling awful inside, such an awful horror that gnaws somewhere in your stomach. I thought, how will we live after all this? Who will we, those of us who survive, come to be because of this war? This isn't forgotten, do you understand me? It can't be unseen.'

*'But gardens are for plants, not plastic,' says indignant Grandpa Pig. Oink-oink.*

Katyusha turns up the volume on the tablet. It's impossible to talk. Katyusha's waiting for us to pay attention to her. Sasha asks her to wait a few more minutes but Katyusha doesn't want to.

'I want to play. Will you tell her how we used to play with Papa? We went to the park with Papa. Did you tell her about the park? Will you play with me?'

'We will. But let's talk first, okay, Katyusha? The nice lady came here specially to see us.'

'Enough talking, enough, we need to play.'

Sasha convinces Katyusha to drink cocoa with waffle cookies. Katyusha sits down across from us. On her tablet, Peppa and her classmates are going to the theatre for a Christmas pageant. Katyusha's satisfied.

Sasha says, 'Our first train went to Dnipropetrovsk, did you know that city's called Dnipro?'

'My grandmother lived there.'

'She's Ukrainian?'

'She's Jewish.* But the little place she's originally from was in Ukraine.'

'Well, so my mother-in-law lives in Dnipro. So we got there at night and spent the night right at the train station. There were crowds there, too. Everybody was already beside themselves, everybody's tired, nobody had any strength. On the third try, my husband stuck us on a train to Lviv. And I immediately had two feelings: joy that Katyusha and I were being saved and horror that I might never see my husband again. He's now standing in front of my eyes, waving, crying and smiling. But Katyusha and I left and that's that. And I don't know how to live. Now I only live normally in my dreams, things are only good in my dreams. I see my husband in my dreams. I recently dreamed that we went to the sea. And you know, the sun was really shining. And the water shone. I've never been to the sea. We were planning to go when Katyusha's a little older. I'm so curious to see what it's like. And I want to show it to Katyusha. We'd started saving money. But then – the war. And now I dream, I dream of that sea. Sometimes it's calm. But recently, about three days before we arrived, I dreamed that the water's rising and rising, and I can't walk anymore, and I don't know how to swim. I look around but don't see the shore. I only know that Katyusha's waiting for me with Papa. I start to feel panicked, I shout, I'm attempting to swim, and I wake up. I wake up all wet, sweaty. Katyusha's sleeping next to me. And I started calling my husband; I didn't get through, I wanted to tell him the dream. You know, if you tell a dream right away, it won't come true if it's bad; it's good that you came, I told you.'

She loses her train of thought. She stops but continues a little later.

'You see, what I wanted to say is we're peaceable people, we have peaceable professions: I'm a seamstress, my husband's in

---

* 'Jewish' was listed on the 'nationality' line of a Soviet passport. [*translator*]

construction. I want to come and rebuild my city, the one you destroyed. But I don't know when this will all end. And I can't go back home with Katyusha while you're bombing us. So you came here. You tell me: When will this end? Do you know anything?'

I know nothing. I'm twirling Katyusha's Peppa Pig, the one who's larger, in my hands. She suddenly oinks and sings right in my hands. The unexpectedness startles us all.

'She's singing, she's singing!' Katyusha's happy.

'See, we thought she'd broken,' says Sasha. 'But she didn't break, she was just tired. And we don't need to fix her, she just needed to rest a little.

'Maybe life's like that, too? Maybe it will fix itself? We just need to wait a little and somehow recover? And then everything will improve. But I understand nothing will improve as long as there's a war. Who can stop all this, do you know?'

'Mama, that's enough, Papa will fix everything, Papa will come and fix everything for you, enough talking now, let's play,' says Katyusha. She's finished her cocoa and seems to be tired of cartoons.

Sasha doesn't hear her.

'I have no idea what will happen next, it's so scary. That's the scariest. I should at least say something to my little daughter, but what will I say? That I don't know? That I lose my mind when her papa doesn't call for a day or two? That the neighbour woman identified her husband by his hand? That my godson Bohdanchik's father is missing in action and his family hasn't known for many weeks what happened to him? And imagine this irony of fate: my godson's mother wanted to divorce him before the war, well, their relationship wasn't quite holding together. And then the war. And he's a firefighter in Izium. And your soldiers came there and did things in that city that I'm afraid to talk about. And she's apparently neither a wife nor a widow and can't talk properly, can't speak about things. Explain to me, why is this happening to her, to us? It's all unforgivable. Unforgivable. I don't know another word for it. I don't want to hate but I can't stop. This hatred is eating me up, I feel sick, but I read about what else you're doing to us and I can't stop.'

Katyusha abruptly sets the tablet aside and stands between me and Sasha. She doesn't touch either of us but she throws up her hands and suddenly says, 'Enough talking about that!'

Pause.

Sasha's the first to ask her: 'About what, Katyusha?'

'About that! Enough! Now! Enough talking about that now! Talk, talk, enough, enough, I can't, enough talking! Be quiet, that's enough. Enough!'

Katyusha's crying and attempting to hit me and Sasha. Sasha takes Katyusha in her arms and firmly presses her to herself. Katyusha's fists pound at her chest, head and shoulders.

That goes on for several minutes. Katyusha finishes crying just as suddenly as she started. Sasha sets her daughter on the floor. But Katyusha again, now calmly and deliberately, says, 'Enough talking about that.'

'What should we talk about, Katyusha?' I ask with an adult's unseemly hope that children are pure and innocent, and will know better, learning straight from God.

'About goodness,' Katyusha answers.

'About goodness?'

'Yes.' She shrugs her shoulders. And without much of a pause or segue, she says to her mother, 'I want to sleep, pick me up, I can't stand.'

Sasha picks her up just in the nick of time. Katyusha's already sleeping.

'You need to leave,' Sasha tells me over her shoulder.

We get ready to go. We leave.

In the doorway, Sasha sticks sandwiches into our hands. 'Eat these on the way. I made them for you. Forgive me that it worked out this way.'

# 15

# Roaming

The war isn't visible in Russia during February 2022. There's something troubling in the air, though: people are nervous, coming unhinged, acting rudely to one another and ever more frequently avoiding conversations about what's happening. They don't call the war a war, they call it 'that', 'those events' or 'what happened on the 24th'.

In everyday speech, people almost immediately started to call the 'frontline' a 'ribbon' and the combat is what happens 'beyond the ribbon'.

## 6 March 2022

On the tenth day of the war, I end up in the same third-class train carriage as Kostik. We're riding to northwestern Russia, to Pskov. There will be 20 hours of travel and conversation.

It becomes clear almost immediately that he and his two comrades are returning 'from beyond the ribbon'. But his companions collapse on the bunks and turn away as soon as the train sets off. I'm left with Kostik.

'Who's going to greet you at the station?'

He shrugs.

'Your mother?'

'Well, she might.'

'Your father?'

'Never saw him. We grew up with our mother. We went to my grandfather's once. He lives in the north, near Magadan. Strange person. Came to Kolyma when he was young and worked in construction. He was digging a basement for a building one time and hit on a ditch of firing squad victims. It's permafrost there, see? All the bodies were almost unspoiled. There were women and even children. They said my grandfather lost his mind then, almost killed his wife and kids, boozed for a long time and stole.

'Seems like he served about ten years, got out and left the city. Started living in the forest.

'My mother brought me and my brother to see him when we were little, to show us to him. She tells him, "Pa, I'm on my own, having a hard time, come to us, live with us, help raise the boys, I don't have anybody else." And he gave her a look and says, "You fool, you yourself don't understand what you're asking. I died long ago, why should I, a dead man, come to your children?" '

Kostik jumps up to have a quick smoke in the vestibule. It's cold.

I'm standing with him. He says, 'I basically went into the army just because I didn't know what else to do. I thought I'd go into the army, think a while. I signed a contract in December: I have a girl-friend and wanted to give her an iPhone. They deployed us near Belgorod in January. The drills weren't drills, it was more wandering around. It was cold, no chow, the commanders were nasty, nobody understood anything. Just when it seemed like we'd settled in and adapted, then it was, "Get ready, training!"

'What the hell kind of training, what was going on? We never figured that out. But they loaded us into trucks, gave us weapons and ammunition, it wasn't like they were giving it to us for drills. Some of the guys tried to ask questions but their mouths got shut fast.

'I wrote to my mother, "We're on the move, out of touch for now." She sent me a heart. I didn't write to my girl. I'm thinking she can wait.

'We rode a long time, standing still more than riding. It's warm in the truck, the guys're sleeping. When a person sleeps, he looks like himself as a child, did you know that? But for some reason I didn't sleep. I wanted to have a look at the road outside the canvas but it was dark. Then there's suddenly a text jingling on my phone: "Wel-come to Ukraine! Roaming's convenient with Beeline!" I'm blown away, what the fuck is up with the roaming?'

He's rubbing his eyes as if he's showing how he'd rubbed them on the night of 24 February in a warm army truck that's entering Ukraine.

His hands are dirty. Dirt has penetrated deep under his finger-nails. He draws a hand over his face and stubble scratches under his palm.

We go back into the train carriage. He opens his duffel bag. Takes out blue rubber flip-flops. Changes into those from combat boots covered in brown mud. Takes out a package of spice cookies and offers them. I decline. He takes one for himself, putting the rest back.

The duffel bag smells like a campfire, mud and some other intan-gible smell of war. That smell can't be described in words but anyone who's ever been at war recognises it flawlessly.

I ask him, 'On leave?'

He picks dirt out from under his nails.

'No. We decided. I decided. We basically refused.'

He's silent for a few seconds and looks at me. In the end, he forces this out: 'We're deserters. We refused. They told us they'll put us in jail now.'

Kostik seems to be the leader among the three. The other two are no longer lying on their bunks, faced away. They're sitting and lis-tening attentively to what he says. Kostik says: 'They told us there'll be a court martial. And we'll be put in jail. As deserters.'

I ask why they ran away anyway.

'Our commander went up in flames.'

People walk by; Kostik keeps quiet. The others keep quiet, too.

After waiting for people to get far enough away not to hear him, he continues. 'We didn't know that would happen. They told us it was like a forced march: we walk, there's tanks behind us, air sup-port, the local population greets us, nobody opposes us.

'It wasn't like that. We ended up in hell, see? Every tree branch hated us and shot at us. We were basically all alone. You don't believe it?

'It was chaos there, I'm telling you the truth. Not one general. There was nobody to command, they're all running around the place, firing and shouting because they're scared. We ran into our own guys, gunfire broke out and right then the enemy opened up heavy fire on us. Long story short, they hit our commander with a rifle grenade launcher. And he burned up right in front of us. Somebody just burned up, see? And so we turned around. Nope, guys, we didn't sign up for this. And then this one politically informed dick appears out of nowhere. They'll gun you down, he says, send you through the platoon. But we didn't give a shit anymore, right guys?'

The guys are looking out the window. The train's moving, swaying slightly, and it seems like they're nodding. But they're not nodding. They're just looking out the window.

'Long story short, we backed out. Outside the ribbon, everybody somehow understood. Well, sure, they said it's like I pissed my pants, I'm not a guy, all that. But the ones that saw what we saw – and I won't tell you everything – they'll understand us and not judge. But when we made it to Belgorod, things got started. Oh, we'll show you, they'd say, it'll be the firing squad, who'd let you go? They took our cards and said there wouldn't be any money for February either. Long story short, I got dick, not an iPhone. But fine, at least they didn't put us in jail.'

The conductor offers tea.

'In Moscow they helped us contact this one woman who works on soldiers' cases, she said to breathe because nobody's going to shoot you, no matter what. She helped us buy tickets. We're going to the public prosecutor on the ninth. We'll see.'

I ask him if he would have signed the contract if he'd known they'd send him to war.

Kostik keeps silent. The train rolls along, clacking. But he's silent. He's looking at me. Round-faced with bags under his eyes, scared. Smelling of war.

'I thought I'd just earn money, I don't understand anything at all about politics.'

Tea. A newspaper seller walks through the train car. Newspapers stick out of a metal basket. Headlines about the war – which the papers call SMO, special military operation – sneak out and grab the eye.

Kostik says, 'I apologise if I holler during the night, you wake me up, don't be shy. I dream about that same incident all the time now . . . Anyway, no details, but wake me up if I holler.'

He didn't shout.

In the morning, on the approach to the station, our train stopped to let an oncoming train through. The oncoming train was carrying IFVs, APCs and other military equipment.

'War's always hungry,' said Kostik.

His mother and girlfriend met him at the station; one of his buddies was met by his grandmother. Nobody met the third. He smoked and shifted from one foot to the other while the other guys hugged their loved ones.

Kostik wrote to me later that the court proceedings went well, that all three managed to break their contracts, nobody was punished and they just lost their money for January and February.

He left for his grandfather's after mobilisation was announced; his girlfriend didn't go with him.

One of his fellow soldiers 'fell off the radar'. It's unknown where he is and what happened to him after the proceedings.

Our other fellow traveller in March, Kostik's second buddy, turned out to be from a military family. After being at home for a short time, at his father's insistence, he went off to war as a volunteer. 'That probably means it's his fate,' Kostik wrote to me in his last text. We haven't communicated since.

## 24 March 2022

I've been added to a Zoom conference with 62 women participating: they're the wives, sisters and mothers of Russian soldiers who've found themselves 'beyond the ribbon'. It's a collective call so a lot aren't using video, though the majority aren't hiding their faces. A half-hour goes towards everyone learning how to use Zoom: sound on and off, video, background. Sometimes I hear a child running, someone's TV in the next room or the sounds of shouting matches.

Their husbands, brothers and children are the very same career Russian military, contractors and even conscripts who were in the vanguard of the invasion into Ukraine in late February 2022.

Towards the end of the war's first month, the fate of more than half these men is unknown. There's envy for the women who know their loved ones are in captivity. They're alive.

Some send video screenshots to the chat. There's someone with his head completely bandaged and stumps instead of arms, followed by a photograph of a woman with a nice-looking brown-haired man in a military uniform on the spit of Vasilevsky Island.

A message: 'This is my husband K.C.Ya. Born in 19xx, helicopter navigator, severely wounded, presumably in Mykolaiv Oblast, I know nothing further about him. If you're able to find him, tell him I love him very much and will wait for him.'

We talk and talk with crying women. They complain about the lack of information, about fear, about threats from the military units their husbands were attached to; they compile lists and give them to the Ukrainian side in spontaneous chats; they create and delete petitions; they argue among themselves about whether there's any point in going to Ukraine to get their men.

They basically don't raise the topic of war. They're overwhelmed by grief and fear.

I finally tell them that the main way I can help them to is make their story public, to speak about them, their sons, husbands and brothers. That's the start of a long and difficult journey of searching, of trying to begin speaking with the Ukrainian side about those who are alive, those who are injured. And about the dead.

I ask them to let me know who among them is prepared to speak with me a couple days later, in a public interview, on the record.

The mother of one of those who is missing in action writes to me on behalf of everyone.

'We decline the interview. The high command came to the military unit. They explained that they're doing everything possible and they showed papers, but Ukraine refuses an officer exchange. They said to be patient for a while, there will be an offensive soon and they'll be freed. Please forgive us for the inconvenience.'

Only three women out of 62 will agree to interviews: mothers of three contract soldiers. Fate will never bring me together with the rest.

The war becomes noticeable in Russian cities in May. Now you can run into it at any Russian train station: a crowd spiffily dressed for summer going about its business but then, plunging into the self-absorbed crowd, are black-and-green *soldiers, soldiers, soldiers.*

Grown men around 40 and completely youthful guys. With homemade knee protectors, hand-me-down army boots and body armour bought in a second-hand store. They buy everything themselves. Sometimes they borrow to buy it. Mums buy for the completely youthful ones.

## 2 October 2022

At the baggage drop-off area in Moscow's Vnukovo airport, a crowd implores the woman at the counter to let a passenger, a volunteer serviceman, take a helmet and armour as carry-on luggage.

Too heavy, the employee says.

But he's going to war, they say.

I record that in my journal. I write: 'My Motherland gathers and sacrifices its own children to a mysterious dragon, all in order to save its previous life and escape its own death. But why do you need that escape and that life if you have no more children?'

Since the armour truly is going to war, the woman at the counter, by the way, lets it on the plane. The guy and I end up in the same row on a plane to Pskov; he's by the window, I'm on the aisle. The sun's illuminating his face. He's young, handsome and broad-shouldered, with a wedding ring on his right hand. Two in camouflage greet him at the airport. It's obvious from the conversation that they've all served together. Now they can go together to their former unit and hand in documents for volunteering 'beyond the ribbon'.

Sasha greets me. He says it's mainly professionals who come to be volunteers: they're special forces, airborne, assault troops. He says war's a job, too. And then there's this: you don't go to the first doctor you see for an operation, you need the best. I'm even jumping up and down, eager to respond, but I keep quiet, remembering before it's too late how many years I've known Sasha. There's also the fact that we've been planning to spend the day together.

Sasha and I have known each other for a long time, through my journalistic work, and we maintain a good rapport despite knowing each other's views. But even the strongest families are crumbling because of the war in 2022. And so, knowing Sasha, I keep quiet, just in case.

And Sasha says, 'So why aren't you asking me what I think about all this? Or do you only talk with whiners?' Sasha lost his leg in Donbas six years before 2022. He has two Chechen wars and several special operations under his belt. Sasha served in an assault battalion on special assignment. He was three years short of his pension. Sasha complained about that then. Now he regrets that he can't go to the new war.

Sasha drives a car for the disabled. That enrages him. He says, 'And where were all of you when it started? In 2014, in 2015? Did it sway you when we were being destroyed? When children were shot? When houses were bombed?'

I say, 'Sasha, nobody was shooting anybody before 2014, before the Russian military showed up in eastern Ukraine.'

'That's what you think.'

Sasha lights a cigarette.

'You just don't understand geopolitics. This whole story's not about people. We, my people, we're soldiers. A person doesn't live long, an empire lives eternally. The enemy wants to tear down our empire. We should lay down our life and save the motherland. Have you heard of that, not sparing anything? That "all" is life, you can't not give all, see? The war, it's checking us, to see who's shit and who's not shit, who's hiding and not giving their all, and who'll go under bullets and right to heaven.'

'But why, Sasha?'

'What do you mean, why?'

'Why go under the bullets if you can *not* die and *not* kill.'

'You explain that to them.'

Sasha parks the car by a grey five-storey building, the oblast's psychiatric hospital which in spring 2022 became a military hospital for the most seriously wounded. Sasha insisted I had to see the hospital. He thinks this will change me.

There are several people by the hospital who've brought parcels to their loved ones. Among them is a woman with little hand-made pies and a jar of soup; she's telling the nurse at the service window that she's a soldier's mother. She gives his first name, surname and date of birth.

I automatically figure out his age is 19. The woman hands over a bag with the food, leaves and sits on a bench.

I sit next to her. Sasha stays nearby, smoking.

Her name is Lyubov Ivanovna. She's not the soldier's mum, she's his grandmother. She says, 'I still haven't seen my Gennushka. They say he doesn't have eyes, either of them. He'll be blind now, disabled. They say he has a concussion, too, but again, I haven't seen him. We need to get him back somehow, have a look, but for now all they do is talk, talk, talk at us. Nothing comes of their conversations. Of course the doctors are smart, but we just don't believe anything, you understand yourself what kind of country we live in, the authorities are crafty.

'But we'll see when he gets out. Now there's a word: concussion. My father came back from war concussed. From the Great Patriotic [War], when we were fighting against fascism. And now we're off again, only now it has a different name, the Great Patriotic Special Military Operation, there you go. But the point's the same. It's absolutely us against the whole world. They hate on us, but for what? What did we do to them?

'There's so many coffins in the city already, so many wounded, so many disabled. And it seems Genka will be disabled but who'll help him? I'm already old.

'I'd heard that if you had money, you could pay somebody off and not go to that war. But where would we get the money? His mother's in jail and there's nobody else. So he went . . . He went.

'But what can you do now? They should just hand him over to me, his relative. I'll look after him. I looked after my father, looked after my husband, but he was just a drunk without any war at all, that's how it worked out. And I'll look after Gennushka as long as I can. Works out he's a hero. His motherland sent him off and he spared nothing for her.'

I offer to give Lyubov Ivanovna a ride to the city. She declines. She says she'll sit here for a while. She'll wait, just in case she runs into some nurse she might be able to ask about Genka. Or relatives of other wounded might say something. The last bus from here is at 5pm.

I wave to Sasha: Let's go!

'Why so soon?'

'Just because.'

'Eh, journalist lady, dear journalist lady,' Sasha sighs.

I ask why he doesn't use a wheelchair or agree to a prosthesis rather than going around on crutches without a leg for six years.

'I don't know. Is that unworthy or something? I don't want to consider myself disabled. I boozed all good and proper after my discharge. Thought I'd never come to. But I somehow survived, thank God. And now I lead military training for the young guys in our division. There's nobody, they're all at the front. How about that, even Sashka came in handy. Maybe we'll still live a little. And show the likes of you how to love the motherland.'

'You think I don't love it?'

'I think you basically don't know life. In life it's either you get them or they get you. If we hadn't attacked them, they would have attacked us.'

'If they'd attacked us, I would have understood that this is my war, too. But not like this.'

'I pity you.'

'I pity all of us.'

At the beginning of the war, Russian president Vladimir Putin promised 12 million roubles to the mothers and widows of each who died there.

That's 200,000 dollars.

And 20 one-room apartments for a small Russian city like Pskov, for example, where there are about 20 military units.

True, the longer the war goes on, the smaller the number of families who will manage to receive money for their dead child.

Fathers rarely receive payments and coffins from 'beyond the ribbon'. Fathers rarely see off soldiers who go 'beyond the ribbon'. And never grandfathers, although it was the slogan 'Thank you, Grandpa, for the Victory' that revived interest in war and the perception of war as some sort of special valour, honour, even privilege.

## 26 April 2022

'Kirill doesn't have a dad,' says Ira. She says that either defiantly or with the desperation of a single woman. It's hard for me to interpret. I'm seeing her for the first time in my life.

Just as we're sitting ourselves down to talk for an interview, she recalls her pills and goes back to her jacket. She has a Russian tricolour and a St George's ribbon pinned to the lapel. Ira takes cardiac drops and a handful of pills out of her jacket pocket. She puts drops in a glass of water. The smell of heart drops spreads around the room. It's both homey and clinical. Bitter.

'Well, Godspeed,' says Ira, and we begin recording.

'On 26 August 2021, the day he turned 20, my son Kirill Chistyakov went to the military recruitment office on his own. He considered army service his duty. He'd gone to cadet school and wanted to go to the military academy after the army. That was his goal. He wanted to realise it.

'And I didn't get involved in male matters, I supported my son in everything. He's the pillar of the family. I also have a younger daughter, but Kirill is Kirill.

'He ended up in artillery. And it seemed like everything had turned out well – he initially served near Petrozavodsk. And then in November they issued him a "Call Mama" SIM card and he called me and announced they were transferring him to serve in Luga, that's in the Leningrad Oblast. But the big thing is that Kirill changed troops. It turns out they transferred him from artillery to military intelligence. I don't get involved in male matters; intelligence service is intelligence service. I was just upset that he was now further from home.

'He called at New Year's and we talked. And I came to see him in January 2022, for a meeting. So that was 27 January. He called me when I was planning to go, Ma, he says, they don't feed us very well, bring chow for everybody to eat. I brought enough for 40 people. Your mum's a good one, that's what the guys said. That's what he told me, meaning he was bragging. I gave him a smartphone as a present that day, too. We made a video for his grandmother, sent it off. You know, people always talk about the maternal heart. But I didn't have any premonition: we laughed, took selfies and that was it. Well, no. For some reason, on that trip I asked him to show me the tag he had on a chain. And I took a picture of it then. Why?'

Ira drinks big swallows of water with the heart drops. I hear the glass knock against her teeth, see her hand shake and how Ira tries to hide the shakiness. 'Almost ready,' she says.

She closes her eyes tightly. She sits like that for a few seconds, with her eyes closed, then commands, 'That's it, on we go.' And on we go.

'So it turns out I last saw my son on 27 January. He called me on 31 January and said he should receive money on his card, 40,000 roubles, since he'd signed a document saying he'd serve in a division under contract, receiving a salary. He said all the guys in the division signed and that's good, the army's like a job for him now, they pay him money.

'Kirill called on 1 February. We're leaving for training in Kursk, he said. I say, where's that. He says to google it.

'I looked and damn, of course it's far. But he promised to call. He called a week later, the connection was bad. He said he's in training all the time, in the fields: slush, mud, his feet are always wet because the combat boots leak. But he was glad there was a bathhouse so he could wash.

'I ask, "Are there a lot of you there?"

'"Ma," he says, "well, we're in the field all the time, how can you tell?"

'On 22 February, he says, "Ma, we're going to the border for training, a month, the commander said there won't be any connection."

'"What border," I say?

'"Ukrainian," he says.

'For some reason I got mad. What border? Why would you go there? Why no connection? Why are you lying?

'But he answers me so calmly, says the commanders told them about the training, they were going to reinforce the borders. Basically, he says, you figure on me being a month without a connection but the commander promised leave after that, so expect me then. And he added – I didn't like this – that he'd put all his personal belongings (military identity card, phone, money, bank card) in a box that his commander took.

'I started shouting, "But where's your tag, the tag, where is it, show me!"

'He showed me. For some reason I calmed down.

'And then came 24 February. Somehow, I didn't pick up on things at first, didn't add one plus one. But then the mums from our division started asking questions in our chat. And it gradually came to me. Like an icy shower.

'I decided I'd call the division, clear things up about what's going on there, why they sent my son and others just as untrained to a real battle. This was their special operation, that means there should be specially trained people there. Let them fight the war.'

I ask her, 'If Kirill had been better trained, would you not have objected to his participation in the war?'

Ira reflects, 'Well, did our president and our defence minister have data about how they were preparing to attack us, that they were threatening us? Were there data? Not everything's so simple there either. Well, I can't sort out politics. I never had time. I was raising children.'

She asks to take a break. Turns on her phone. Messages come in, plinking, interrupting each other. In March 2022, Ira organised a chat for relatives of service members who found themselves in the zone of the special military operation, as Russia called the war against Ukraine. Ira calls it that too, however.

'Can I answer the girls?' she asks.

Ira listens to voicemails where crying women tell how they're searching for their children or husbands. She answers by incanting words of consolation and support. In my presence, she records six voicemails with advice and consolation during a 10-minute break. She says, 'Everybody has the same thing. A child's missing but we're dismissed – in the division, in the ministry, everywhere – because we're nobody.'

I ask her to tell me what else she knows about her son Kirill. She says, 'On 14 March 2022, he made a videocall to me from Ukraine, from an unfamiliar number. I saved that number for myself. And later used it to find both his serviceman buddy and his fiancée on social media. He died on 28 March, that boy, everything was confirmed.

'But he was still alive then. Everybody was still alive. Kirill called on video and the mortar shelling started when he called. The sound of automatic-weapon fire was audible. "What's that," I say? "Where are you? Do you have armour?"

'"Ma," he says, "I've got other stuff to worry about now, like my combat boots ripped back in Kursk, I wound them with wire, and they still fell apart, but the other day they brought humanitarian aid to the village here and I got myself some sneakers."

'He started showing me those sneakers but the sun was really bright, I didn't see anything.

'"Son," I asked, "how are you eating, who's responsible for you there anyway?"

'"Some of the locals feel sorry for us and bring food," he says. "But it's usually hard, they don't even sell water in the store, they weren't expecting us here."'

Ira drinks water. I scrutinise her: long hair, strong-willed face, bags under her eyes, nose with a scaly, red tip. That's from tears. She's been wiping it with a hankie.

She shows screenshots of the video conversation with Kirill. Why did she make those screenshots? Her nails, which have grown out, click dully at her smartphone screen. There's a photograph of Ira, Kirill and his younger sister Elya on the phone's wallpaper. It seems like New Year's; there's a Christmas tree in the background.

Ira says:

'Last contact was 22 March, from a basement, from a Ukrainian number. He didn't say anything specifically, only, "Ma, just don't watch the TV and don't believe what they say there. It's all lies, Ma!" I asked what, exactly, was lies, I asked what he was doing in that basement, I asked:

*How did you end up there?*
*Where are your commanders?*
*What did they tell you?*
*What's your plan?*
*When are you coming back?*
*I asked . . .*
*I asked . . .*
*I asked.*

'Then I asked him, "How can we get you out of there, son?"

'"Come on, Ma," he said. And he hung up.

'Based on the number he'd called from, I later found a woman, a Ukrainian citizen. She was very afraid to talk with me. As I understood it, she left through Russia for, as she put it, "Lesser Europe", I don't know where that is. She said she has an infant and she's afraid. She confirmed to me that my son and a few other guys lived at her house until 26 March. She'd hidden them. But then couldn't. I asked them to leave, she said, because it wasn't safe for my family. I asked her to meet with me, I said it was important that she tell me everything, it seems like I shouted that it was important because there were casualties.

'"Who died?" she asked.

'I told her the names. She burst out sobbing. She sobbed very hard. And hung up. She sent a message later: "Mala Rohan. Don't ever call here again."

'She shut off her phone. I couldn't get in contact with her again.

'I passed her information on to the Ministry of Defence, to our division, and I started writing to them, saying to answer me about what was my son doing in Mala Rohan. What kind of place is that? What happened there?

'They ask me how I know that, say it's all secret information.

'On 11 April 2022 at 14.10, an officer called me from the Ministry of Defence and told me that Kirill is in captivity on Ukrainian territory. And that's official.

'On 12 April at 7.30, there's another call from the Ministry of Defence. Your son, Kirill Chistyakov, has been declared missing in action, they say.

'On 16 April at 13.20, they called me again saying he's in captivity on Ukrainian territory.

'I was already puffed up with tears by that point and I say right into the phone to make up your mind already! What, he's in captivity one day and then on the run the next, is that it? A day in captivity, then escapes here and then captured again? What kind of superman do I have there? Can you explain to me how that is? Who's giving you information?

'They give it to us from the division, they say. So I run to the division. But nobody there talks with us, the parents.'

Ira's hand draws a map of the Mala Rohan area on her knee and she talks about the battles that took place in late March of 2022 in Biskvitne and Tsyrkuny, how many were taken prisoner, how many were killed. She'd reconstructed those several March days down to the hour. She has all the videos of all the prisoners and all the corpses in the Mala Rohan region on those days. Her son is not in one single video.

I ask her what she thinks, why this war was necessary.

'Well, basically, if they call a war a war, the questions go away on their own. Then it works out that we, our guys, are defending the motherland. That's if it's a war. But if it's a special operation and our children, husbands and brothers are going missing there, then we want it to be seen differently.'

'So what's the difference?'

'The difference is that during a special military operation the law on protecting prisoners of war isn't in force. This is a war in its essence, but in name, it's a special operation to destroy fascism.'

'Do you believe that?'

'I haven't lived in Ukraine, I don't know.'

'Have fascists attacked you?'

'No, no . . . I've been to Kharkiv, to Crimea, in the 1990s, to Mykolaiv, and was even in Lviv, at a restaurant. But that was a long time ago. Maybe something's changed? Maybe we don't know everything and some kind of anger at us really has accumulated?'


## 27 November 2022

Two days before this – meaning on 25 November – Vladimir Putin, the Russian president, met with women who were introduced as mothers of Russian soldiers fighting in Ukraine.

'Your guys chose that fate,' President Putin told the women.

After learning of preparations for the president to meet with mothers, Ira Chistyakova put in several appeals asking to be given an opportunity to participate. By November 2022, Ira had managed to bring together around a thousand mothers of service members who were missing, dead or in captivity. They also wrote letters requesting that Chistyakova represent their interests at the meeting with Putin.

But Ira wasn't there.

'I don't know who those women are who met with the president. I should have been there. I would have told him what this war has become for us and about its costs, and I would have asked him how our children ended up there, what for, and who sent them there. And why on earth we went there.'

During the seven months since we last met, Ira has lost weight, begun to look drawn, and become sharper and more severe. She no longer takes either sedatives or heart medicine. There are no more ribbons on her jacket lapel and I ask her why she'd been wearing them.

'Kirill got them even before the army, around Russia Day. And so I decided, well, consider it a superstition that I'll wear them until he comes back from the army. But later, as long as the war . . . But I took them all off later for some reason. Well, really, how will that help me? I need to find my son.'

I ask Ira how she'd gotten on during those seven months that we didn't see each other.

She says, 'I found him.'

She's breathing very fast so as not to cry. She told me before the interview that she'd decided not to cry, no matter what. Now she's breathing and holding back tears.

'How?' I ask.

She says, 'During those seven and a half months, I went 25,000 kilometres on foot, in cars, buses, trains and hitching. I rode with long-haul truckers and the military. With everyone who agreed, who appreciated my perspective. I was everywhere: Donbas, Mariupol and Mirny. Makiivka, Kupiansk, Bakhmut – I was everywhere. I was under bombing and shelling. The ones who sent our children there, those who got out of it, those who pretended nothing happened – they should be sent there. But I went on my own.'

'Why?'

'I was searching for my son. I rushed off after any sign, any information. But nothing worked out. All the threads broke off. But I had to take that route. Because I needed to see with my own eyes what war is, what destruction is, what catastrophic death is, what maimed people are – adults without legs, children on crutches or with fingers missing. Until a person has seen that – and not on that diabolical television screen, where they don't even call Ukrainians people, they're just Ukrainofascists or Banderites – in person, they won't understand how much grief the war brings. All mothers' tears are salty. Ours and theirs. And nobody gave birth in order to give back for slaughter. Nobody, believe me. Nobody.'

Ira keeps silent and breathes.

She catches her breath and continues: 'I was near the front line for two months. I bawled for two months without stopping. And this is what I can tell you. They'll answer for every teardrop because every cat will pay for the mouse's tears.'

'Who will answer for this?'

'They will. The ones who pulled us into this, who pulled in our children, who unleashed the war and made us believe this was how it had to be.'

'You think so?'

'I'm sure of it. You know, I never thought I'd be like this. But they woke up the sleeping Ira, who didn't care about politics, who went with the flow and didn't see anything beyond the mortgage. I woke up. I won't forget anything they did. And I won't forgive anything.'

Ira opens a map on her phone, where the populated places she visited have little green circles around them. She says:

'I returned to Karelia from Donbas but was only at home for two days. See, if you're a mother, if your child's between heaven and earth, then I don't know how you can keep on living without getting to the bottom of things, without finding out exactly what happened to him, without putting all your efforts into helping him.

'Basically, I rushed from home to Rostov-on-Don where there's a military genetics lab at the morgue. It's been in operation since the Chechen War. People had written to me that my Kirill was apparently there. And they sent a photo: a blurry screenshot from a video of uncertain origin. But I knew I had to verify everything. Basically, I came to that morgue on 10 August and spent six days there. I looked at all the boys who'd died since April. More than 400 were unidentified. I found two from Kirill's platoon; they'd been dead since March. I won't tell what I saw.

'I don't know how some people identify their boys: the bodies are mangled badly during artillery shelling, sometimes there's a hand, sometimes there's only a finger left. Some come there and just take a bag and bury without asking, "Is this my child, the right one?" They take the bag and bury, take the money. I can't explain that. And they told me to take the money, take it, you have a daughter. And if Kirill's found, well, you'll live. But how can I take money for a live son? And I didn't give birth to him for the money. Or to bury him. I don't understand that logic. Among the bodies in Rostov, I identified another of Kirill's fellow soldiers, an orphaned boy from Petersburg. Well, the women and I buried him, I went there. We said goodbyes.

'But I didn't find Kirill there.

'I went down into that morgue like it was hell. Spent a week in hell. But I didn't find Kirill.

'I was so glad. Only I didn't have the strength to be glad.

'You know, there were moments when I prayed and just repeated to myself, *Lord, Lord, don't stop my heart. Give me the strength and courage to find him.*

'And sometimes I'd pray by myself, shut in the kitchen, wailing, *Change my place and his, I don't need this life!* But one time my daughter came in. Mama, she asked me, what about me, am I really not your daughter?

'Then I promised myself I wouldn't cry anymore. I won't cry until I find him.

'And the Lord heard me. I saw video of one exchange on the Internet, they said they'd exchanged one from Karelia. I thought then that if he's one of ours, I'll find him and learn everything about Kirill from him, I'm absolutely sure.'

We take a break. It's getting dark outside. Ira's standing by the window and talking on the phone with her daughter. Her daughter Elya's 12 but Ira's already used to leaving her at home alone because Ira's been searching for her missing son almost as long as the war's been going on.

I'd asked Ira about this in April but I ask again.

'Why, in your opinion, was this war necessary, have you figured that out?'

'No. I travelled everywhere and didn't figure it out. But I figured something else out. I figured out Ukrainians.

'Look, I'm a patriot of my country. And I'll remain one no matter what happens. And if someone barges through my door and wants to harm me or my daughter, I'll kill that person with my bare hands. Nothing in me will falter. How did they – I'm talking about Ukrainians now – feel when we came in with tanks, planes and weapons and bombs, huh?

'But you can't reason about those things here, laws come out every day about how we can only

*Keep quiet,*
*Keep quiet,*
*Keep quiet.*

'And they threaten you with prison or national contempt for every word, for every maternal question. And you'll have to recognise absolutely every mother, every woman whose child, son, brother, husband is there, "beyond the ribbon", as a traitor. Because we won't keep quiet.

'And I'll tell you this about the war. If we're destined to defend ourselves, then we should defend ourselves here, in our own country, in our own motherland. If we're destined to die, then only here, on our own land. But not to lie somewhere in someone else's land. We don't need someone else's land. We haven't even learned to live normally with our own.'

She walks away from the window. And I notice all the more how she's changed. I tell her that. And tell her I can't imagine the obstacles she's overcome.

Ira nods. She says:

'I had three photo albums with a hundred photos apiece: a lot of Kirill's, photos with his guys, his fellow soldiers. I took those around to the prisoners of war, the ones who'd already been exchanged; to the guys who "crossed the ribbon" to go on vacation; to the injured; I went everywhere. And nobody recognised Kirill. And they didn't recognise the guys from his regiment. But I felt in my heart that that Karelian guy, our guy, would help me. I searched for him for two weeks, through friends, through the Internet, through the authorities. Well, the authorities, obviously, didn't help me. But I found him. To be more exact, I found one person who's not indifferent, who contacted me and told me where that former prisoner of war resides, 140 kilometres from our city. I went there with the mother of one other boy who'd been missing in action. The man didn't live at that address but we found him. He didn't want to talk but I shouted at him through the fence that I'm a mother, I'm searching for my son, and I won't leave until we talk. I have the right.

'He opened the gate for me and took the album. He turned and turned pages and suddenly poked at a picture of Kirill and said,

"Oh, the kid." The floor really went out from under my feet, there it was, you know, that sense when you've fallen through somewhere.

'I grabbed his arm and said, "Come on, come on, where did you see, where did you see him?"

'He says, "He was sitting in a basement with me in Kyiv." He says, "I don't know his name, we weren't allowed to talk there." But he, that person, confirmed that my son is alive, healthy, not concussed, not wounded. And he later identified two other guys from my album. I notified the parents right away.

'We sat and talked for a short while. He told us to leave quickly, he had a lot to do and not much time. He's already had a rest, bathed and was planning to return to the front. I just opened my mouth, like how could that be?

'He warned me, said, "That's not for you to know, woman."

'Even so I didn't leave empty-handed. I'd made him write down his testimony and that he'd seen Kirill. More specifically, he himself couldn't write, the fingers on his right hand had been broken, they didn't move well, but he signed everything. I took a picture of him with that paper.

'And I sent that photograph and that statement to the Russian Defence Ministry. That's how I did their work for them, found my son and brought them something that was all prepared. Just do an exchange.'

## 14 December 2022

I'm riding 140 kilometres from Petrozavodsk to search for Ira's acquaintance. I convince myself that I should speak with that former prisoner of war myself, clarify certain details. I make it to the spot, find the yard and the building and introduce myself, but he doesn't want to talk with me.

'Fuck off,' he calmly says. He spits. 'Nobody fucking needs you at all, garbage journalists. You scrounge around, sniff around, spy. Shit, what do you need anyway? We're defending the motherland

and we'll drop dead for it if we have to. We're under enemy fire, under bullets, but you? Fuck off out of here right now, got it?'

He takes a log in his hands and makes a show of how he's planning to throw it at me. I take a few steps away. I ask why he wasn't staying at home long. He answers, 'And why would I want to be here? There's no work here, there isn't dick. Just boozing. And I already signed a contract. Warring's normal man's work. Somebody's got to do it. And I know how.'

I say I've heard he apparently had broken fingers.

'The bones healed up,' says the former prisoner of war. And he adds, 'Listen, I'm losing my patience.'

I reply that I wanted to talk with him, among other things, about being a prisoner, about Kirill and about his views.

'There's nothing to say,' he says, cutting me off. 'People are spilling blood there. And you shut your yap.'

It's chilly outside. But I feel the sweet smell of a wood-burning stove. Somewhere, a dog chokes on its howl.

I walk through the village. It's not very big and it ends, as expected, in a cemetery. They're burying someone there, a priest is singing 'Eternal Memory' and the women are crying but there aren't many mourners.

A hundred metres from the mourners there's a man standing with a shovel and eating an apple. After looking closely, I realise he's not really eating, just having bites of food: there's a bottle in his jacket pocket that he drinks from every now and then. He's glad to see a conversation partner in me. Skipping the introduction phase, he immediately says, 'I get a fucking kick out of these people: they just live on, like nothing happened, you stick their ugly face in it: there it is, the coffin, a little coffin, that one's here, he made it here, but how many didn't make it? And how many have been put in the grave there? Yes, you look around, shit, what have we done, shit? What kind of slaughter have we fucking pushed on the whole world, I'm fucking amazed, what, does nobody see it or what? Did your eyes fall out? You, shit, do you even think what kind of payback there will be for all of you for that? And your kids? And

their kids? But no . . . Why should we think, thinking – let somebody else think. But we just curl up to protect ourselves, mum's
the word. But shit, you look around, look around. You just have a
sober look around at all these ruins and burial grounds. And
acknowledge this thing that you did it all, you bastard, you. Your
hands smashed it up. And you'll answer for it. And nothing else
matters.'

He holds out the bottle for me; I refuse. He finishes it himself.
Puts on his hat and leaves, pressing the shovel in his armpit. An
unseen rooster shrieks somewhere not too far away.

The bus will come soon. It's time to go.

In November 2022, the Russian Ministry of Defence officially
acknowledged Kirill Chistyakov as a prisoner of war. But he didn't
show up on the exchange lists.

In January 2023, Ira Chistyakova received information from several sources in Ukraine that her son Kirill Chistyakov had never
been in captivity but had died near Mala Rohan in March 2022.

Several of those who wrote and called offered private services to
Ira for identifying Kirill's body using DNA and offered, for money,
to send the genetic material outside the country.

Those people demanded upfront payment for their services.

The Ukrainian military department where Chistyakova had officially appealed with her enquiry recommended that she personally
come to Ukraine to search for her son, dead or alive. That's impossible to do, however, since entry without visas has been prohibited
since the beginning of the war and nobody that Chistyakova is in
contact with was prepared to send a soldier's mother an invitation
to Ukraine, let alone guarantee her safety.

In February 2023, the Russian Ministry of Defence notified
Chistyakova that they don't know where her son is and suggest he
be officially declared missing in action.

Ira refused. They offered her 50 per cent more money than the
other mothers. After yet another of those proposals, Chistyakova
threatened the military recruitment officer, saying she'd use all the
'coffin' money they'd offered to buy actual coffins and send them to

Moscow. They stopped offering her money. Then, in the summer of 2023, they issued a certificate saying her son is a veteran of the Special Military Operation. As she says, 'I don't have a son but I do have a document.'

I say, What do you need it for?

She says, I agree, what the hell do I need it for. But it's like it prolongs Kirill. Get what I'm saying?

I say I don't get it.

And she says, thank God you don't need to.

# 16.

# The Chocolate Bar

On its outskirts, the Polish city of Łódź looks like any provincial Eastern European city, with its rectangular city blocks and broad streets linked together by sizeable intersections with traffic lights. Department store. Movie theatre. Stone monument. Four-storey brick buildings interspersed with prefab five-storey buildings. Towards the outskirts, there are more and more five-storey buildings.

Tatiana happens to live on the second floor of one of them. On the first floor is a Żabka, a franchise convenience store.

Tatiana has a one-room apartment with a balcony.

Three strangers and a Scottish terrier settled into Tatiana's apartment during May 2022. Now there are made-up mattresses for women on the floor of Tatiana's apartment and a corner is partitioned off with a curtain. The man who sleeps there, behind the curtain, introduces himself as Uncle Sasha.

Tatiana herself now sleeps in the kitchen. And a new kitchen has been temporarily fitted out in the hallway. When I walk into Tatiana's apartment, I unknowingly stick my bag in a skillet. Everybody laughs.

Tatiana is tall, beautiful and shy. She's a psychologist from Tula, in Russia.

Tatiana emigrated from Russia to Poland in 2014, soon after the annexation of Crimea and the beginning of combat in Donbas. She says she couldn't watch how calmly her countrypeople regarded the seizing of foreign territories and a war unfolding in the neighbouring country.

'I left out of shame. It seemed important to me to preserve my dignity, normalcy, if you will. It was a blow for me when I realised my country's citizens were prepared to pretend nothing had happened, that they'd stick their heads in the sand for the sake of preserving their own comfort zones. It's a quiet psychosis on the national level. I didn't want to be a part of it,' says Tatiana.

After selling her apartment in Tula in 2014, Tatiana divided her money into two parts. She bought the tiny apartment in Łódź and set aside the rest 'for my life until old age itself'.

Tatiana and I are standing on the balcony: only there can we speak calmly if all the residents of her apartment are at home. Tatiana says, 'With my views, which I wasn't planning to hide, there was no place for me at home. Nobody here especially needed me either. I lived quietly. I told myself that I'm living out my life, meaning I'm waiting, simply and calmly, for old age and death. I was doing well: I read books, went to parks, travelled a little and planned to get a dog. Nobody knows me, I don't know anybody, it's life with a clean slate. After the war started, I thought, but maybe that all happened in my life so I'd end up in the right place at the right time? I went to the shopping mall that had become a centre for helping Ukraine. They brought busloads of refugees there and I said I'm a single person, full of energy, that I have neither work nor children, but I have tons of free time and am ready to work morning to night to be useful, to atone for my guilt . . .'

Tatiana goes silent because there are peals of laughter breaking out in the apartment.

Tatiana looks affectionately through the balcony window into the room. She says, 'It's inconceivable but they laugh a lot. Sure, they also start crying later and don't stop. But my life's very simple now: I laugh along with them, I cry with them, they need me. That gives my life meaning. So it's still unknown who came to help whom. Let's go inside.'

The women are bustling around and setting out tea. Uncle Sasha comes out and we meet properly.

They invite us to the table. There are only two chairs, so some of us stand or sit on the arm of an easy chair. The head of the household is Tyson, a Scottish terrier. Inna holds him in her arms and constantly gives him more food.

'Eat, eat, sweetie, eat, you're my dear saviour.'

Tyson eats an oatmeal cookie from a reclining position. He doesn't hop down from Inna's arms. Inna, who's not very tall, has wavy ash-grey hair and lively eyes; she often pops outside to smoke.

'He's been like this ever since Mariupol itself,' says Inna. 'Tyson pressed into me and hasn't let me go ever since we all piled into Sasha's car and started driving. And I hold on to him, too. I cry **a little** when I'm with him at night. **Or probably more than just a little**. He and I are left, just the two of us. I wouldn't be here either if it weren't for him.'

Inna goes silent and looks at some spot inside herself. She's silent and all the others at the table are silent, too. Tyson's snuffling audibly. He wiggles in Inna's arms and again asks for a cookie, returning his human to reality. Inna says, 'And you know, everything in my life suited me: I worked as a train conductor and my husband was at a factory, we had our own apartment. It was the second marriage for both of us. The kind of love, how can I tell you this, that's late, the last one. We loved each other with all our might, so much it sometimes felt shameful. Like sinning in your youth.

'He's no longer here so I can probably already say that now because it's like a reminiscence and I'm not bragging, right?'

She's not asking me or Tatiana or Sveta and Sasha, her Mariupol neighbours who became travelling companions and witnesses to the scariest days of her life. She's asking Tyson. Tyson licks Inna's face and hands, lies on his back and sprawls out.

I say, 'Like a cat.'

Inna's offended for Tyson.

'No, you tell her, I'm not a cat. I'm just a dog who came from the war. I'm allowed everything now, I'm afraid of everything now. You know, when we were on the run, we rode 900 kilometres in Sasha's shot-up car without stopping once. And Tyson lay with me, wrapped up in a little blanket. When we first got here, he was nervous, whimpered, cried and probably remembered everything we'd been through. Then I'd get the little blanket and he and I would go to the car. I'd put him on my knees and he'd fall asleep. And I'd sit and remember what life was before the war. Our good fortune.'

Inna's crying.

Tatiana stands, embraces Inna, enveloping her, and waves a hand at us, signalling, *Get out of here, we need some time.*

Sveta, Uncle Sasha and I go out on the balcony. Where else?

Uncle Sasha shows us a black KIA under the window that was pretty well hit with bullets. He says, 'We probably wouldn't have gotten away if not for that car. At a checkpoint, when we were leaving, the Kadyrovites took off one licence plate, the front one, and threw it in the gully.'

I ask, 'Why?'

He laughs in response. He laughs for a long time, starts coughing and uses his hand to wipe away the tears his laughter brings to his eyes. He says, 'You're so funny, damn, the questions you ask. Why? Because they could! Whoever has an automatic weapon is the boss, that's how they're made.

'They put us on our knees, one of them walked around and poked with his weapon: Banderites, fascists, we'll shoot you now. But he was apparently in a good mood. He just knocked off the licence plate, got out the tape, and stuck their Zs all over the car. He did that sticking with feeling, with enjoyment. Then he says to get the fuck out fast, I'll count to ten, then I'm going to shoot. And he really did shoot at us later. But we'd already floored it.'

Uncle Sasha shows pictures on his phone of the KIA with Zs stuck on it.

'Sasha, what are you scaring the young woman for, you tell her how you became our provider, how you saved us all from a hungry death.' This is Sveta talking. She pushes her husband in the side and they both start laughing. They cough. They light cigarettes. Uncle Sasha says:

'There was a school in front of our building. To be honest with you, I don't know what they needed it for but it was like this: either the AFU is sitting there holding a defensive position, or it's Kadyrovites, then the Kadyrovites are dislodged – that's Azov, then it's DPR but the AFU knocks them out quick because they were the most unstable of them all, they were removed quick. But before they were removed, they came to our houses, taking some things or just breaking and ruining them and they kept saying, "So we lived eight years with shelling, our kids and women are sitting in basements, now you'll feel what that's like." But what do we have to do with it, did we attack them? We wanted that?

'We didn't want it to be like they had.

'Maybe there were some in the city who wanted that but after Russian soldiers came and started poking at us, there, that was it, nobody wanted it. What kind of Russian World is it that they're denazifying old women until they die? Why do we need that kind of Russian World?

'Long story short, they fought and fought for that school then, bam! They all left. Well, I went over there, I'm thinking maybe those warriors at least left behind something for us to eat, what's so valuable there that they fought so many days for the school?

'It was really tight for us with food in those days: we were on the outskirts, cut off from humanitarian aid and everything we had was long gone. Things were already bad.

'Anyway, I go inside and it's bedlam in the school, the kind of bedlam, Katya, that makes your heart sink. I walk around, wandering, some places there's bloody rags, some places the desks are shot up, one combat boot lying there, the chalkboard's in splinters, globes, flower pots, everything! And here I see a first-grade alphabet book lying around. Well, I think, I'll take it. I snap it up! And under it I see there's an untouched can, round, so big. Well, I think, is it herring, is it military potted meat? I bring that to the basement, so happy, and we had this one guy there, former military, who starts hollering, "What're you doing," he says, "you old buzzard, you brought us death! It's an unexploded mine!" And he tosses it away, right out of the basement. And it exploded. So I'm standing there, scratching my turnip, thinking, so I really am an old buzzard, an idiot, what can you say!'

They laugh again.

Tatiana comes out on the balcony. She says Inna's had a rest and is ready to continue.

Uncle Sasha and Sveta stay to smoke. Tatiana and I go back inside. Tatiana will sit next to Inna, in case Inna doesn't feel good. Inna pats Tyson as she speaks.

'My husband considered himself charmed, that nothing would happen to him. And that this was all basically a mistake. They came, they'll realise we're not Banderites and not fascists, the main thing is to stay calm. They're our brothers: they'll come, see, figure things out, confess and go back. You and I will get through all this, he'd say. What's this about denazifying us, it's all some kind of stupidity.

'And we never went anywhere, not to any kind of basement. We lived at home, sixth floor. I did sleep in the hallway; I was afraid. But my husband slept in the bedroom.

'Water got scarce pretty fast. First we drank what we drained from the air conditioners, then that was gone. We tried to keep ourselves in good order, though, not let ourselves go. We'd collect ice from puddles, both for ourselves and to wash the dogs' paws. The water melted, we boiled it and made tea. We somehow washed the dogs' legs in beer, that happened, too. Well, there was no chance of going out because there was shooting.

'But my husband would tell me, "Inna, don't be afraid, it'll all end soon. It's not a war against people, they somehow got things mixed up." Anyway, we tried to live a regular life.

'Basically, we lived on the outskirts so they captured us first. And everybody where we were tried to strengthen their position. There was constant shooting, you get used to that fast. I tried not to be afraid. I wasn't alone, I was with my husband. That gave me some sense of protection. And dogs discipline you, too: shelling or no shelling, they have to pee and poop, so we'd go outside. We had two dogs. Tyson and Lada, she's a terrier, too, but a different kind. A Westie. White. My husband always told me, Tyson's yours and Lada's mine. And that's how they stayed for ever.'

Inna goes silent. Tyson turns to her, wagging his tail. She pats him. Tatiana says, 'Innusha, you can do it . . . You'll tell the story and it will let go of you. Go ahead, honey. But don't tell it if you don't want to, it's not required.'

Inna says, 'I want to tell it. Let them know. Let them record it. They'll be judged for it later. For my husband, for my dog, for all of us, for our life that's gone and won't ever come back.'

Tatiana nods and takes her by the hand. Inna says, 'Tyson was very restless that morning. He pulled me out for a walk at seven in the morning. And we have a curfew until eight. But I say to my husband, "Vlad, what can you do, the dog's a living creature, you can't torture him." Anyway, I went out to the yard with Tyson, he poops, I'm sorry, and I bend because there's shooting. And I'm stooped over him like this and I see for myself how a Kadyrov tank drives into our building's courtyard, turns and shoots. It shoots right into our apartment. Where they're sleeping. I'm shouting and Tyson's just looking at me, he's doing his business. Once they've started to poop, dogs can't stop.

'It's weird, isn't it? I probably can't tell you how it all was, you'll never feel what I felt.

'I'm just standing and seeing my building burn and inside it are the ones I love more than everything on earth. And I can't do anything, I'm just repeating, "Vlad, Lada, Vlad, Lada . . ."

'I apparently shouted, did something, darted around the yard, I don't remember anything. I only remember that later, when I'm in a basement, Sveta gives me tea and I'm shaking. And then Sashka, the fool, came in with that mine of his. Which is called defusing tension.'

I can't figure out if she's laughing or crying. Inna's just shaking hard. Tatiana stands and throws a blanket over her shoulders. She strokes her and says, 'That's everything, everything, honey, that's already everything.'

Tatiana says, 'Let's go, honey, we'll have a smoke. It's all done, now you can just talk, you don't have to talk more about that.'

But Inna keeps talking on the balcony.

'You have to understand, we had a residential area, the objective was sleeping, we don't have either an army or other strategic object-ive. The PortCity entertainment centre and the Metro hypermarket, are those military objectives?

'And that tank, I saw how he drove in: he saw it was a building. Did he have a watch? Did he see it was seven in the morning? A person was sleeping there! When a person sleeps, they're warm, they're vulnerable. And Vlad's Ladochka always came in to him towards morning. There was nothing left of them. I found nothing. I don't have a grave, a keepsake, nothing. Only this video.'

She takes out her phone and shows a video the neighbours filmed. There are campfires in the video, people are cooking something on them, children are romping around alongside them, then the camera abruptly turns to the left and on the screen there's a flame breaking out of an apartment on the sixth floor. The video ends.

Inna puts away the phone. 'I watch that video all the time and attempt to understand what they were feeling.'

Sveta hugs Inna. Inna puts her head on Sveta's shoulder. These women didn't know each other before the war, though they lived in neighbouring buildings.

Two weeks after Vlad and Lada died, Inna, Uncle Sasha and Sveta decided to bust out of Mariupol. The only possible route from the building where they'd been living went to Russia, via the tiny village of Old Crimea, not far from Mariupol.

Uncle Sasha, whose car they decided to escape in, brought the women to a checkpoint and returned to Mariupol to get a few more people from the basement. He now says, 'Well, of course, it was a **little bit** hairy: the road was being shot at from all sides. But I convinced myself that if I die, I'll die heroically and my women'll compose beautiful songs about me later.'

But nobody laughs. Inna says, 'We had to leave by driving through those Kadyrovites who were hard at work near us. We could already recognise them. By both the accent and the uniform. Sveta went over to talk with them but I couldn't. They were standing there, swaggering and obnoxiously forward.'

Sveta says, 'They asked about Inna and I say, "Your tank shot right at her husband." And they say, "Why're you lying! There wasn't anybody in those buildings, just AFU snipers, we were working on them." And then when he was walking away, he started yelling, "People like you are killing our friends, our comrades here, what are you doing demanding your rights, go back to your homes. Your AFU made you a human shield."

'And to be honest, I told him a certain something, something like, "Who invited you and your comrades here anyway, are they killing you or what? And maybe they made us a human shield but we're not hacked off, we're supporting our country and we're against you, the invaders and orcs."

'But it seems like I didn't say that out loud. I only thought it. You know, I've never been more scared in my life than that. I'm not bashful. I don't respect cowardice. I've always entered the fray and I don't mince words. But he was standing there, huge and bearded, and behind him was power, an army – your country's huge. And I started feeling very scared. I'm still ashamed that I didn't say to his face everything I was thinking. I said it to myself.'

Sveta buries her face in Inna's shoulder. And now Inna's already talking and Sveta's just sobbing and adding clarifying words.

Inna says:

'They indulged in everything: undressing, taking off Tyson's clothes, they prodded at everything there. What are you looking for? You might ask. They read phones: all the texts, all the pictures. They read, brazenly looking you in the eyes and watching to see how you reacted when your personal stuff's right there, out loud.

'Then they made us give interviews. About Ukrainian soldiers' crimes and Russia's noble mission to liberate an oppressed people, shit.

'I talked and my tears just flowed. I felt so sick to my stomach but I had to get out. And so I say what they ask, I thank them for liberation but in front of my eyes the whole time is that tank turning, shooting and everything instantly catching fire and burning, burning before my eyes. All my life, all my purpose, everything about me that's gentle. And the voice of that correspondent woman who came to the checkpoint to interview us for propaganda:

'"What's your attitude towards the special military operation Russia's conducting?"

'"My attitude's positive. I approve of the actions of Russian President Vladimir Putin and the Russian armed forces . . ."

'Sure, of course I approve it. I'm so glad you liberated me. We're all, the whole country, so happy you barged in on us that we could just shit ourselves. Thanks to you, this kind of freedom came so freaking easily. Thank you, thank you, liberators, you liberated us. What, I'm hesitant to ask, though, is it that you liberated me from?

From my husband, family, home, everything. So now I'm a free person, in your opinion, is that right? Sometimes I come to my senses and have the impression that I've just watched some kind of movie, that this didn't happen to me, it wasn't with us. It still hasn't all hit me. Sometimes it hits me during the night. That's how I'm very slowly coming closer to a realisation of what happened. But I won't understand it. They came, destroyed life, liberated me from my home, liberated me from my husband, liberated me from my happiness. Thank you, liberators. Damn you.

'At the end they made us pull the SIM cards out of our phones, took them, and then shot our phones: that was my whole life with Vlad, that was the last I had left of that life. And I burst into tears and a Kadyrovite comes over. I have this bag, my passport was in it, and he sticks a chocolate bar in there and slaps me on the shoulder. "Don't cry, woman, everything will be fine."

'What will be fine? What? What???

'I bit my lip so as not to answer. I think I could have strangled him. But we left.'

We're standing, all four of us, on the balcony, and it's almost as crowded as rush hour on a subway or trolleybus. It's seemingly cold but we don't feel it. Tatiana's outsized arms are embracing Inna and Sveta. They're both the height of her shoulder and it works out as if Tatiana's towering over them.

Inna presses her head to Tatiana's arm and says, 'I hated Russians until I met Taniushka. They only let us out of Mariupol on the Russian side. We're driving and I hate everything: the cities, stores, buildings, people. We got to their refugee centre and they gave us this thin hot soup and said, "Eat!" And then one woman there says, "Can you really be so ungrateful?" But why should I be grateful for a bowl of soup? I had soup but where is it? I used to be glad for a new phone, when my husband gifted it to me, but now I'm supposed to be glad about a bowl of soup?'

Now Sveta speaks,. 'And there was this one **woman** there who served in the cafeteria, she **spoke** Ukrainian, she was always repeating, looking at us, why are you **all** coming, **all** making your way here, prices went up because of you. And I wanted to tell her, "Open your eyes, woman! It's not because of us, it's because of that grandpa of yours sitting in a bunker or **wherever** he's hiding there." But we kept quiet, we were supposed to be grateful, shit.'

Uncle Sasha has a coughing fit.

'Come on, let's go, let's go for a walk! That's enough, that's it, *basta*! We didn't stay there, right? That's it!'

Right then, everybody starts laughing again and telling, interrupting each other, how at the refugee site they were given documents for a train that would have brought them to another refugee site in the Tula Oblast, where they would have gone through additional filtration and received refugee paperwork. But they ran away from their escort, literally along the rails at the Taganrog train station in the evening. They smoke, brushing away tears and ash, interrupting each other, describing personal and group heroism while in search of petrol for the KIA and food.

Tatiana suddenly says, 'Eh, why did I sell my apartment! You could have stayed at my Tula apartment.' And, all together, they roar with laughter again.

The tea inside went cold long ago. Tyson's scratching at the balcony door from the inside. We go back in, bringing with us the smell of cigarettes, a summer evening and rain. We take seats. Inna picks up Tyson. And after touching my shoulder, she asks, 'Tell me, you know more than our people: what do you think, will Mariupol be Ukrainian again? I'd really want to go back home. But I have no need for Mariupol if it's not Ukrainian. If it's not, it can go away.'

# 17

# Blackberries

August is blackberry-picking time. At dawn the fleshy blackberries are saturated with moisture but haven't yet softened in the full sun. You reach a hand between the leaves, touch a berry, turn it lightly and it easily detaches from the plant. You put it in a basket and reach for another. I've tried speeding things up by picking blackberries with two hands but it doesn't work. You can only pick with one hand.

'Each berry requires its own personal attention,' Paola says with a laugh. 'Don't you hurry. Forget about everything and try to enjoy it. My blackberry bushes were created for enjoyment – there's not one prickle.'

I attempt to focus on the blackberries.

But I end up just thinking about how it turned out that people dreamed up blackberries without prickles but couldn't make a world without war.

Paola and I have known each other for many years. Six? Seven? Ten? I don't remember. Every year I wait for summer to set in so I can go to Paola's farm in the very heart of Italy's Campania, pick blackberries and talk about how the year went.

For the first time in my life, I want us to keep silent.

Paola says, 'It's so good that you came.'

I nod.

'I've been waiting for you.'

I twist a berry.

'I need your help. I have three families of Ukrainian refugees at my house: three mums, five children. I need you to speak with them.'

The berry bursts in my hand. Reddish-black juice runs down my fingers.

I ask Paola, 'Are you sure they'll speak Russian?'

'They speak Russian among themselves. We called for a Russian interpreter from Terracina when they were having an especially hard time.'

'Yes, of course, I'll speak with them.'

Paola empties the first basket of blackberries into a plastic box.

She says, 'We'll finish with the blackberries and I'll tell them you've come. They'll be glad, Katerina. I've been telling them over and over, all the time: when Katerina comes, she'll talk with you.'

'And what's going on?'

'They cry. We all cry all the time. It's all a big ordeal. My husband and I nearly divorced because of it. It's turned out to be really hard.'

'What, exactly?'

'To sympathise. Not in the sense of hanging a Ukrainian flag in the window. But every day. They live with us every day. See what I'm saying?'

I do seem to understand. But I keep quiet and pick blackberries.

The sun rises. Roosters crow. Somewhere in the distance, a cow moos. Or a buffalo. In Campania, people raise buffalos and make proper mozzarella cheese from the milk.

'They don't like mozzarella, can you imagine,' says Paola, 'and they don't like pasta either, they don't like anything. A completely different mentality. We don't understand each other. Can you imagine, they're here all by themselves, in a world where nobody understands them but everybody prepared themselves to feel sorry for them.

'In the beginning of your war, everybody collected and brought items. We didn't have as many refugees as in Eastern Europe, like in Poland or the Baltic countries. After all, it's harder to get to us. But they made it. If you'd only seen how surprised people were here. Some of them arrived in expensive cars, some were well dressed. I don't know what people expected, that they'd arrive in rags, dirty and with eczema, huh, Katerina?'

We sit down for a quick rest. The two of us have picked four boxes of sweet blackberries. Paola drinks coffee and smokes. She says, 'I'm not asking you why you're [all] keeping quiet in Russia.'

'Thank you.'

'But I don't believe, no matter what they write here in our newspapers, that everybody living in Russia is for the war.'

'It's not like that, of course.'

'Then how did it work out this way, Katerina?'

'I ask myself about that every day.'

Paola strokes my shoulder.

A tanned little boy, about ten years old, comes out of the house.

'This is Vitalik,' says Paola, introducing us, 'Elena's son.'

She tells him in Italian to bring me in to his mother. He nods.

He takes me by the hand and leads me into the house.

Three women are standing in various poses in the kitchen; one of them is cooking something.

I tell them who I am.

Silence.

I say I'm a friend of Paola's, that I come to this farm every year and to this area in general because I love these places, that the sea is wonderful here.

Silence.

I apologise for speaking Russian. And add, just in case, that I understand Ukrainian, I have relatives there.

The woman in the middle of the kitchen shrugs and introduces herself.

'Elena.'

Right then she adds, 'So we're cooking something up before it starts.'

'Before what starts?'

'The heat. It's so hot here that I can't even go outside.'

'And I don't even want to,' says another woman. She's standing by the exhaust fan and smoking.

We introduce ourselves. She's Yulia.

The third woman turns away. I don't understand if that's on purpose or not. She's looking out at the yard. Children are playing in the yard, splashing themselves with water. In the summer, Paola organises something like a day camp for local kids. They're taught to take care of animals and plants, gather honey from hives without fearing the bees, interact with ponies without riding them, things like that. The camp is called *Tenda Verde*, the green tent. That all has a new purpose now: the refugee women's children are learning Italian and forgetting shelling, checkpoints and bombings, while they're also being distracted from the loss of home, something that doesn't appear to look as harsh as shelling but wounds no less.

I tell the women I think the place they've ended up is the most wonderful in the world. I say I know every little street in the surrounding cities here and if they have questions, I'll tell them everything, translate everything, take them everywhere.

I say something else, too.

'Oh, we don't need anything,' says Elena.

After a silence, she adds, 'We don't need anything. We don't really want anything anymore. The kids seem to have acclimatised normally, they chatter like the locals, the landlady's kids taught them.'

'What about you?'

'We're just living along with our heads in our news. Everything for us is there. You go to bed at night and read *they* have sirens there and that rings in your ears. I brought things with me but in my mind I didn't move, I'm still there, in my kitchen and—'

Yulia interrupts Elena.

'You have to understand that they, these Italians, they all come to see us. Learn the language, they say, get jobs. They brought us on some kind of trip, like to introduce us to local professions. But I don't want to be a baker! I don't want to shape any of their rolls, I don't want to speak their language, see? And they get offended. Volunteers call us, they say that's not polite. That's how impolite we are.

'But the fact that we have four duffel bags of winter things and there's no shelves to store it all? What's with that? My child needs to go to school, where does he go? You can't figure out where the closest school is in these parts. You can't get there on foot, see? Where do I bring the little one in September?'

'Let's buy you a bicycle,' I say.

'Give me 2021,' says Yulia. She's looking me in the eye.

The woman by the window who didn't introduce herself sighs and hugs her shoulders. It seems like she's cold. But the sun's already sizzling, the heat's around 30 degrees.

Elena stirs the contents of the pot.

'Our Yulia doesn't know how to ride a bicycle. And anyway the heat here, I don't know how they ride. The main thing is you have to ride along the road the whole time, gives you the fear of God. But the ones who don't have a car, they ride.'

There's a sour-sweet smell: meat and potatoes with prunes, like my grandmother cooked.

I ask Elena, 'Where are you from?'

'Dnipro, Dnipropetrovsk, do you know it?'

'I do.'

'That's where I'm from, we're all from there,' says Elena. 'I taught dance. I used to be a ballerina. So I taught kids to dance, I had my team, we went everywhere. My husband earned decent money; he was in business. We had an apartment, a car, everything. I didn't want for anything. Why do I have to start all over now here, without my husband, alone, in a foreign country? My cousin, she went to Russia, not because it's easier for her there, but she says it's more understandable.'

I ask where her cousin is.

Elena rummages around in her phone and shows me the address. It's the outskirts of Moscow.

I ask her to tell her cousin I'll be in Moscow soon, maybe I can be helpful.

Elena says her cousin doesn't need anything, that an organisation, the Lighthouse Charity Foundation, helped her.

I don't stop to consider if I should or shouldn't say this right now to these people, but I go ahead and say, 'That's a foundation that I help. I was there at the organisation recently, at their site where they give out humanitarian aid.'

'And?' I don't remember which of them asked but it seems like it was all three.

I ask Yulia for a cigarette and also smoke out the window. I don't know how to say things. How can you explain in just a few words that in the centre of the capital of the country that started the war on their country, two storeys of a brick building that belongs to the Moscow city administration are taken up by an organisation that helps Ukrainian refugees but was opened by people who used to help terminally ill children? But I utter those very words. And add that when I was at the distribution site for the Lighthouse Charity Foundation ten days ago, I saw people who hadn't come for things but for food: buckwheat groats, sugar and canned goods. And some people haven't seen meat since early March. I get wound up and for some reason I tell these three women what a wild feeling gripped me at that humanitarian aid distribution site.

Expensive foreign cars drove past: Moscow's a rich city and this was almost the very centre. But alongside me stood people who didn't have elementary things, people who were literally starving.

They didn't interrupt me and I grew bolder. I also told them about how helping refugees is the only way for many Russians who are against the war to express their protest.

'So there are people who're against it?' Elena asks.

I say there are many.

She puts her hand on her hip and says, 'Somehow, I haven't heard about them. But my cousin said volunteers there told her right away that politics is a no-no. You know, it's like in the American army. Don't ask me, I won't fuck with your head.'

Everybody laughs.

'Mokryna, Mokryna, phone call!' shout three boys and one girl as they run into the kitchen. They hand a phone to the listless young woman by the window. It's a videocall.

The man in the phone is speaking Ukrainian; the woman immediately starts to cry.

Elena turns off the cooktop gas; Yulia pushes at my back. 'Let's go, let's go, it's Mokryna's husband calling.'

We go out on the terrace. They close the door tightly behind us and both light cigarettes. I've ended up with them as a sort of accomplice and they give me a cigarette, too. I'm worried along with them but don't know the reason.

'There's this story,' says Yulia, 'there's no brief version. But the shorter version is that Mokryna's from Mykolaiv. But her husband Albert's from Vinnytsia. Got the difference?

'Basically, that Albert, he's a military man, well he's Azov, right? Not a shocker for you, is it? And Mokryna's a simple girl, she loves him. But things didn't work out for them with kids. And so they scraped together money, decided on IVF. They got her ready for half a year. There were difficulties, his service, he came and went, you don't belong to yourself. They had an appointment for 25 February. Well, what more can I say?

'And so, the shorter version is that Mokryna left with us, brought her little brother and sister with her, she's raising them instead of her parents. And that Albert, he fought and fought and got injured.'

I gasp. Elena pokes me in the side, appealing to me to pull myself together.

'And so thanks to that injury of his, see, he ended up at home. And she asked him,' Elena nods towards the kitchen, 'to find out how things are with their eggs and sperms. If there's any chance, you got me?'

I take a long drag on her cigarette so as not to say too much.

It's getting hot.

Paola loudly calls the children to breakfast. And Mokryna opens the door, inviting us to come in.

'Well?!'

'Well, that's it, I'm going for ovulation.'

'So it's saved?'

'It's saved.'

'Oy, girls, so shall we down one or what?' Elena suddenly says.

A bottle of grappa appears out of nowhere. I automatically look at the time: 10am. A little early, of course, but in theory, it doesn't matter anymore.

We drink to Mokryna going to Dnipro and getting pregnant.

We drink to everyone going home and ending the wandering.

We drink to regime change in Russia and for everybody to stop thinking Ukraine is Russia.

We drink to me going to Dnipro and finding the addresses where strangers hid my 12-year-old grandmother from the Stalinist repressions in 1937.

And then for some reason I talk about how after Dnepropetrovsk (that's what it was called in those years) my grandmother went to Kharkiv, where she enrolled at Kharkiv Aviation Institute, and how her trousers fell off her because of malnutrition. My grandmother ran cross-country for the institute's team and held up her trousers.

And then Mokryna tells how she ordered clothes for herself on Amazon for her whole pregnancy and didn't bring them with her, she left them in Dnipro.

And then Yulia talks about how her relative from the Russian city of Mineral'nye Vody wrote, saying to stay patient a little longer and they'd be liberated.

We pour again.

Mokryna – who's tall and brown-eyed – turns her shot glass in her slender fingers and asks, apparently not addressing anyone in particular, 'But what if I get pregnant and the war doesn't end? Then what's it all for?'

'But people have babies for no reason,' says Elena. And she adds, 'Somebody has to live normally.'

Mokryna's the first to start crying. Through her tears, she says, 'Albert said we should have a son and he'll get revenge. But I don't want, I can't and I won't have any baby who's going to continue all this, see?'

Yulia hugs her.

'You shouldn't talk like that, Mokryna. He's alive, he agreed to a child. And thank God.'

'But I don't want to fight more. I can't hate anymore, see?'

Elena hugs them both.

'Our children will hate their children. It'll be like that to the seventh generation. And we can't do anything. However much they did, none of it will be forgiven.'

I don't remember the point when I started crying, too. I just remember that the four of us were crying and hugging. And I say to Mokryna, that 'Mokryna' – which in Russian is rooted in 'wet' – is also like *lacrima*, 'tear' in Italian. That makes us cry even more.

And I can't remember any another episode in my life when I was that drunk at 10 in the morning.

The children come in and out of the kitchen. Paola comes in and brings us food.

Someone switches the burner with the sweet-sour meat on and off, and at that moment we're discussing how Italians don't eat soups, not to mention borshch, that instead of sweet beetroot they eat the leaves, though not everywhere; they don't have sour cream and nobody knows how delicious it is to cut up tomatoes and onion, then dress them with sour cream and vinegar.

'Their vinegar is different,' Elena says defiantly.

That seems to be the last thing I remember from that morning.

We're sitting, hugging, in a hot Italian kitchen: Elena, Yulia, Mokryna and I, who have somehow, incomprehensibly, ended up in their embraces. Each of us cries for her own reasons and we're not ashamed. We pick up on each other's weeping and briefly catch our breath so we can continue crying.

I don't know how long we cry. We just stop when all the tears are gone.

It suddenly feels both easy and awkward. I don't have that level of closeness with any of my girlfriends I've known for decades.

Reeling, I leave the kitchen and see Paola. She says, 'Thank you.'

I mumble something in reply and as she sits me in her car, she says, 'Thank you, thank you, Katerina. We don't understand any of that at all. I saw how the girls were themselves with you. How you cried. They don't cry with me, I'm a stranger. But you – it's odd because you're allegedly the enemy – are one of them. You know,' Paola says as she stops the car. 'I realised something now about how if someone attacks you, that doesn't necessarily mean that you're good. It's just that the attacker is even worse. This isn't about any of you specifically. It's just an observation.'

She puts the car in motion and continues.

'We expected the refugees would be as sweet as kittens. We thought that if we extended a hand to them and gave our unnecessary things to them that would be all.

'But everything's deeper and more terrifying. And we don't delve into your problems, we have plenty of our own. It's like this for us: two Slavic peoples quarrelled very close to our borders and that's dangerous.

'I understand everything, I see the grief that's seething in your cauldron and spilling over, flowing and reaching us, too, of course.

'But I'll never be able to understand them as deeply as you.'

'I'm glad I can at least say that to you.'

'There's still one problem because time and patience are all we can actually give to people who've escaped death in Ukraine by some miracle. At the beginning of the war it seemed to me that this was the simplest, it's what definitely won't run out, it's something everybody has.

'But I see how both those are coming to an end. But the war isn't ending.'

In January 2023, a Russian missile landed on the building where Yulia and her family lived before the war. They weren't there so neither she nor her husband nor her child were harmed.

Elena acclimatised in Italy and isn't planning to return to Ukraine.

Mokryna insisted that I not state where she stayed to have her baby. Yes, yes, she got pregnant.

## 18.

# The Cat

In May 2022, a message arrives: 'Hello, it's Marina from Mariupol. I told you about cockroaches. Can you talk?'

I can talk.

'We're in Wrocław and you should come here. There are women here. There are women here that your soldiers raped. You should see this. If you're not afraid.'

I went but the women in the Wrocław dormitory for refugees were already gone. I met with Liza. She's a volunteer who's been working with refugees since late March, initially in Warsaw, now throughout Poland. This evening, Liza brought a family to Wrocław, where they'll now live, to integrate, as they say in official language.

Liza will travel on to Dresden in the morning to get the women I came to see in Warsaw. But Liza doesn't even want to speak with me about that. For that matter, she doesn't want to speak with me at all.

Liza, who has fiery red hair and is dressed mannishly, pointedly places a folder with documents on the front seat and shows me the back seat. She didn't really want to drive me but Marina convinced her to.

'Just nothing about guilt feelings and never-ending 24 February that keep torturing you, okay?' says Liza, immediately beginning to use familiar pronouns. I nod. 'The whining and remorse has fucking worn me out,' she summarises, and steps on the gas.

It's a little over three hours to drive from Polish Wrocław to German Dresden.

I calm myself, thinking, *It's possible to just keep silent for a while.* And we keep silent.

Liza placed the documents face down but I know the files contain the stories of Ukrainian women raped by Russian soldiers in Bucha, Irpin, Borodianka, Bakhmut, and more.

In April 2022, these women managed to escape the war by coming to Poland. By the time they were in Wrocław, several learned they were pregnant. Initially, nobody thought about the strict bans on abortion in Poland. They now solve that problem with Liza's help.

Three and a half weeks ago, Liza brought the women to Germany for paid abortions and rehabilitation. Now she's going to pick them up and bring them back.

It's raining and we're not driving as fast as Liza would like. She swears.

Liza lived in Kyiv before the war and worked with women who'd survived violence: she placed the victims in shelters and arranged for psychological and legal help. The organisation where Liza worked collaborated closely with similar Russian organisations. Some contacts still remain. We have acquaintances in common. But that doesn't help.

Liza cuts off all attempts to begin speaking with her about the women whose stories are described in the folders lying on the front seat.

'You'll hear it in court,' she says, cutting me off.

She softens about 30 kilometres later.

'Listen, we don't have the right to speak with them about anything either. The International Criminal Court and their authorised representatives are conducting an investigation. The girls, meaning the victims, can't be questioned until the investigator's done. Those are the rules. But the investigator still hasn't come to them. So I sometimes just listen when they really need to vent. But I don't ask questions. When we were going to the Germans, well . . . we went for the procedure and one cried so hard, she was even shouting. She's 35, dreamed her whole life about a child and then this. But, she says, I won't keep it, I can't, as soon as I see the eyes, I'll remember *those eyes*. And I'll hate the child, wouldn't be able to hold it in my arms. And she's crying. Well and then everybody in the car started sobbing, too, even me. Each for her own reasons. Would you give birth to a baby like that?'

★

There's 30 kilometres to go. The rain's abating. Gas station. We get out for coffee. We stand and smoke in the parking lot by Liza's car, a small, peppy jeep with a Ukrainian licence plate and Ukrainian flags on the front and back windows. In order to say something, I say, 'Great car.'

'It's not mine.'

I should probably ask whose it is. But conversation with redheaded Liza is thin ice. Any question could turn out to be the one that makes her just toss me out of the car. And so I keep quiet and look at Liza. The wind's blowing her red hair, which the sun is making even brighter. Liza keeps one hand in her camouflage trouser pocket; the other holds a cigarette. Liza's nails are polished black. She finishes, puts out her cigarette and we ride on.

'Want a joke?' Liza asks. And without waiting for my answer, she says, '"Dear Grandfather Frost, this isn't at all what I had in mind when I asked you for constant travel, getting drunk and finally being able to smoke and swear in front of my mother next year." Funny?'

'Funny.'

'Not a damn thing funny. In the first days I was always repeating to myself, "this isn't happening to me". It can't be that I've completely lost control over my life and no longer manage anything. And that's me, me! I've controlled everything my whole life.

'I got this car from a guy, my college classmate, who went off as a volunteer. He came by and said, "Do something good using this car, help people." And those really were the first days. When everybody was running from parking lots into the subway in such a stupor, hiding from bombing. I took the keys and I'm looking at him and thinking, why'd you come to see me anyway, why? I can't deal with myself, now there's a car, too.

'I just got my licence in January, I'm basically afraid at the wheel. But the eyes are afraid and the hands act. We have friends who own a few restaurants and in the first days they decided to cook food for people, for homeland defence and others. And I figured out then, "Ah, so that's what I need Seryoga's car for." And I started driving around with food. There was one really sketchy point. I'm driving and the Russians had just hit our TV tower, I was really close. And I'm looking out the windshield, there's this explosion, a cloud, fire. And I started shouting out loud from fear. I stepped on the gas just so I wouldn't stop and crawl under the seat. And then suddenly, this feeling of absolute unreality came over me. Liza, is this really you? Are you in *Lara Croft*? Is this really your life now?'

From a motorist's point of view, the border of Poland and Germany isn't defined at all. There are fields, fields, fields and some low-rise towns along the side of the road. An EU traffic sign about the nearing border. Gradually there are more German names than Polish ones. And then they're all German. We're in Germany.

'Why did you leave Kyiv?' I ask Liza, understanding that it's easier for her to speak with me while she's holding the wheel.

'The answer will be funny now,' says Liza, looking at me in the rearview mirror, as if she needs to gauge my sense of humour before answering.

Liza gets mixed up on a roundabout, swears, and has words in Ukrainian with the GPS. Then she recalls what we were talking about.

'I left because of a cat. I had a pregnant cat. There was a point when I was driving around the whole city in Seryoga's jeep, gathering up and feeding all the animals people left behind when they ran from the war. And then it was like something suddenly hit me over the head. How will I feed five cats if there's a humanitarian catastrophe in Kyiv and my cat has kittens? Then I also wondered, damn, how would I go to a bomb shelter with those cats, and what if they're like Zoska? Zoska's my cat. She totally lost her mind in the bomb shelter. Long story short, that really was an incredibly spontaneous and very strange decision but can I not justify myself?

'If you want, think I was just afraid and the cat and all that are my justification.

'Driving was so scary for me. I'd only been driving for real three

weeks of my life, around empty Kyiv, I didn't understand anything
and only knew the rules purely theoretically.

'Anyway, I left Kyiv and was antsy the first two hours.

'Basically, I made stops to cry.

'Here's something else from the "funny things about me" list. In
May 2021, I bought an apartment in Kyiv and finished renovations in
December. And the whole time, the thought irritated me that of
course this was great but the whole bourgeois lifestyle wasn't my
thing. I beat myself up for being spoiled, getting too settled and
being stuck in my own comfort. Basically, on New Year's Eve, I
made a wish to change my life, get out of my comfort zone. I
wanted to leave the apartment so my mother could live there.
Because she was still living with my brother. I thought if she has the
experience of independent life maybe they'd come unglued from
each other. I was the one who was so independent, blowing out of
the house at 15, like the wind, and always on my own. But Borya's
different. He's always around Mama. He was.'

We're silent again. Dresden's coming up. For some reason, I tell Liza
I have a daughter named Liza. And also a brother, Andrei, and a sis-
ter, Natasha; they live in Kyiv. And my Uncle Sasha, too, he's also in
Kyiv, he—

She cuts me off.

'And what? How has that helped you? How will that help all of
us? How will that help all of us?' she repeats mechanically, no longer
questioning at all.

We're entering Dresden.

Redheaded Liza looks at me in the rearview mirror.

'I didn't want to take you. I agreed because I wanted to say to
your face how much I hate you, all of you who are so sweet, so
empathetic, so "it's not me, it's all Putin". I thought I'd say that and
somehow feel better. But no. All of you always have some kind of
excuse: relatives, a good resumé, little children, your charitable
organisations.

'It's just that none of that matters. It basically doesn't mean anything, see? All of you – your other brother who's not Ukrainian, some classmate of yours, your former or current colleague or the guy you kissed under the stairs at school – it doesn't really matter who specifically – but you're all coming and killing us. And then you write on your social media how bad you feel, oh-oh, we're so proper, shit, how is this all possible, it's not us, it's some kind of other Russians. It's you. I wanted to tell you that, Katya.'

Traffic light.

'I've been through all the stages, from harsh hatred and wanting to follow Borya to the front to total apathy. Then I went on antidepressants and it eased a little. There was a point when I thought about hardcore escape, leaving town for Portugal or something to lie there and look at the sky, forget everything: who I am, where I'm from and what you did to us. But I want to remember. If I have kids, I'll tell them what you did to us. And how we didn't give in, I'll tell them that, too. Our children will be proud of us. But yours will curse you.'

Liza stops the car and gets out alone to smoke. She smokes, leaning against her jeep and looking at the sky. I can't see her face, just her red hair bobbing and flying in the wind.

After smoking, Liza takes out her phone and makes a call – she finishes speaking in the car, and I hear, 'Just don't say anything about me. I'll be there in 15 minutes.'

She hangs up.

We drive.

I ask, 'Are you staying the night?'

'It's wait and see. I don't know. There are complications.'

A turn, a fork in the road, swearing at the GPS.

It seems like the GPS has lost its mind, constantly repeating, 'Return to start point.' But redheaded Liza isn't driving by the directions. She's just driving so as not to stop, she needs this additional stretch of the trip to finish talking. And she says, 'Mama always loved Borya more. And he loved her more, too. It was idyllic for them. I'm not like that. I left home at 15. And always did everything myself. But Borya was such a sweet sweetie of a guy, he's our responsible one. I was really little when our father died; but Borya's nine years older than me. And then he got this self-important idea that now he's father to us all. For our mother, Borya was always the smartest, most responsible and most handsome. I didn't understand. It drove me crazy that, holy crap, the guy's 30 years old and he's still living with Mama. And they always did everything for each other: just so long as everything's good for Mamochka, just so long as everything's good for Borya.'

Traffic light.

'With his brain, Borya could have been anything he wanted. But after studying maths and mechanics he did his army service and got into trading. He sat at his computer and made endless cash. I thought he'd move away somewhere, Thailand or even America. But he bought a house beyond Lebedivka and brought Mama with him. Mama started a garden, some tomatoes, strawberries, flowers. At first Borya was online half a year, on some sites for whack-job fans of elite gin, then he went to London and to Norway, and took courses. And then – you don't know whether to laugh or cry – he spent insane cash on equipment and started making his own gin. He grew his own juniper, I think he brought his own seedlings from somewhere in Finland. He picked the berries himself. He'd say it seems like it's all simple: juniper, potato and sugar. But he could lecture for hours about berries that were or weren't the right ones, and how to tell them apart. Long story short, some kind of bullshit. I never understood that. Some friends, designers, made Borya a branded label and, to be honest, he fucking wore everybody out with that gin: gin for New Year's, gin for Christmas, gin for birthdays. Borya didn't need money so he was doing all that from the heart. I didn't go to that suburban idyll of theirs very often. But I can't lie: the house was beautiful.'

Traffic light.

'After the war started, not now but in 2014, Borya helped the army. Humanitarian aid, money. Sometimes he brought parcels to the front line himself. Some of his army friends were fighting there. Basically, there were people he knew.

'In February, he told our mother he never thought it would get to this but he couldn't stay at home in a situation like this, especially given his experience. I don't know if that experience was useful or not. Borya died near Mariupol. Not even a month and a half had gone by. They told us almost immediately that he'd died but they had to search a long time for his body. My mother went there, identified him and that was that. And I was thinking the whole time that it was too bad Borya died, not me. It would have been easier for everybody. Basically . . .' And here Liza stops the car and turns to me. She's looking right at me for the first time and is speaking with me rather than the rearview mirror or the emptiness in front of her. 'My mother's already in Dresden now, she knows you. It's actually her that convinced me to take you. She wants to talk with you, don't ask what I think about that.'

She turns around and we drive off. And it's in utter silence that we reach the Centre, a spacious apartment on the outskirts of Dresden, where families of refugees from Ukraine have been living for several weeks at a time since March 2022. Psychologists work with some of them. Some need medical help, some are simply catching their breath before moving on.

Before getting out of the car, I ask her, 'What about the cat? Did she have kittens?'

Liza's surprised, as if she'd already forgotten about the cat. But she answers.

'She had kittens. Five, how about that? I gave them away to people who'd decided to stay here for ever. I gave them for house-warmings, for happiness, there's a superstition.'

We get out of the car and walk up to a five-storey brick building. Liza keys in a code and goes up to the second floor. The door to the apartment is open. The first thing we see is a woman on all fours, her back to us, holding a floor rag in her hands. She's finishing scrubbing the hallway.

'Why am I not surprised, mother?' says Liza.

The woman stands and turns. She keeps raising and lowering hands red from hot water, unable to decide whether or not to hug Liza.

'My daughter,' she says, not budging. 'My dear daughter,' she says, this time in Ukrainian.

Liza's shoulder pushes me aside as she walks forward to hug her mother. Liza's tall and her mother ends up at her armpit. Her mother's crying. Liza seems to be crying, too. I don't see that but I see her shoulders rise and fall. Women come out of the rooms: one's in a robe, another's in a tracksuit, and there are children behind them. For some time, the women watch Liza and her mother crying in the middle of the hallway. Then they walk over and hug them, stroking their shoulders and hair. The younger children join in with the women's crying. Soon the whole hallway is crying. And everybody in that apartment has grounds to cry.

Liza's the first to free herself from the crying knot of women. She says a few names and asks them to get ready. One of the women asks, 'Oh, Liza, come on, at least have some tea for the road.'

'Here we go,' snaps Liza.

The kitchen table is set with tea, streusel cakes, sweets and cookies.

'Liza, will you have something to eat?' her mother asks her.

Liza introduces us: 'Olga Timofeyevna – Katya.'

The women bustle around in the kitchen, which smells of food. Some are passing along items and notes to go to Wrocław, some are simply exchanging phone numbers.

Liza turns to me.

'You didn't see anybody here and you didn't hear one single name. It's not for journalists. She' – Liza nods at her mother – 'is for journalists. But you have no right to anything else, got it?'

'Liza,' says Olga Timofeyevna, attempting to step in.

'Ma, don't interfere. Let's go, we need to talk.'

They leave the room. I'm left in the kitchen, among several women. I want to look at them but can't find the strength within to raise my head. Fortunately, five-year-old Vovchik comes running into the kitchen and helps me out of a hopeless situation. He and I play, so I look busy.

The women offer tea, coffee and even borshch. I agree to

everything. Liza comes in and also starts on some borshch. Their love for Liza is palpable: they give her more bread and sausage, ask how she's feeling. Everybody relaxes a little at the table as they discuss news and people I don't know. Liza answers questions in detail. But she abruptly sets her plate aside. 'It's time.'

The women leave the kitchen and then appear in the corridor, already dressed, with their bags. Everybody hugs and kisses, and there are again tears to be seen.

Liza and I exchange glances in the doorway. She wishes me success and says, 'Just don't torture my mother too hard.'

Olga Timofeyevna goes out to the car to see off Liza and the women who are travelling with her. She returns with documents, the same files that lay by Liza on the front seat. They need to be passed along to a volunteer organisation here in Dresden. Although it might seem to outsiders that almost everything that happens with refugees outside Ukraine happens on its own, the reality is that there are large and small organisations all over where volunteers try to keep track of every story and every family, while doing their best to resolve the problems that arise.

The organisation from Poland where Liza volunteers sent documents for an organisation that helps refugees in Germany. The documents have the histories of three women who spent almost a month in Dresden. They helped two terminate pregnancies and performed a complex operation on the reproductive organs of a third, after which there was rehab.

Liza took folders with reports about that.

Olga Timofeyevna returns to the kitchen. I don't know if it can happen that a person ages in an instant. But it seems like the life went out of her after Liza's departure.

I ask if she wants to postpone our conversation until tomorrow. She shakes her head.

She says:

'You know, I've always been your fan. And Borya, too, my son. Liza told you she has a brother? Had. Borya died. Borya was a person who wouldn't harm a cat. He and I were very close. He loved your programmes, too. Remember – this was before Crimea – when you made an appearance at our university? Borya and I came to have a look at you.

'Katya, I'm not Ukrainian by blood. My kin are all from the Urals, my parents came to work in Kyiv, this was back in the Soviet time, and so that's where I grew up but I'm not Ukrainian by blood. My husband, though, he was Ukrainian. So it works out that Liza and Borya are half. But we spoke Russian at home. And with friends. For some reason it was more customary in our circle to speak Russian. I never thought it would get to . . . to . . . I don't know how to put it, Katya. To the limit? But that's somehow too literary.

'It seems like I'm losing my mind. Hatred is driving me out of my mind. I'm not a person capable of hating. It's hard for me to maintain such a degree of it in me, it's eating me up inside. But do you know what I'm feeling? I'm feeling like I've lived my life completely in vain. I loved Ukraine but I also loved Russia. We have relatives who've stayed there in Pervouralsk. And I cultivated in my children a love and respect for Russia, as a second motherland. You can't expect such treachery, such barbarity, such brutality from someone you love. You simply don't expect that. We weren't ready, Katya. Then came 2014. And Russia arrived and took what it could reach for itself. In Russia that probably didn't seem like too much because you're a very, very big country and it probably went unnoticed for you that a whole piece of land that you call your own is overflowing with blood as your boys die, too. But we saw ours dying. There's not such a large population in Ukraine to squander like Russians do. There were dead, wounded and maimed wherever you poked around. No, it didn't touch us personally.

'Borya, thank God, had already done his service before 2014 but he had an officer's rank and the service branch was decent. Borya was a paratrooper. Did Liza show you a photograph?

'Of course she didn't show you. Liza's resentful, jealous of him, even dead. But there's nothing you can do there. As a mother, Katya, you understand it's impossible to choose one of two children. But Borya became my closest person in the world after his father died – he was hit by a car – just before the New Year, can you imagine?

'I thought then that nothing would be bitterer. But that happened.

'Liza got out of hand, in denial, after her father's death. She was her father's daughter. But I didn't have either the strength to hold her back or the disposition to lessen her temper. Borya wiped away all my tears. He pulled me out of it. You probably wonder why I'm telling you this?

'I'm telling it so you can know us better, after all, we're your enemies. We and those Banderites and fascists being destroyed in your name.

'When one motherland started out-and-out destroying the other motherland, my son went to fight for his motherland that found itself in danger. I don't know how he would have acted if Ukraine had attacked Russia. But I also can't imagine Ukraine would attack. Russia attacked us. Russia came and ruined our life, destroyed our homes. I'm completely certain what happened in Bucha could certainly have happened in the settlement where Borya and I lived. Nearby, too. And anywhere. That shouldn't be, it's unforgivable.

'And so my son went to defend me.

'In February, after the big war started, I wrote you a letter, Katya. It most likely didn't reach you. I wrote to you about how – since they came to kill us in your name – that means everything you've done was in vain. That means you did something wrong. That means you made mistakes somewhere, too. Or we made a mistake believing you. I don't know everything, I don't know your whole life . . . All I know about you is what I can read on the Internet. But you or your friends aren't nobodies in your country. And if what came to kill us developed in your presence, in front of your eyes, during your active work years, that means you did something that allowed it to grow. That means you're part of this, too.

'Don't answer me, you don't need to. I don't want to hear your justifications. That won't change anything. I simply want you to know that Borya was killed on 26 March in close fighting not far from Azovstal, by a shot to the head. The bullet entered his eye. The guys didn't abandon him on the battlefield, thank you to them for that. Borya's body ended up at Azovstal. He was there when

Mariupol was being destroyed, when people were dying around there, when bombing was going on.

'They informed me of Borya's death in early April but I didn't believe it. I was sure he'd been taken prisoner, that he had a concussion, that he didn't remember. I watched all the exchanges, I went and talked with prisoners, I asked everybody about Borya.

'On 3 April, Vitya called me; he was with Borya in that battle. He told me how my son died. He came to see me in Kyiv – the commanders gave him leave – and he sat like this with me, telling me, minute by minute, how Borya died. I didn't believe it at first. But Vitya took my hands in his, shook me and said, looking into my eyes, "Olga Timofeyevna, I honourably swear that I saw all this with my own eyes, you have to believe it, otherwise you'll lose your mind, I've seen mothers who lost their minds searching for their dead sons."

'In late April, they exchanged Borya.

'I identified Borya's remains in Kyiv. I vomited for a week after that. I won't tell you the details, I'm not a sadist. Going through that is hell for a mother.

'I don't know why I'm alive now, it's definitely not for Liza, although I believe that one day she and I will talk about everything and grow closer.

'Borya will never have children, I'll never have his grandchildren. Maybe there will be some from Liza. I'll try to be a good grandmother to them.

'I'm now learning Ukrainian. When the war's over, I'll only speak Ukrainian. That's my tribute of respect to the country that didn't give in and didn't break when you so traitorously and despicably attacked it.

'I'm in several chats where mums search for their missing sons. These are Ukrainian chats. But sometimes Russian mums land there, too. They're some of the most desperate, some of the ones who aren't prepared to exchange their child for money, as your leadership suggests to you.

'I listen to those mums' voicemails, read their messages, watch the videos and, you know what I think, Katya? I think I know for certain what my son died for. And no matter how painful it was for me, I'm proud of Borya and understand he's a hero. But your sons, what are they dying for? Have you asked yourself that question?

'Or asked them?

'None of this is forgivable, Katya. And don't try to brush it aside, you're complicit in this, too.

'That's what I wanted to tell you.

'And now let's drink tea. You can stay the night if you want. The room where the girls Liza took were sleeping in is now available.'

19.

# Salo

'I can't cook at all anymore. It really turns my stomach to see a skillet. I don't cook at all at home. I only have yogurts in the refrigerator. I eat yogurts.

'You can see there's basically nothing in this apartment. I can't force myself to start feeling at home. I bought curtains before you came. Nothing else.

'But in my last Kyiv apartment, as it happens, I bought curtains in February 2022, as the final stroke of renovation, who needs all that now?

'It seems like now I can't stay anywhere for ever.

'I'm mentally stuck in Borodianka* on that black day, 10 March 2022: I'm standing in the summer kitchen of somebody's house with a skillet in my hands and rendering salo.† The skillet's bouncing because there are tanks driving towards us and they're making the whole earth shake.

'Something happened to me at that point, a sort of madness I can't explain. Oksana, I told myself, let the sky fall to the earth, but you finish rendering the salo! And I rendered it.

'The house rattled, everything shook, it wasn't just scary, it was terrifying. They were shooting. One shrieking bullet went into the moulding of the kitchen window about 50 centimetres from me. But I was rendering salo so as not to get distracted.

'And do you know what I was thinking about? I was wondering what we'd done to make everything go wrong and when that happened.

---

* Borodianka is a town on the Zdvyzh River, northwest of Kyiv.
† Сало (salo) is, in simplest terms, salted (and sometimes smoked) pork fat that may also contain some meat and/or skin. [*translator*]

'No, I'm not talking about myself, not about how, of all the possible places in Ukraine to save ourselves from the war, we'd gone to Borodianka, towards the tanks. That's fate, what else can you say. I'm talking about something else.

'I'm from Donetsk. Your propagandists keep shouting, "Where were you for eight years?" We were at home, with Donetsk, we were with our country. But where were you? You were taking away our country and our home. That's the simple answer. But there are no simple answers in life.

'Basically, tanks surrounded us, assault troops were shooting, planes were swooping down and bombing us, but I was rendering salo and recalling our life before 24 February 2022.

'I was born in Donetsk 30 years ago, just after the collapse of the Soviet Union, which I don't remember. I grew up in Ukraine. I had everything there: home, parents, friends, work, I had joy. I was joyful, I remember that well.

'If it's important to you, we spoke Russian. Nobody banned it, there was never any of that. They taught Ukrainian in schools. I speak two languages fluently. Almost everybody 30 and younger speaks two languages. Of course our parents don't speak Ukrainian as fluently. Our good life ended in the summer, or perhaps the early autumn, of 2013. People in military uniforms started showing up in Donetsk. We didn't understand where they were coming from, who they were. People in the city said they were our own, from Donbas, concerned people who were very worried about the fate of our land. They'd take walks in our parks, two or three at a time, approaching and politely starting conversations with us: "Good afternoon, we're worried about the fate of this region of ours. We and you are Russians, we need to defend the Russian World." And they gave us leaflets. But do you know what the problem was? We didn't hear their way of speaking as our own, the way they sometimes pronounced the letter "o" is how people speak further north, in Russia. And that looked strange: they're worried about us though they're not from here themselves.

'But we were living our own life, we were in a hurry to live. We had other things to think about.

'And so, while we were living our life, they took over the regional administrative offices in Donetsk and our Donbas television tower. Which means that we used to watch Ukrainian news but after the takeover, they started showing what was allegedly our local news. And the picture changed a little.

'No, what am I saying? It changed overall, not a little.

'There were hardly any entertaining programmes in those new broadcasts. It was just news. Their tone was unsettling. Several times a day they'd say an assault was being planned for Donetsk: the Banderites were coming, they were going to mistreat the local Russian-speaking population and they'd been taught how to do that in special camps in western Ukraine. That all sounds bonkers the first 10 or 20 times. But it wasn't 10 and it wasn't 20 times. It was 10 or 20 times each day. People who clung to the television – people like our parents, for example, people over 50 – started changing right in front of us. Conversations got started.

*'About how they'll capture us,*
*'About how we're proud and won't tolerate violence against us,*
*'About how we don't want to pay taxes to Kyiv anymore,*
*'About how we should defend the Russian World.*

'This is right where I first heard that phrase: *Russian World*. It was now constantly on TV and the radio, and people had started saying it. And it later turned out that we should defend it. That "Russian World".

'There was a referendum a while later. Nobody understood what questions they were discussing but the general point was that Donbas needed independence from Ukraine. And there were two boxes to check: yes or no.

'I didn't go to that referendum. I thought it was all some kind of raving, a diversion for pensioners, that they'd make some noise and stop.

'But I was wrong. Right after the referendum, on TV they started calling for people to take to the streets: a demonstration against Ukraine, a demonstration for seceding from Ukraine, a demonstration for the Russian World. Our city, which had always been about comfort, about being able to earn money and steer clear of politics,

suddenly became utterly politicised. People started talking at public
transportation stops, on transportation, everywhere, about that
"Russian World" that needed to be defended. The Banderites were
no longer a figure of speech. People now spoke about them seriously, too. But I still thought none of this could be for real, that the
topic would somehow change.

'People I knew unexpectedly told me there'd be a demonstration
of young people from Donetsk who were against Donbas seceding.
There was a peace-loving message there, that, yes, we're Russian-
speakers but we're Ukrainians, we don't want to secede, we're for
European values, we love our country. I saw the slogans my colleagues were painting at our office. People in IT, advertising,
design . . . All those young, starry-eyed kids whose lives would be
worthless in less than a year.

'Anyway, they took their signs and went out to the street. I
stayed in the office; there was work. About 30 minutes later I hear
shouts and shooting. I peer out the window and see people with
assault rifles running down University Street. And my IT people
are running away from them, scattering. Somebody tosses a
smoke grenade. The network's down. And now you can't figure
anything out.

'Everybody runs into the office about 40 minutes later. They said
no demonstration happened: people in balaclavas showed up, they
started pushing, kicking and stirring up people in the crowd and
then they raised their assault rifles and started shooting.

'My dad met me after work and I attempted to tell him what happened. Right away he said, "Yes, I know everything, it was on TV.
People went out to defend the Russian World and Donbas's independence but the fascists and Banderites attacked them and broke
up our demonstration."

'"Pa, hold on, this whole story, it was about defending the *unity*
of Ukraine. It was my friends there, it's us, we want to be Ukraine."

'"What can you know, **dear daughter**, I saw it on TV. People were
walking, carrying Russian flags and the damned Banderites started
getting in their way."

'And then it occurred to me that we'd basically ended up in

different universes. And this was my own dad! I couldn't get my head around that.

'But events were unfolding fast and there was no more time to get my head around things because there were now lots of soldiers in the city, they'd started shooting more often and later that was very often, then the incomings started, and then . . . And then we got used to them. We learned to determine distance, determine the type of weapon. The city started descending into the hell of war. And you know this one other detail? Airplanes stopped flying to the city.

'I loved watching airplanes. You tilt your head back and watch, imagining the people there, who's flying where. The Donetsk airport – the best in the world, which greeted so many guests for the European Championships [Euro 2012] – was destroyed in the first months of the war and it stopped being a place for joy. It became a grave for people.

'We learned to live with that. We got used to lying down to sleep and not being sure we'd wake up. That changes the psyche irreversibly. You actually stop living. You function.

'But I broke loose.

'I went away to Kyiv, to visit friends for two weeks. I had a return ticket. But the bridge the trains went over to Donetsk was blown up the day after I left. I still had the ticket but there was no longer a way home.

'I started all over again in Kyiv: a job and a rental apartment. But it was like I'd ended up on the other side of the Moon. People in Kyiv thought Donetskites had surrendered to the Russians, that they're separatists and don't want to be part of Ukraine. People told me that we don't know Ukrainian, we hate our country and want to join Russia.

'Television was working in Kyiv, too. It was different. But also powerful. And that stunned me.

'On the mundane level, everything revealed itself when I had to find an apartment: they wouldn't rent to Donetskites. There were a thousand reasons. From saying we didn't shoot back when the Russians came to us to saying we didn't have money and couldn't pay for ourselves. But the main reason – I only figured this out later – was pain. As a result, I rented an apartment in Boryspil.* And you know what? There's a cemetery nearby. And so every week at that cemetery they buried boys who came in coffins from Donbas. They were called up after high school – well, if they hadn't managed to apply to college or couldn't get in – and sent to the front, then returned in coffins. Young mums, girls from their schools and girlfriends walked behind the coffins. And hatred was growing and growing in each of those people. In the first place, of course, towards Russia. Well, and Donbas, right along with it.

'I think it's good my windows faced that way. It didn't allow my life to normalise. I saw other people's pain every week but didn't get used to it.

'I went to see Papa in Donetsk every couple of months. That was a very dangerous trip in 2014–15. One time they stopped us at a checkpoint, saying to wait until the battle's over. We waited then drove off. It was snowing, New Year's was coming. We raised glasses of champagne but they were shooting outside: either fireworks or other people. Imagine, you can get used to that, too.

'My city had emptied out. It looked like a house whose people left after misfortune showed up. But its smell was preserved, certain things were still lying in their places, carelessly tossed: it was like the owner would come back soon, he'd remember what he'd forgotten and come back.

'But nobody was coming back. They were just leaving, no end. And those who stayed had turned into shadows of themselves. Nobody was shouting on the street now if an incoming hit a bus stop and somebody died. They just gathered the shards, business-like, loaded the person into an ambulance and rode on, going about their business. Can you imagine the level of depression my fellow residents, my people, my loved ones, reached? It's called *being doomed*. Everyone who'd stayed in the city had *made peace with* that.

'I stopped going to Donetsk after Papa died.

* Boryspil is a small city about 30 kilometres east of Kyiv. It is home to Ukraine's largest airport. [*translator*]

'I felt bitter and ashamed but I felt relief because I no longer had to see that. Although the shelling had lessened in the last couple of years and life had started to take shape, little by little, if you can say that about a place that all life had left . . . An acquaintance once even said, "Oksana! We had a traffic jam for the first time in Donetsk today. Can you imagine that! There's more cars now!" That was in the fall of 2021. You know what happened later.

'Everybody knows what happened later.

'The world crumbled.

'And in my personal little world, I had to run from war again. That's how I ended up in Borodianka: in a tracksuit and old trainers, with napkins and a plastic bottle of water. There were a few of us in the house. My Donetsk knowledge about how to insulate a basement turned out to be very useful. We sat in the basement for several days and there was a child with us, a four-year-old little girl. She and I played the game of who can keep quiet the longest. I attempted to at least prepare her a little for when soldiers would enter the house, when she'd have to sit quietly and not give herself away. Sometimes I thought, my Lord, what am I doing, they'll find us anyway, kill us anyway, they've come to kill us. Their supreme leader told them that our country, our people, I, that little girl, don't exist. He didn't simply tell them that, he conveyed that to them over TV. And so they're coming, on their way.

'At some point, it simply got unbearable to sit in the basement. And we asked the landlady if we could do anything around the house. It fell on me to render salo. That's how I ended up with that skillet in my hand. There was a battle going on outside, helicopters flying overhead, the world had shrunk down to that damned skillet and I'd grabbed at it as my chance to survive. If I close my eyes now, I see salo bubbling, sputtering and frothing, I'll return again to what I was thinking during the four awful hours when the tanks were entering Borodianka.

'They went past us, to the centre, went into a school and the city administration. All the major awful events took place about 800 metres from us.

'Then we made a decision to run, figuring there wouldn't be another chance.

'We wrapped the car in white sheets. Everybody who'd been in the house got in the car; there was no room left for things. And we started off towards the highway. I rode with my eyes squeezed shut until the point the driver said, "That's it, there's the AFU."

'Our people really were already there; we joined a column and made it to the Zhytomyr highway.

'And after that, everything was the same for everybody: brief moves, overnighting in other people's houses, other people's clothes, warm food from volunteers, shelling and bombing somewhere nearby and you're like a hunted wild animal so you're moving in order to survive.

'People say a lot about the hatred that we Ukrainians feel for you. I think I'm still a long way off from reaching hatred. For now I experience rage. They came, they destroyed, they took joy, light, life, they trampled. What for? Just because you can?

'At one volunteer site, there was a woman standing in slippers and just a sweater. She had a child in her arms. I hadn't noticed where they'd come from. But in the light of a torch it suddenly became obvious there was blood running down her leg. A volunteer ran over and started leading her out, calling to a doctor, and asking, "Wounded?" And she's just crying, crying. Anyway, they poured her some tea, calmed her and found a jacket and hat for the child. And then she says, "Oh Lord, how embarrassing, everybody has the war but I have my period."

'And a few more of us women at the warming site started crying along with her. That doesn't seem like anything in particular, but what rage. That can't be forgiven.'

# 20

# Honey

On the 183rd day of the war, 84-year-old Svetlana Alexandrovna Petrenko, a native of Ukrainian Bakhmut (Artemivsk), lost her mind.

Put differently, one might say Svetlana Alexandrovna lapsed into childhood. She'd begun thinking that this was not 2022 and that this was not the Ukrainian city of Zaporizhzhia, where she'd evacuated with her 66-year-old daughter Lyudmila after Bakhmut turned into smouldering ruins because of the war Russia had unleashed against Ukraine.

Svetlana Alexandrovna's consciousness shifted her to 1942, when German Nazi invaders occupied those places. The most common phrases Svetlana Alexandrovna started repeating were: 'Mamochka, do we still have honey? They won't kill us, Mamochka?'

Svetlana Alexandrovna lost her mind on a packed bus that was carrying women, the elderly and children from Bakhmut (Artemivsk) to Zaporizhzhia. Svetlana Alexandrovna was sitting by the window and her daughter stood next to her, after boxing her in with other people's bundles and bags.

As the bus made a turn, Svetlana Alexandrovna began shrilly shouting, 'Mamochka, I'm scared, Mama!' Lyudmila pressed her mother's head against her own belly and closed her mouth. Lyudmila was later ashamed of herself for doing that. But she was very afraid Svetlana Alexandrovna would keep shouting and then they'd be taken off the bus.

But they weren't.

Svetlana Alexandrovna cried and cried into her daughter's belly and called for her mother. 'Mamochka, Mama, will Papa never come? Did they kill Grandpa for ever? Mama, what will we do if the honey runs out?' She repeated that, sniffling.

Lyudmila knew that story. When Svetlana Alexandrovna was in her right mind, she'd told Lyudmila the story many times, about how the Nazis captured Artemivsk (as it was then called) and shot her grandfather because rumour had it he was hiding partisans in a shed at the apiary.

Svetlana Alexandrovna was four years old in 1942, so she most likely didn't know if there'd been partisans or not. But her grandfather was shot in front of her and her mother. She's remembered that her whole life. Svetlana Alexandrovna's story always ended with the shooting scene. 'He threw his arms up like this, started wheezing and fell backward. And that's it. But his beard moved as if someone invisible was tugging it from behind.' Lyudmila remembered that story in all its details. And now she saw how her mother had fully plunged into the circumstances of those years and transformed from an 84-year-old to a four-year-old. Svetlana Alexandrovna cried, pressing into Lyudmila as if she weren't the mother but Lyudmila was, and Svetlana Alexandrovna was a little girl, Lyudmila's daughter. She cried and was afraid the honey would run out and then the Nazis would kill them. After they'd shot several citizens of Artemivsk in 1942 – one being Svetlana Alexandrovna's grandfather – the Nazis turned to the locals, asking who knew how to handle bees. That person turned out to be Svetlana Alexandrovna's mother. The Nazis exchanged honey for milk, bread and the possibility of remaining among the living. The never-ending explosions returned Svetlana Alexandrovna to that time.

'I can't bring her the rest of the way,' Lyudmila wrote on WhatsApp to her daughter Zhanna in the city of Sokol, which is in northern Russia's Vologda Oblast.

'There's no other way, Mama, try,' Zhanna replied.

Zhanna had married and moved to Russia even before Artemivsk became Bakhmut. After Russian troops invaded Ukraine in 2014 and began the war in Donbas, Bakhmut ended up being closer to the line of contact than other Ukrainian cities. Zhanna had suggested many times that her mother, Lyudmila, and her grandmother, Svetlana Alexandrovna, leave. She had also suggested moving to Russia. But the women flat-out refused. 'This is our land, our graves are here. And we'll lie down here, too. That's how people's lives are arranged and don't you forget it,' Svetlana Alexandrovna said into the phone to her granddaughter. 'The rest of us have to live right even if you won't.'

The conversations about moving ended there.

And then the war started.

On the 186th day of *that* war, at the height of the summer of 2022, Lyudmila talked with the head of the internal medicine department at Zaporizhzhia's municipal hospital, which was, surprisingly, working according to its former schedule and treating patients with highly varied illnesses unrelated to the war.

But Svetlana Alexandrovna's haze was associated with the war. She'd apparently begun seeing fascists around her and feeling like a four-year-old at the point when a missile hit the home she shared with her daughter, completely destroying everything they'd kept and loved there all those years. Miraculously, the women survived. They were out of the house, getting humanitarian aid, at the time of the attack. Svetlana Alexandrovna began crying and tumbled on her side when she caught sight of the smoking ruins. People then ran to them and a commotion ensued. Svetlana Alexandrovna and Lyudmila were transferred to a temporary shelter in a former dormitory, where they were examined, fed, dressed and shod, and told to prepare for evacuation the next day. In all that commotion, nobody noticed that Svetlana Alexandrovna had begun losing her mind.

'When I heard her calling for her mother on the bus, I knew immediately that was the end, see? And there was nowhere for us to go because we had nothing there but ruins,' Lyudmila told the head of the internal medicine department at the city hospital in Zaporizhzhia.

He nodded, patted Lyudmila on the back and promised to provide medical treatment for Svetlana Alexandrovna for a couple of weeks. The din of exploding shells was audible outside.

'I can't say I believed him but I needed something to do,' says Lyudmila. 'So I started looking into how we could leave. At first I told everything as it was: I have a daughter, she lives near Vologda and her gramma and I want to go to her. Her grandmother's an old lady, it's difficult for her to drift around to unfamiliar places. But it turned out that it was only possible to go to western Ukraine with international volunteers. Or to Europe. They didn't bring anyone to Russia. Other volunteers, Russians, brought people to Russia. But they were on the other side of the front. If we're here, they'd have nothing to do with us: to them we're on the Banderites' side.'

After evacuation from Bakhmut, Lyudmila and Svetlana Alexandrovna were referred to the care of Caritas, an international confederation of Catholic relief organisations whose volunteers used microbuses to bring refugees from Zaporizhzhia to Poland, Lithuania and Latvia.

'Nobody will go to Russia,' the young volunteer woman told Lyudmila. 'It's the aggressor country.'

'Basically, I called Zhanna and told her, **dear daughter**, we don't belong anywhere. People here have their routes that Gramma and I don't fit. It's too bad we even got tangled up in this. And also too bad we evacuated. We should have stayed at home. It's not so scary to die there,' says Lyudmila.

The couple of weeks during which the head of the internal medicine department promised to treat Svetlana Alexandrovna were coming to an end. Volunteers from Caritas came to see Lyudmila every day and asked where she and her mother had decided to go: the 'expiration date' for refugees in Zaporizhzhia was pressing. Lyudmila had already been living in a transit apartment longer than the norm.

And then Zhanna decided to come and see her mother and grandmother. She left her children and husband behind and attempted to force her way to Zaporizhzhia. But she didn't advance beyond Belgorod. She was detained at a checkpoint and interrogated for a long time.

'The military man who interrogated me, I think he was a major, put himself in my place and introduced me to a well-known war correspondent,' says Zhanna. 'He promised to help by bringing my mother and grandmother to Rostov in some sort of truck via the Donetsk Oblast. I'd meet them there and take them to my house by train.

'That correspondent and I wrote to each other over Telegram and had already started talking details: how my grandmother and mother would be delivered to the line of contact, how to accommodate them in that army truck and how to transport my grandmother safely so she wouldn't get scared.

'But that correspondent disappeared for a few days and later called me one night and said, "That's it, Zhanna, the evacuation's cancelled, the Antonov Bridge was blown up, there's no more connection with Kherson, our troops are wrapping up. Long story short, we really have other things to worry about. I'd definitely advise you go to Europe. It's calmer."'

That's how Zhanna found out back in the summer, much earlier than the news media, that the Antonov Bridge was no more and that the position of Russian troops in Kherson and its environs had changed radically.

'We're humble people, I hadn't thought extensively about any of that. Do I need that?' says Zhanna. 'I was just listening to that correspondent and recalling news stories on our TV where they talked about how "We don't abandon our own" and were always showing some kind of reporting from populated places our army seemed to be capturing one after another. And that everybody greeted, cried over and thanked our soldiers. And only some kind of Banderites were shooting back. And you know, here's where suspicion started to creep in. My grandma and mother, aren't they our people, too, after all? So why doesn't anybody want to take them out of there? Or let's consider that bridge. Why don't they talk about that in the reporting if there's already nothing left of that bridge?

'We're always enduring and enduring because that's what the government asks us to do – they always need something from us – but it's our personal issue when it turns out we need something.

'My head was exploding as I sat in a Belgorod hostel, scrolling the news on my tablet. I was getting the sense that we'd all become victims of some big scam, that we were all going about our business – well . . . survival, right? But some huge scam was being readied behind our back.'

Zhanna's wearing a green sweater with orange lilies and a plunging neckline. As she speaks, redness creeps out of that neckline, along Zhanna's chest and neck. It covers both her chest and her neck and, finally, her whole face. Zhanna's ablaze. She has never before allowed herself to say anything unsavoury about the Russian authorities. It's not even that. This is the first time she's discussing the authorities with someone.

Zhanna says, 'Mama called and said they'd release Gram tomorrow. And that there are two routes: either back to Bakhmut or, with Caritas, to Warsaw or Riga. In those days, they were no longer bringing anybody to other cities.'

Lyudmila touches her daughter on the shoulder, asking to have a word. She shows a photograph of Svetlana Alexandrovna on her smartphone: she's smiling at the camera, wearing a dark blue and green robe. She and the head of the internal medicine department are standing with their arms around each other.

Lyudmila says, 'Just imagine, that doctor pulled her out of it. He returned our old lady to us all in one piece. But he said she needed calm and calm. And where do I get that calm? I take him by the arm and I say, "Doctor, give us some kind of medicine for the road, I just need her to obey me and not be afraid." Well, he gave me a package and a half of Phenazepam. That's why I didn't tell you his name, see? At that point, I had no understanding of where we were going. Zhanna was now in charge of us.

'I just gave Gram the pills and she was happy the whole time, we were the only ones who were nervous. I basically don't know how I got through that. But my daughter said, "Mama, you can." And I could, as you see.'

Lyudmila's crying. Zhanna strokes her on the head. 'Oh, Ma.'

We're sitting in a warm and crowded kitchen in Sokol, a monocity in the Vologda Oblast. Svetlana Alexandrovna's wearing a dark blue and green robe, standing by the stove and frying cheese pancakes.

Zhanna says, 'The hardest part was teaching my mother and grandma to lie. They were supposed to tell Caritas they'd decided to go to Warsaw. And that was it, period, they didn't need any Russia, even for free.

'And Mama's saying to me all the time, "But Zhan, what if I can't or what if Grandma gives it away?"

'And I told her: "Mama, I'm not asking for something supernatural, just lie! It's like it's for the sake of life, a white lie. Nobody will suffer, do you get that?"

'Anyway, they put them on a bus and I found the people who went on to kidnap them off the bus in Warsaw and . . . Well, it works out they were stolen from those volunteers, right?'

Lyudmila and Svetlana Alexandrovna cross themselves, synchronised.

Lyudmila says, 'I was afraid for Grandma, that she'd either go off her rocker again or tell them the whole truth, the way it was. But our bus arrived during the night, Grandma was sleepy from the medicines and tired anyway, so it seemed like she didn't understand what happened.'

'Yes, I understood, I understood, so why are you embarrassing me in front of people?' says Svetlana Alexandrovna. She laughs and flips cheese pancakes.

Now Zhanna speaks.

'Just don't be offended but I can't tell you all the people who helped deliver my grandma and mum here. But there were Ukrainians and Russians and Belarusians. And you know what amazed me? They didn't feud when they helped us. Nobody told me I'm an aggressor or that my grandma and mum are Banderites. People just helped. They took them off the bus in Warsaw, brought them for a couple of days of rest, fed them, warmed them up, then sat them on a bus to Minsk and then a car to Moscow. People did all that, see? Not governments, not those war correspondents, but people. If I just tell you their names, will you write them? It doesn't matter who they are? But what if they happen to read your book and see themselves? You write them.'

And she lists them: 'Tatiana, Katya, Maxim, Lena, Nikolai Sergeevich and Olya.'

Lyudmila interrupts her daughter: 'Can I say something separately about Olya? She met us in Minsk. And she brought us food in her own containers. Everything hot, piping hot, all wrapped in towels, with her sweater on top. I say, "Olya, how will we return the containers to you?" And she laughs, "Well, somehow." And so we left.'

Now Zhanna speaks.

'I met them in Moscow, my hands and legs started shaking. The three of us got up and stood there, hugging. It was Mama who thought I knew how to get them out of there, that I'd thought everything up, organised it, that I . . . I . . .'

Zhanna's searching for words. But she finds a kitchen towel and covers her mouth with it so as not to cry. The word comes, and Zhanna says, 'I didn't know how everything would end. I just suddenly realised that nobody needs us but us ourselves. And also that I want to live with Mama and Grandma, I'll get them or die trying.'

The women hug and cry again.

Zhanna's husband Valery comes in, making it suddenly obvious how small the kitchen is.

'Well, here we go,' says Valery's bass voice. 'The deadly womanly waterworks!'

Everybody laughs.

Valery says, 'Tell the correspondent about your sabotage work instead.'

Everybody laughs again. Zhanna say, 'I brought Mama and Grandma to the plant, to show them to my boss, she's the one who told us people have to wear the letter Z, well, on a pin, that's what they do all over Russia now, it's a sign of fighting Nazism. So I brought Gram and Mama in, to show them they're not Nazi women at all, that Gramma herself suffered from the Nazis. And Gramma told them about the honey and about how her grandfather was shot, right, Gram?'

Svetlana Alexandrovna nods. 'I told them, why not?' And she portions the cheese pancakes out on plates.

'I don't know if that had an effect or not. But they allowed me to not
wear a pin,' says Zhanna. 'A few others don't wear them on the floor.
But nobody talks about reasons, they're afraid of management.'

Now there's bustling around the table: the women are serving
sour cream, jam and honey to Valery, me and each other.

Everybody eats.

Over tea, I ask, 'What comes next? What are you planning?'

'What can you plan, we'll somehow live out a life,' says Lyudmila. 'But there's nowhere to return. You just have a look, have a
look. This is the building where we temporarily lived in Zaporizhzhia, with Caritas. And this is the corner the bus to Warsaw took
us away from, well, see the post office? See it?'

She's scrolling through videos. The first has a smoking crater
instead of a building. The second shows the grey-black skeleton of
a building in front of which lies a POST OFFICE sign that canister
shot had battered pretty thoroughly. There are other videos and
photos of destruction; there are almost no people to see. Looking
at the changing photos, I think about where all those people went,
where they are.

I hear Lyudmila's voice through that shroud: 'And they even
wrecked the cemetery in Artemivsk. Even our people's graves no
longer exist. Nothing's left.'

I keep silent and she's thinking I didn't understand.

'It's Bakhmut, that one,' Lyudmila clarifies.

'Yes, yes, I know, Artemivsk is now Bakhmut.'

We all keep silent. Zhanna stirs her tea with a spoon.

The dog sleeping under the table barks, briefly and muffled; he's
dreaming of something.

Three boys are chasing an enamelled bucket instead of a ball outside on the icy football field that Zhanna's apartment window
overlooks. Snow is falling, thick and monotonous. It's grey outside,
though the sun is at its zenith. It won't get brighter.

We all go still and it's as if we're falling asleep a little at the kitchen
table, softening from the warmth and the absence of the necessity

to say something, run somewhere or do something. In a daze, we look out the window at the boys, the bucket and the snow.

Svetlana Alexandrovna touches me on the shoulder. 'Child, do you like honey?'

I shudder.

'I wanted to give you some for the road, we have a lot.'

## 21.

# The Magic Swan-Geese

The city of Hamburg, located on the Elbe River, seems as large and sturdy as the container ships that continuously visit Germany's busiest port.

Hamburg is cold, windy and deserted in December. People save themselves by going all out to decorate the city for Christmas, giving it a cosy and cordial appearance, warming it with themselves. By evening, that's almost successful: people crowd around little Christmas huts and there are scents of sausages, mulled wine and Christmas trees.

But everything reverts back in the early morning, when the Christmas market is closed and the streets are uninhabited, dank and grey.

To warm up, I go into a church that turns out to be the Protestant church of St Catherine. A morning service is under way.

The priest is reading from the Gospel of Matthew. I listen attentively to the moment when the disciples are frightened after seeing Jesus walk on the sea. They're thinking He's a ghost so they're very confused and ready to run. He feels that. He stops them with his hand.

He says, 'It is I. Don't be afraid.'

*'Ich bin es; fürchtet euch nicht!'* says the priest.

The organ begins playing as I'm walking out of the church. I pause on the threshold. It's too bad, I'd have liked to listen for a bit. But I need to hurry and so I walk towards the train station. That's where I agreed to meet with Danil, by the taxi stand. He'd written that I'll definitely recognise him since he's in a wheelchair.

I wave my hand as soon as I spot him and run to greet him. I slow down a little when I'm a few metres away, to hide my surprise at how much he's aged compared to his avatar on Telegram.

I explain it to myself: the war.

I get a grip on my emotions, approach, hold out my hand and, just in case, ask, 'Danil?'

The frightened person in the wheelchair waves his hands at me. 'Nein, nein, das ist ein Fehler. Ich brauche nichts von Ihnen!'*

I lose my nerve and withdraw my hand. I look around. Check my location with the location on my phone. Everything's correct. A call: 'Hey! Stay where you are, I see you, I'll be right there!'

He shouts to me and speeds from the other side of the station, pushing off from the ground with one foot, bent forward slightly and holding the hand rims of the mechanical wheelchair on both sides.

Tall, brown-eyed, light-haired. Wearing a dark blue 'Mariupol 1960' jacket.

He immediately explains about the jacket. 'We had this football team in the city. My mother worked there as a nurse. Not with the main team, with the youth team. I nicked it from her when I was leaving the city. As kind of a souvenir.'

We ascertain that the train station has two taxi stands. They're on opposite sides. And while I was looking for him *here*, he was waiting for me *there*. We laugh and decide to go to Starbucks. I offer to make his life a little easier and push the wheelchair. He snorts.

'Please, there's no need to push anything. I even get a kick out of riding on my own. If people are going to push me, I'll get totally lazy and turn into a whiner who hangs on everybody's neck. There's actually lots of those temptations. People offered me money twice while I was waiting for you. Makes me crazy.'

'Listen, well, people don't know how else to offer their help to you. Money's usually simplest of all.'

'I want least of all for people to pity me. I don't need pity. I want to live on equal terms, see?'

I do see, what's not to see?

We come around the station from the other direction and again meet the German in the wheelchair, the guy I took for Danil.

* No, no, it's a mistake. I don't need anything from you! (German)

I say, 'Guess what, I took you for him.'

'You what? You really can't see we have nothing in common?'

We laugh. The person in the wheelchair gives us the thumbs up. It seems like he's also glad that we met and are going to a café, or rather that I have to run in order to keep up with Danil's wheelchair. He's moving very quickly.

The ramp at Starbucks goes to the entrance but then cuts off before the three downward steps leading inside. Danil makes a show that it's easy for him to hop up to the counter inside on one foot. I pretend it's not hard at all to carry his wheelchair in there. I notice that his wheelchair has a broken handle and ask, 'Why didn't you tell anybody you have a broken wheelchair?'

He answers, 'It's nothing, I won't have it long. They'll be putting on a new prosthesis soon and that'll be it, meaning I can tough it out.'

The barista asks if it's for here or to go.

'For here, of course.'

Here at Starbucks, after all, there's Christmas music, there's the smell of gingerbread cookies and cinnamon. It's warm here. Warm for Hamburg, of course.

We chat as they make the coffee. Danil was evacuated from Mariupol via Rostov-on-Don, the city of my childhood, and the volunteer told him there's a resemblance between Mariupol and Rostov.

'There's basically no resemblance,' says Danil, outraged. 'Your streets there are all squiggly and rutted and they take people who the hell knows where, like they don't know the rules, but the big thing is it's another city, it smells different. Well, why am I saying this, you understand you don't have the sea there, and that's the least of it! If there's no sea, there's no pier and if there's no pier, that's not life.' He searches in his phone and shows me the Mariupol pier, lighted by a full moon.

I say, 'You can only take a stroll on a pier like that if you have someone with you.'

'To be honest, that's not required. It's so beautiful you can go by yourself. It's really very beautiful in Mariupol on a summer night. It was. It's too bad you haven't seen it.'

The coffee's ready. We ask where the tables are. The young

woman smiles and answers that their tables are on the second floor. No, there's no elevator.

The expression on my face must have changed because Danil takes me by the elbow and quietly says, 'Forget about it, let's not make a fuss about rights, we just won't go to Starbucks anymore. We'll just go sit outside now, okay? You won't freeze? Are you warmly dressed? I, for one, am very warmly dressed. I basically never freeze, I'm warm in any bitter cold.'

It somehow works out that he begins the interview, not me. He says, 'Should I tell you right away how this all happened or are there other questions?'

I understand that I want to go as long as possible without finding out how this all happened and what, exactly, happened. I want:

*To drink coffee,*

*To walk around Christmassy Hamburg,*

*To compare my Rostov and his Mariupol,*

*To discuss with him which is better: Melitopol dark red sour cherries or Melitopol light red sweet cherries, and to finally ascertain which bay near Mariupol brings you to deeper waters so you're not just walking the whole time in a knee-deep sea.*

Long story short, I suddenly realise I'm a coward. I just don't have it in me.

*I don't want to talk about the war.*

*I don't want to talk with him about the war.*

*I want to pretend this war just never happened.*

*That it only seemed to happen.*

As we drink coffee, though, and I attempt to formulate my first question, we simultaneously receive identical messages because we're subscribed to the same Telegram news channels. The news is that Russia has, right now, begun shelling Ukraine yet again.

It won't work to pretend nothing ever happened.

Danil's 21. The scars on his left arm, caused by shards, aren't visible under his dark blue 'Mariupol 1960' jacket, though I know about that injury. It's impossible not to notice the absence of a left leg below the hip. And so I say, 'Let's start at the point when the war was already going but you still hadn't left Mariupol. Explain why.'

'That was a question of principle. Well, why? It's my city, my pier, my drama theatre, my streets, my Veselka park. I didn't want to leave. Nobody was expecting me anywhere, I wanted to be at home and I stayed. I wasn't alone, either. There was also the little one, Mama, and Mama's boyfriend. They were my company.'

'More specifically, the little one and I stayed in our apartment in the 23rd micro-district* but Mama had gone to her boyfriend's in Kirovsky.†

'But she didn't go immediately. There was shooting but life was still the usual until roughly 3 March. I still went to work on the 3rd but there was no more work at all. They just handed out groceries – I worked at a supermarket – and said, adios, everybody go home.

'I brought Mama to Kirovsky and said I'd come for her on the 6th or 7th. Public transportation was no longer running, you had to go on foot. From Mama's boyfriend's to our apartment was a brisk 50-minute walk. Otherwise it was a little over an hour.'

'I came back to the little one. She couldn't be left on her own. It was scary.'

Danil calls his stepsister Katya 'the little one'. She's 15. He finds a photo of Katya on his phone, it's a selfie of her and a girlfriend. He says, 'By the way, you asked why people don't leave: the little one has a friend in Mariupol and neither of them goes anywhere without the other. Is that a substantial reason in your opinion or what?'

I don't have a chance to answer. Danil's putting the phone away. He says, 'Katya and I were sitting in safety. I'm still convinced that our apartment was the safest place in Mariupol. We'd sit in the area between apartments when there was incoming. And when there wasn't any booming, we were calm at the apartment, did our own things.

* An administrative subdistrict in western Mariupol through which troops entered the city.
† A northeastern part of Mariupol located near Azovstal, which was subjected to massive shelling during the blockade of Mariupol; there were hard-fought battles in the area.

'And I thought I wouldn't go get Mama since it was dicey to leave the little one on her own. But 8 March arrived. And then – bam! – Mama comes and says, "Pack your things, we're going to Kirovsky." I say, "Mama, that's illogical. You're bringing us to the tenth floor of a 12-storey building next to Azovstal. Nobody's going to hand over Mariupol, you can see not one stone will be left standing. They'll pass us by but they'll stay to the death in Kirovsky. And it will a total shitshow for us there, Mama."

'What do you think, did she listen to me? That's right, she didn't listen. That happens with women. Once they've made a decision, no logical arguments work. So the little one and I packed up food, took bags and tromped off towards Kirovsky. It was about an hour and a half to walk, if you stop and rest.

'What else are you interested in?'

I say, 'Just tell me more.'

But it turns out he suddenly has to write a text message immediately.

Then put sugar in his coffee and do something else.

Then he abruptly says, 'Want to hear something freaky? I don't have phantom pain in my leg anymore, that was only in the first couple of months, it really isn't nice. But now all that's left is this freakiness. Sometimes either my knee or calf or heel itches. And if I get thinking about something, I forget and try to scratch. So what are you interested in?'

I say, 'Can you tell me what happened next?'

He says, 'From what point?'

And for some reason he smiles. Danil has a nice smile, it's broad and very calm.

'Listen,' he says, 'what's next was just happenstance. It's hard to explain.'

'If you don't want to or it's difficult for you, you don't have to tell it.'

'No, nothing's difficult for me! I basically don't reflect on the subject. It's just this story is kind of a coincidence, see?'

We keep silent. A few stray snowflakes fall from the grey sky. A homeless man comes and goes, clinking a glass with coins. A

Christmas carousel for children begins its work somewhere on the city square. And gusts of wind bring us 'Jingle Bells'.

And Danil says:

'It's all simple. It was on 19 March, at nine to nine-thirty in the morning, something like that. We were sitting in Mama's boyfriend's apartment. More specifically, the little one was standing in a corner of the hallway, I was shielding her. The load-bearing wall was apparently in that hallway, so it worked out to be the safest place. Mama was sitting on a chair by the entrance to the kitchen. Her boyfriend was a little farther away, closer to the window.

'They'd been pounding Kirovsky long and hard that day. We'd already spent several hours in those positions. And about 15 minutes before "my" incoming, Mama says, "Danil, sit down, sit for a while. You're probably tired."

'And so she and I change places. I sit down and she stands alongside the little one.

'You know death always comes in on soft paws. You'll never hear the shell that flies at you. And I didn't hear mine.

'You just blink – once – and there, now you're lying instead of sitting. There's a hellish chirping in your ears and something smells nasty. That's how an incoming smells. Probably the powder.

'At first I thought I'd gone blind. There was total darkness. Then the dust and smoke started to settle and I saw that the wall of the room had simply come down, that the sun was shining brightly through a gap, there was nobody around and it was quiet, I didn't hear anything but a shrill sound.

'I forced myself to crawl away from the light, towards the stairwell. I forced myself not to panic. I just crawled into the stairwell because that was about where Katya and Mama should be. Mama's boyfriend had been killed, that was immediately obvious because he'd been standing closest of all to the wall that was now gone.

'I crawled out into the stairwell, crawled up to the window, rolled on my back, raised myself up a little and sat. I saw Katya, who had a shard in her leg but nothing serious. Mama was totally okay. But she started screaming when she saw my leg. And my head hurt, it was just splitting. And I say, swearing, to be honest, because it was that kind of moment.

'"Mama, you're a medic, why are you shouting? I have a charging cable in my pocket. Put a tourniquet on my leg and remember what time you did it. Then go into the apartment and find something to put one on my arm."'

The clock on Hamburg's town hall chimes. He swallows some coffee and keeps silent, so as not to shout over the clock.

I ask, 'But how do you know all this: the tourniquet, noting the time . . .'

'I'm a nurse's son! It's just somebody had to be calm at that point. And I became that person. You know, I told myself then, "Say goodbye to your leg, Danil, but don't scare anybody." And it turned out that I managed Mama until the point the soldiers arrived. Katya went downstairs and said what happened to us: one 200, one 300.* The soldiers came quickly.'

'Which soldiers?'

'AFU. We were still on the side where the AFU was in control. They had a commander, awesome guy, he and I got to be friends later. But he gave me a hard time at first. "What the hell are you doing here? Everybody got a notification yesterday to go down into the basement, that there'd be shelling."

'Well, I cursed him out, too. "Where did you go? Who did you warn?"

'That guy sent for the soldier who was supposed to have run through the stairwell to warn people.

'He says, "Guys, sorry, it's my fault. I only ran to the seventh floor."

'I'm looking at the commander, like, "Any more questions about why we're not in the basement?"

'They kept quiet. They called for one of their doctors, who somehow dressed my leg specially there. I was already starting to freeze from blood loss so they covered me with a space blanket. In

---

* The code '200' is for someone who has died. The code '300' is for someone who is severely injured. [*translator*]

the process, I even managed to joke with that guy, the Ukrainian commander, and he was surprised: "Where do you get the strength?"

'And I'd thought to myself that I didn't have much of a chance. If I give in, then I'm giving in for now and for ever. Well, I decided that for now I can't give in.

'They brought me downstairs and opened some apartment on the first floor. I lay there for a little while but there was a lot of shooting so they brought me down to the basement. Mama and the little one were already there. The AFU said they'd send me to the hospital once the shelling let up. But the shelling just wasn't ending. Want to hear something freaky? Mama told me there was an incoming about an hour after they took me out of the basement. Almost everybody died.'

He obviously needs a break. Danil reaches for the cup of coffee, continuing to smile at me. I notice his hand's shaking.

'You're freezing!'

'No! My hands always shake, ever since I was a kid.'

I touch his hand; it's icy.

'Danil, you're frozen.'

'Let's talk here about everything, then we'll go where it's warm. Shall we finish up this topic already?'

I nod.

He says:

'The story was that there were AFU artillery observers on the roof of our building and one of the neighbouring buildings. The Russians were hammering at them. The shelling got quieter the next day, somewhere around lunchtime. The soldiers found a car for me and convinced a guy from the basement to drop me at the hospital. Mama and the little one decided to go back home. Meaning to our house, in the 23rd micro-district. They still live there. They called yesterday, told me the new authorities apparently promised to install radiators for them. But that's all like something from another life for me.

'So we drove a long time that day. The road to the hospital in usual times would have taken about 10 or 15 minutes, but if you go this way there's mines and if you go that way the bridge was blown up. The city was like the zombie apocalypse, with burned-out buses, cars, corpses and craters, so we were zigzagging. I didn't particularly look to the sides because it made me feel sick.

'We somehow made it to the hospital but it was dark there. There was no more hospital.

'We turned around and went to the emergency hospital, another hour weaving among mines and ruins. I don't know how we didn't get blown up, but then we're suddenly driving up to the Magic Swan-Geese* hotel and restaurant – we had such a place. There's a wooden fence around it. And a Ukrainian military guy's face, really solid, with big cheeks, suddenly appears out from behind that fence. He's shooting up into the air, stopping.

'"I won't let you in. It's Russia over there, DPR, soldiers. Basically, Russians.'

'He and the driver start bickering in very raised voices. I just hear the driver yelling at him: "I got a guy in bad shape, a 300, he'll die now, let us in, bastard."

'In some corner of my consciousness, I understand that's about me. That I'm the 300 in bad shape. And I can die. I can't say I was overly scared. But that was probably the only point. I later got so I didn't care what happened to me. I looked at the Magic Swan-Geese and there was such a strange feeling in my chest: either pitying myself or pitying everybody, or not feeling sorry for anybody and damn it all, let it end soon. The driver took me out of that condition when I suddenly heard him yelling at the soldier, "Fuck off, I'm driving in and that's that!"

'And the military guy's yelling, too. "You're driving, I'm shooting, I warned you."

'But we peeled out and he didn't shoot. And we went to the hospital. There were four more checkpoints, Russian ones, along the

---

* 'The Magic Swan-Geese' is a folk tale that famed ethnographer Alexander Afanasyev included in his eight-volume collection of Russian fairy tales and folklore. Similar stories exist in other languages, including Lithuanian, Latvian, and Estonian. [*translator*]

way. We went through them. They peered in, saw me, and there were no more questions. A car from the second checkpoint escorted us, so they wouldn't shoot.

'In admissions the surgeons started examining me immediately. And the doctor asked me to move my leg.

'I moved it. He says to amputate. And I'm like: good.

'You actually said "good"?' I ask.

'You think I could argue? I understood everything, this wasn't news to me. It's just that in March 2022 saving one person's leg in the city of Mariupol would sacrifice the lives of 15 others. They were in admissions, too, and they were also bleeding profusely. That's all there is to it.

'Actually, that's not all. The doctor asked me to move my arm, too. I lifted my hand for about 40 seconds. That was so frigging painful. But I'm mentally saying to the doctor, "If you tell me you're going to amputate my arm, I'll bust you up with one arm and one leg, I'll find the strength." It was like he heard my thoughts because he said, "Well, the arm can stay." "Oh," I said to myself, "thank you, kind soul." They put me right on a table and took me away for an operation.'

He lifts the sleeve of his 'Mariupol 1960' jacket and I see four diagonal blue scars: four breaks from a fragment wound. The bones somehow knit together after that. He says it's nothing, the arm works and that's the main thing, and soon there'll be a prosthesis instead of a leg.

I ask what the prospects are for getting a prosthesis here in Hamburg.

He says, 'I'm waiting for insurance. That remains to be seen. Life has taught me not to guess.'

I ask, 'What do you think of Hamburg?'

He says, 'It's fine. I'm getting used to it.'

He says he'd counted on them being able to make the prosthesis in Saint Petersburg and initially went there but they refused him. Russia lacked the technologies Danil needed. He describes his journey to Hamburg: bus to Rostov, train to Saint Petersburg, car to Riga, bus to Klaipėda, ferry to Kiel, bus to Hamburg. The refugee camp where, according to him, he's been lucky with neighbours.

'Criminal elements usually flourish in camps like that. But we have a nice room: a family with two kids, a husband and wife without kids, a family with three kids, an African-American grandmother and me.

'Then they gave me a status and now I'm living in a nursing home. Pretty much everybody there is in a wheelchair. I'm waiting for insurance. Paperwork is required all the time there: documentation, proofs. That basically eats up all my time.'

I ask, 'Who do you blame for what happened to you?'

'Do you truly believe I should think about that? Well, what's the use if I find out and name him by name:

'*The one who didn't run all the way to our floor.*

'*The one who was the artillery observer on the roof of our building.*

'*The one who loaded the ammo that hit us.*

'*The one who gave the order.*

'*The one who led in the troops.*

'*The one who started the war.*

'*Who?*'

I don't know how to answer him. I ask again. 'Who do you yourself think it was?'

'I believe it to be the circumstances. We didn't choose them. It just fell to us to be the city where the offensive tripped up. They sacrificed us. They didn't spare us. We didn't leave and both sides used us in the fight. We weren't like people, see, but like justifications during war or like gambling chips. They used us to pay when the war stalled, that's the lot that fell to us. That's what probably happens, that's war?'

'Will you go to Mariupol?'

'Not anymore. I said goodbye on 29 May 2022. That was my last day in the city. I bathed in the sea, in the bay, which I really love. And said goodbye. That's it. I'm no longer there and won't be there.'

'Even if it becomes Ukrainian again?'

'That's really not the issue. You know, if a person goes through the sort of hell that we went through, it doesn't make a difference who the authorities are. Don't you see?

'I'll tell you that when it's very painful, what's most important of all to you is that *it stops being painful*. Whether that's a pill or a syrup, a sedative or they simply cut off a leg.

'Whoever's known unbearable pain like that will confirm it.

'We survived it. We as a city. We as people. I don't know if people have enough strength to live through that hell again if Mariupol's recaptured. They probably do. I know a person can bear everything. But now it's just important that they stop shooting. That they allow people to live calmly, without fear. Even for a tiny bit, a little while. Mama and the little one are in Mariupol. I invite the little one here but she doesn't want to leave. Mama, too. The apartment there is theirs, everything's dear to them. But I won't go there if it's Russian, Ukrainian or something else. It's just that it used to be mine. But not now. Don't you see?'

He smiles again. He says, 'Never mind, don't worry about it. You weren't there with us. You won't understand.'

A red-headed guy in a puffy down jacket approaches us.

'I'll introduce you, this is my friend, also Danil, he's from Kyiv. We met here in Hamburg. We're going to hang out, will you come with us? We've already finished about my leg and about Mariupol. Can we talk about something else now? Do you think about the future at all?'

# 22

# The Textbook

'Are you judging me? Come on, tell me, are you judging me? Everybody judges me. You, too?' Rita reels as she stands. Both her hands are pressing at the table. Rita wants to say something else and awkwardly swings her head, a motion that makes her round glasses, like Harry Potter's, fly off her. They fly off and land right in a glass of wine.

Lady Gaga's 'Bloody Mary' is blaring for the whole bar to hear.

Rita sits down. She pulls her glasses out of the wine glass and wipes them with a napkin. She nods to herself as if she's continuing an internal monologue, but there are no audible words, just a repetitive chorus at full volume.

'Rita,' Him-chan shouts, getting up from the table and rushing to her. But it's too late. Rita's already crying.

Him-chan strokes her shoulder and back, and wipes away her tears. Rita sits on Him-chan's lap, embracing his neck with both arms and laying her head on his shoulder.

Rita is full-figured and curvaceous, with freckles and a mane of thick red hair. Him-chan is dark-skinned, small and black-haired.

'The most real Korean. From Korea. The south, of course,' as Rita told me about him. And she wasn't lying.

Rita's sitting on Him-chan's lap at a bar in Vilnius, the capital of Lithuania.

She cries, cries uncontrollably, and then suddenly nods off.

It's 24 February 2023, the anniversary of the war. And Rita's birthday. She turned 26 today. And she and Him-chan married today.

The bar's emptying out. Rita wakes up. We walk, or, rather, Him-chan and I lead Rita along the Vilnius paving stones. Snow's falling.

This is a leisurely snow, it's as if it doesn't want to fall. Each snowflake hangs under a streetlight. It resists, evades, arguing with the power of gravity about its fate, as if it knows that nothing good awaits it on the ground. And so it wants to extend this February, this winter and this evening of Rita's.

'This February will end,' Rita says, suddenly speaking up. We're stopping under a streetlight. Rita takes out and lights a cigarette, which gives her trouble. She has a coughing fit. She throws up. She washes off with snow. Rita's mascara is smeared under her eyes. That's visible in the streetlight.

'This February will end no matter what,' Rita repeats, more certainly. 'And we'll understand everything. Actually, you'll all understand everything. I already got it. That's why I won't be here anymore. Consider me no longer here.'

Rita throws up again.

The English vocabulary that Him-chan and I have in common is enough to agree that the two of us will lead Rita to their rented apartment.

'I've never seen her so drunk,' says Him-chan.

'It's all my fault,' says Him-chan.

'Fine, it'll be tomorrow soon,' says Him-chan, stroking Rita on the back and saying something to her in Korean. Rita answers. Sharply. It seems to me that they're arguing. But then Rita's crying again. We're already at home.

Him-chan leads Rita to the bathroom. I stay in the kitchen. Splashing water and their voices are audible from the other side of the wall; Him-chan and Rita are speaking Korean.

The kitchen, like all the rest of the apartment, is crammed with boxes, bags and suitcases.

Photographs are heaped on a table. Young people I don't know are having fun, kissing, clinking glasses with the camera and making faces. Some guys are wearing pointy hats and girls are wearing wigs; Rita's in her Harry Potter glasses and a black bat-like wrap with a crown on her head. In one photo, a guy in an elf costume is holding Rita in his arms. Both are laughing.

'So I printed from the phone. I don't know whether to take them or not,' Rita says as she comes out of the bathroom. She's wearing a robe, her hair's in a towel; she looks freshened. Rita sits alongside me. She goes through the photos and says, 'This is 2021. My birthday. We're celebrating in Kyiv. We just got drunk and had fun. These are my classmates, a lot of us lived in the dorm, like I did. I'm from Irpin*, they're from all over.

'That's Seryozha,' she says, pointing to the elf. 'He's from Donetsk. He died in the summer.

'That's Olya. She died fast, in April. A lot of us rushed off to the front in the very beginning. We're medics. We can help . . . We should.'

Rita spreads out the photos.

'Mariam, we called her Marina. She's from the Carpathians, but there's some kind of long story there, they came from Tajikistan, there was a war there then, too, her parents got out. Mariam's at the front now.

'And this is our Lyokha. He's in Kyiv. Works at a hospital. He says they're so shorthanded you can make a career super-fast. He got into surgery and he's already operating. We couldn't even dream of that before.

'Here's Valerka, he's transporting medications.' A blue-eyed guy in a blurry photo is pulling at his cheeks and sticking out his tongue. 'He's been wounded twice, he even has some medal from the president, he was driving along, got hit by shelling and there was a bus of people near him. And Valerka pulled people out and helped them, he got an award. He had medical treatment so he's transporting again. See, they're all, the whole country's at the front now, even the ones who aren't there physically. In some places it's adrenaline, in some it's an appetite for justice . . . But what's justice? That's adrenaline, too, yes.'

Rita sighs and looks down.

'I don't know . . . I can't grasp that. I woke up the morning of the 24th and there was noisy booming below the windows. I thought it was our fools with fireworks. But this one girl, not from our faculty but she lived on our floor, suddenly starts shrieking out in the

* Irpin is a small suburban city just west of Kyiv. [*translator*]

hallway. She's just shrieking and shrieking on one high note, shouting louder than the explosions. That shriek of hers was in my ears until I left Ukraine. And then it went away.

'She was shrieking because she'd gone insane. But her shriek made everybody else insane, too. For some reason I put my silver shoes in my bag to take with me, the shoes I planned to wear for my birthday that night. I wanted the *Frozen* look. My birthday always falls on carnival week in Europe. Ever since freshman year, we've organised a carnival for my b-day. But in 2022, Russia organised our carnival . . .'

Rita takes a cigarette, lights it and smokes by the window. I hadn't noticed that Him-chan had come into the kitchen; he stands and opens the ventilation window.

'He's a good one, isn't he?' Rita's apparently asking, though she's confirming instead of asking. 'Remember, I told you about him. Did you believe me then?'

I believed her. But I hadn't thought I'd end up at Rita's wedding.

Rita and I met a month earlier. She, a flight attendant on a European budget airline, recognised me. And in the course of passing by several times – drinks, food, duty-free – she'd managed to tell me her birthday's 24 February, she's from Irpin, and that she never again in her life wanted to look back and celebrate her birthday or remember the anniversary of the war. That's why she was going to get married on 24 February 2023. Her future husband, who's Korean, told her you need to overlay something good on every bad calendar date. And then the bad will stop existing.

'And do you speak Korean?' I asked Rita then, on the plane.

She nodded with pride.

In Rita's bag, which she doesn't part with, either on Earth or in the sky, there's a paperback Korean language textbook. On the cover is a drawing of a bird sitting on a branch; there are mountains with snowy peaks in the distance.

'Mama and I went to Lviv when I was eight,' Rita says as passengers walk past us towards the restroom. 'And that textbook was in a bookstore. I sobbed and begged her to buy it. My mother was like, what are you talking about, there's some kind of written characters there, let's maybe buy a doll or a magnet as a souvenir. But I was stubborn. It was like I saw a sign of my fate in that bird, that mountain, in everything. And I convinced her. She bought it. And at home I made sense of everything and started learning Korean. Well, of course, that was nuts. Who in Irpin gave a crap about that Korean? But it was so nuts that people didn't even laugh at me. I learned the whole textbook backwards and forwards. I thought I'd learn it and – whoa! – something would happen in my life and it would change for the better. But nothing happened.

Then I found a teacher for myself on Skype and we worked together. Twice a week, without any breaks; I sent her money on PayPal. I only missed a few lessons when I was enrolling at the medical institute, otherwise, never. At the institute, the girls asked me, "The hell do you need that for?" They thought I had some kind of secret. But there was nothing, I was just learning.'

They call for Rita. We agree to meet after the flight; she goes off to work. I stand at the rear of the plane and watch her go.

On the ground, we go to a café, start speaking with the familiar 'you' and I immediately ask, 'How did you become a stewardess?'

Rita corrects me.

'Flight attendant. That's what's correct. But it was basically just an ad. I read it, called, went through training and all that without having come to my senses. I think they took me because they felt sorry for me. They feel sorry for refugees, didn't you know? Theoretically that's not especially pleasant, you always feel like a kitten. But it helps with some everyday things. I don't know what work I would have if not for that ad. But that's what the ad was. I didn't place any importance on it. I guess it didn't matter to me what I'd do. Basically, nothing mattered for me anymore after 24 February.

'I remember how I ran out of the dorm and looked at what was in my bag: silver shoes, passport and a Korean textbook. Well, is that normal? But nothing surprised me, it was important to get my parents, so I went home to Irpin. I wasn't feeling a thing, not fear, not desperation, not bravery. I just knew I had to make it to my mother and father, and get them. And later we'd all go far away from this hell.'

Rita stops. She knocks her palms on the table several times, attempting to calm down. She takes off her glasses, wipes them with the hem of her sleeve and puts them back on.

'It's hard for me to say this and you're probably the first person on earth I've said it to, but I didn't want for a second to fight. And I didn't understand others who were fighting, who are like: "Not one bit of land, not one step back, we'll smash the enemy."

'I got so scared in those first days and, see, it was just like I had a vision or something, of rivers of blood, thousands of deaths. Over what, I wondered. Over what flag's going to hang on my building? But what's the difference?! You have to spare people. But thinking like that is unpatriotic, right? Thinking like that isn't allowed now. Everybody's struggling now, fighting, reconquering. Prison's not far off with views like mine. Do you think it's only in your country that they put people in jail if they don't think the right way? But I'm not rooting for your people.

'I'm not rooting for anybody specific, I'm for people.

'I won't tell you about how I got to Irpin. I saw things then that mean I'm now going to live my life to forget them. I got a ride and a shell hit the car in front of us and I saw the ripped-off arm of one of the car's passengers flying. The actual arm, it flew past like a pigeon. Everybody started screaming, jumped out of cars, rushed to help and pull someone out somewhere but everybody was already dead. Nobody breathing. At the time I was thinking: So I studied all those years to be a doctor – I'm a paediatric ENT – I was supposed to save lives, maybe easing children's breathing or maybe just treating some boo-boos, my life looked sunny to me. But now I'm in the mud, the cold, taking the pulse of a blood-soaked person so I can tell everybody he's already dead, he can't be saved? I learned how to do that? I lived for that? That's my life? Well, no, it isn't.

'I get to my mum and dad's, walk in and say, "Pack your things!"

'They say, "**Or what?** Go where?"

'I say, "We're leaving, all of us, let's go, it's a war!"'

'But my mother just tells me in a calm voice that only cowards bolt.

'And again, "This is our land, we're not taking one step away, let them run over us old people with their tanks. We're not going anywhere."

'My grandmother came out, too. She shakes her cane, yells at me, says, "Where are you planning to run, you don't need to."

'I stayed the night at their place, everything's rumbling all around, the Internet and mobile coverage are already down, the electricity's on and off. And I realised that no-no-no. I can't do this.

'We talked again in the morning, this time with tears. It seems like Mama saw there'd be no life there but my father was standing his ground, neither my mother nor my gram would budge without him. And the Russian army's getting closer and closer: tanks are rumbling, everything's shaking, there's panic.

'You know, I'll tell you honestly, in those days, from the place I was in, staying and fighting looked like "imbecility and courage" pure and simple. I'm not justifying myself, I understand everything, that yes, I'm a coward. But even if I'd been president of the country, I would still have said, "Let's stop shooting, let's save everybody, the rest isn't important, people should simply live." Dumb logic, you say, right? Our president didn't do that and now he's a hero, right? Well, so I'm not the president. People are more important to me than ideas, more important than territories. Because I studied to be a doctor. But I already told you that.'

Rita gulps down her coffee, an entire XL cup of cappuccino, in a few swallows.

I look at her: freckles, glasses, rosy cheeks, a Mickey Mouse wallet on the table. I say, 'So you're really getting married on the 24th?'

She doesn't answer the question. She continues her story.

'I got in a jeep with volunteers. It later turned out to be acquaintances of the singer Svetlana Loboda, helping bring her family out. I was simply lucky, they squeezed me in as the fourth in the back seat. The corridor we could leave on was already bottlenecked. Somebody guided us with a walkie-talkie. And he said you have to accelerate hard and then the car will jump on a hummock and fly over a bog. But it turns out that if you don't accelerate, you won't jump and you'll fall into the bog. And get stuck. Everybody in the car discussed it. There's a risk, there's no risk, is it worth risking and generally what would happen. And I just sat with my eyes closed, thinking about how I want to get out of here at any price, I'm more useful alive than dead, and in war there's only use for people who understand and accept the laws of war. They're the ones that should fight, and the ones who don't want to fight should be brought out and hidden . . .

'Long story short, those were some of my ridiculous, childish thoughts. I'm embarrassed about them. So many people who thought like that are dead now, nobody asked them. But I was lucky because our car took off and we ended up flying over that bog and driving on towards the Polish border. My war – I knew this for sure – would end after lasting for only a couple weeks. I was just praying we could leave. And we did.

'I ended up in Vilnius three weeks later. I was sitting on a bench in a park I don't know the name of. I have my textbook and to calm myself I'm riffling through pages I know down to the last hyphen. Him-chan came up to me and started speaking Korean. We've been together ever since.

'You know, Him-chan says every person has some scripted journey they need to follow and things will only get worse if you deviate. When Him-chan walked up to me, I thought everything I'd been preparing for had happened. That this is it, now I can relax. But he explained to me later that we absolutely had to get married on my birthday, to close things out, to forget the war started on that day. I don't want to remember that. Do you see what I'm saying?'

Rita invited me to her wedding that same day – I didn't believe that up until the day the wedding would actually take place and I'd see it with my own eyes. But the wedding turned out to be a party in a bar: the real wedding will be in Korea. Rita and Him-chan are flying there tomorrow, 25 February. They've already packed their things.

Rita says, 'My mother and father won't speak to me. They think I'm a traitor, that you can't do that. But I want to forget everything and start over again, from the very, very beginning. I'll speak Korean, think in Korean, I'll have as many Korean children for him – she nods at Him-chan – as he wants. He says they can even give me some sort of Korean name. And I'll disappear, dissolve into their country, into their culture.'

I look at Rita and think about how she's planning to dissolve in South Korea.

Rita says, 'I'll just be nobody there, just some white broad their countryman foolishly decided to marry. We all look the same to them but our war is something else, distant. Nobody will ask me about anything anymore. And I won't be wondering about that any longer, see? That's how it'll be. I already wiped all the Telegram channels off my phone and my whole notepad, though I left my mother and father. But nobody else. I laid out the photos, thinking I'll look today and toss them in the trash. That was my life, now there'll be another. Are you judging me?'

'I'm not judging you, Rita.'

I want to pat her, hug her. But Rita flings my hand away and leaves the room. Him-chan follows her and when he returns a couple of minutes later, he shrugs his shoulders in amazement.

'Rita's sleeping.'

He adds as an apology, 'Our plane's early tomorrow, at 6.45. With three transfers to Seoul.'

I recall that Rita told me the name 'Him-chan' translates from the Korean as 'strong'. His name fits him perfectly.

# 23.

# The Kerb

It's 7 September 2022. The Russia–Estonia border crossing. Russian side, Shumilkino. It's 60 kilometres from here to the city of Pskov, from where there are trains to Moscow or Saint Petersburg. This is the new route from Europe to Russia.

The taxi I ordered didn't arrive at the agreed time to take me to the Pskov train station. The driver stopped answering the phone.

It's raining.

I'm running from one vehicle to the next, hauling a huge suitcase and pleading to get a ride towards Pskov. My train to Moscow is in a little over an hour.

The drivers – of trucks, light vehicles and minibuses – decline, with varying excuses.

The rain's intensifying, though it had just started to seem it couldn't possibly rain any harder.

A line of trucks and cars stretches along the road from Russia towards the border crossing: Latvia, Lithuania and Estonia are closing their borders to people with Russian passports and visas. People are trying to make it out.

Several passenger vehicles stand at the side of the road, just beyond the border crossing into Russia. Drivers awaiting their passengers sleep, reclining in their seats.

Everybody's waiting for someone. They're usually taxi drivers. Ever since the war started, though, there are minibuses with Ukrainian licence plates, driven by volunteers, on duty at the border. Some bring Ukrainian refugees from Russia to Europe; others take people from Europe to Russia. Those riding to Europe consider those riding to Russia traitors. And vice versa.

I run from car to car but nobody wants to take me. I don't give

in, I knock. It's a white imported car, the last in the line of those
waiting.

A heavy-set man of about 50 with a childishly ruddy face is sleeping
behind the wheel. I wake him up and ask him to take me to Pskov.

'Will I make it back in a couple hours? I need to greet my people,'
he says. He suddenly smiles and starts to look like a cartoon bear.
'Haven't seen my grandson in half a year. I miss him.'

He doesn't ask how much I'll pay. Zhenya, he says. And holds out
a huge hand as an introduction. There are Russian-language children's books and several kinds of crisps scattered on the backseat of
the car. I ask him where his grandson's coming from.

'From Riga. The kids left right after the war: my daughter's 25,
my grandson's two and a half. The kids. I'm bringing some books
and bought a white cat. Have a look, is that cat okay? The little one
won't be scared?'

I hadn't noticed but there really is a cat sitting between the front
and back seats. It's big and plush. Its indifferent yellow plastic eyes
stare past me, out the window, where it's raining. The cat seems a
little creepy to me. But I don't say anything. Zhenya says, 'I'm tired
of living apart, see? Do you have children? Are they still little? Well,
they'll get older and you'll realise they're still little even when
they're big. But now it works out my daughter's in Riga and I'm in
Kupiansk, I can't help her, can't hug my grandson, she's struggling
there, too, no work, nothing, no money, no friends, they won't take
the little one for kindergarten.'

I don't know that city so I write 'Kupiansk' in my notepad so I
don't forget to ask him in more detail. But he's talking, leaving no
pauses for my questions.

'You don't mind that I started speaking right away with [the
familiar] "you"? Forgive me, somehow I've started to miss people
while I've been on the road. I've been driving alone, I'm alone everywhere, there's nobody to talk with.

'You know, a lot of us are coming back home now. It's hard in a
foreign country. The mentality's not ours, people are different,
nobody there really needs us. And so I say, *It's time to come home,
dear daughter.*" – "*Yes, Pa, it's time, come get us.*"

'Today I'll meet them and tomorrow we'll already be at home. Oh, mother's expecting them. We laid in lots of food.'

I ask, 'Where is it, Kupiansk?'

He says, 'Near Kharkiv.'

Kharkiv's Ukrainian and I ask why he came to meet his daughter from the Russian side.

'Kharkiv, yes. But we have Russia there. They've been with us since 24 February. And what do you think? All our authorities – the military ones and the civilian ones – pulled up anchor the day the war started and went to defend Kharkiv. The Russian soldiers entered the city and called in the mayor to ask, "Will you let us go through?" But how could he not? Was he supposed to run at them with a pitchfork? We're now, what is it, collaborators. I tell the mayor – we know each other, we went to school together: "Genka, after the AFU's driven the Russian army out of here, you'll have to **bolt** ahead of them or you'll be hung up like a traitor."'

Zhenya laughs. Of course he has a marvellous smile. I tell him that and he's pleased. We laugh together. It's raining, we're driving to Pskov, we're two people who were never supposed to meet.

He asks when the train is and (after determining there's time) suggests buying ice cream at a gas station. We both love ice cream. Eating vanilla ice cream in the car brings us together.

I ask how Zhenya's getting on under the Russians.

'A person's like a rat, gets used to everything. We're living.'

I ask what the Russians have changed in Kupiansk. He shrugs.

'They handed out passports. We all have Russian passports now, can you imagine? At first I thought about not taking one but a pass-port's a pension. It's a salary. It's just some kind of everyday life, see? It's not at all about what they think it is.'

I don't understand what he means, so I ask.

'Are you stupid or something? Born yesterday, right? Do you not understand anything they're doing or what? It works out we're now their people, shit, we're their citizens, we're now their shield!'

He's yelling at me and pressing the gas pedal. I squeeze my eyes shut and press into the passenger seat. Spruce trees race past.

*Spruce trees*
*Spruce trees*
*Spruce trees*

Finally, the Pskov city limits. He has to brake; there's a traffic light. He brakes and stops yelling. Clears his throat. I open my eyes.

He says, 'I'm sorry. But it's obvious we're now Russians. We're now the ones they came to defend. "Russian World", have you heard that? I'm now pretty familiar with geopolitics. We're all familiar with it now. With geopolitics and ADS and various weapons, how the HIMARS shoots, where it shoots, how far and did the ADS work in response or not. What the hell do I need that for anyway?

'I'm basically a chemistry and biology teacher, a village teacher. I was exempted from the military in my youth because there weren't any teachers. I was fine working in the school, I even liked it. With the children there, you teach them good sense, then I'd come home from school and work around the farm. When my pension kicked in, my wife and I expanded that work: chickens, ducks, we even have rabbits. Meat, eggs, all our own. Then we started selling eggs and meat in Kharkiv, where my sisters live. We raised them and my sisters sold them. You know, everything had worked out with that recently, we'd started living well. Shit.'

He's no longer shouting.

The traffic light changes.

We ride, silent, for a bit.

He says, 'When the Russians arrived, they took away our SIM cards, meaning the Ukrainian ones. They gave out their own shitty MirTelekom.'

The way he says 'shitty' is so funny that I want to laugh. But I don't laugh.

He says, 'At night, Russian soldiers in our Kupiansk shell Kharkiv, where my sisters are. And the AFU shoots at us from Kharkiv. But the ADS works fine. For us and for them. In the mornings I call my sisters while I'm still under the covers, "**How, what, is everybody**

**still alive?**" We don't know if we'll see each other again and how things will be now.'

I ask what else Russian soldiers have done other than the MirTelekom cards and Russian passports. Unexpectedly, Zhenya laughs.

'You won't believe it, you won't believe it, that's all there is to it.'

He scrolls through photos on his mobile phone. And finds what he needs.

And, just in case I didn't get it, he explains. 'They painted the kerbs in the tricolour, fancy that?'

I ask, 'Zhenya, if you could choose now who you'd rather live under would it be Russians or Ukraine?'

Zhenya answers quickly, without thinking. It's obvious he's asked himself this question many times, so he has an answer.

'You know, to be honest, it no longer matters. I just don't want them to shoot anymore. I want to live a little, see? We had a hard life, we always pulled through, struggled for those kopecks, worked from night until morning and morning until night. In the nineties there was nothing to eat, well, you remember that yourself, right?

'So it was only about ten years ago when everything fell into place and I'd just started feeling like I'm a man who can provide: I can both buy a TV and trade in for a new car. Last year my daughter was left without her husband, so I tell her, "It's okay, dear daughter, come join Mama and me, we'll live fine and raise your little guy." We didn't want for anything, see? We had everything.

'And they say it's all about language, the war's about that, but I'll tell you: whoever wanted to speak Russian spoke it. There were isolated types who were stirring things up, but the people didn't need that. People wanted to live, to live, see?

'But when the war came, I felt like there was nothing I could do: it's booming and booming, warriors are walking around the city with weapons and I can't save anybody, well, I can cover someone with myself, I'm a big guy. And now that's all started to calm down. Now it's more or less calm, there's just booming during the nights no matter what. But during the day, you putter around in the kitchen garden and it seems like maybe there was a bang, but probably not, it's quiet. Or else there's a siren. Or maybe not a siren. That's called phantom sirens, have you heard of that?

'But it's already quiet overall. Children have come back to the city and they play. That gives everything a peaceful kind of look. The soldiers said, "We came here for the long-term, we're not planning to leave here." And it came to me to let it be as it is.

'Russians, then, it's Russians. That's how we'll live. We'll just get our daughter and grandson and forget what this war was.

'Damn it.'


Zhenya and I embrace at the train station. He looks even more like a bear at full height – I'm about as tall as his elbow. He won't take any money from me. And I do tell him the cat is great for his grandson. We exchange phone numbers, though there's no particular need for that. He sees me off at the train carriage and heads back to the border crossing to get his daughter and grandson.


When you're riding from Pskov to Moscow during the night, there's hardly any mobile coverage. It appears early in the morning, not long before the train's arrival. The first news I see on the approach to Moscow is 'AFU in tough battles for Kupiansk'. I check my notepad, to see if I remembered everything correctly. I start calling Zhenya.

I call at 6am.

At 7am.

At 8am.

At 8.30.

8.45, 8.50, 8.53 8.54 8.55.

I get through to him at 9.30. He's happy. 'I got everybody, we spent the night in Pskov, we're racing home!'

I say, 'Zhenya, you can't go back there. It's not safe in Kupiansk.'

He doesn't believe me. He says his wife would have called him and now he'll call his contacts in the city administration.

I say he doesn't need to call any administration. I read the news, reports from the front, to him.

*Ukrainian forces advanced 20km deep into occupied territory towards the north of Izium, in the Kupiansk direction . . .*

*Sub-units of the Russian army are retreating, taking up defensive position on the eastern bank of the Oskol . . .*

*The AFU liberated the western bank of the Oskol and continue their offensive . . .*

*The bridge over the Oskol River, which divides Kupiansk in two, has been blown up . . .*

I tell him he can't go to Kupiansk, don't do it.

He says, 'That can't be.'

He hangs up.

I call at 10am.

At 10.05, 10.07, 10.10.

I call.

Call.

Call.

He finally answers and shouts, 'What do you want? Why are you scaring me? Who are you anyway? Fuck off! Don't call me anymore!'

I don't let him hang up, I tell him he can make a detour to my native city, Rostov-on-Don, on his way to Kupiansk. My parents and my childhood friends are there, we'll definitely come up with something. He can drive where he likes but he should leave his daughter and grandson in Rostov. With that white cat, I add, for some reason. It's doubtful that's what had an effect but he agreed.

Two days later, on 10 September, he makes contact again.

One text: 'Katya, it's fucked up.'

I called. But he didn't pick up.

His daughter, who'd stayed in an unfamiliar city with a small child and a plush cat, also hadn't received any news at all from her father in several days.

We called each other, cheered each other up and read the news.

*. . . missile attacks were carried out on several targets in Kupiansk;*

*. . . in the course of hard-fought battles on the 206th day of the war, the city of Kupiansk came under the control of the AFU;*

*. . . the Ukrainian flag was raised over the city's administrative building;*

*. . . the location of the city's mayor, who collaborated with the occupants, is unknown.*

Zhenya and I have a videocall on 12 September 2022. I don't know how it's possible to lose so much weight in five days but it's hard for me to recognise him.

He briefly tells me his news. A mine flew into his house in Kupiansk and his wife was in the kitchen garden at that time. She was seriously wounded and lost her arm. The house itself is half-destroyed but the neighbours have things worse. Zhenya's farmstead no longer exists; the chickens and ducks were stunned by the shooting and explosions, and are flitting around the city.

He says, 'I don't know how you saw that I shouldn't go there with the little ones. Thank you for holding on to them. God sent you to me.'

I can't say anything to him in reply. I don't know how to reply.

He says, 'Hey, come on, don't cry. Come on, why are you crying? You know what I was thinking about today? Shit, now they'll have to repaint the kerbs.'

# 24

# The Pillowcase

I was born and raised in the Russian south, in Rostov-on-Don.

My family ended up there pretty much by chance: after Stalin's death, the Soviet government ordered the children of enemies of the people – which my grandmother and grandfather were – to establish themselves wherever the supreme leader's demise found them. All my great-great-grandparents, with one exception – my great-great-grandmother who was imprisoned in the gulag for almost 20 years – were subjected to repression by the Stalinist regime and killed. At that time, children of the repressed were called the children of enemies of the people and the repressed themselves were enemies of the people. And thus the descendant of German nobility and the great-granddaughter of a rabbi from a little Ukrainian Jewish town settled in that southern city. They met, they married. My mother was born in Rostov a year after the tyrant's death. As was I, a quarter-century later.

The northwestern part of the Rostov Oblast borders Ukraine. Ever since I can remember, buses and shuttle vans went from Rostov to Donetsk, Luhansk, Mariupol and Melitopol. People in Rostov speak a lot like people living in eastern Ukraine: we have similar pronunciation, call small apricots *zherdyol*, aubergines 'blue ones' and three-litre jars 'cylinders'. Being neighbours over the years, we've intermixed: people from neighbouring hamlets, Cossack settlements and villages married, merged their households and had children.

After Russia and Ukraine became two separate countries, many Rostov residents' relatives ended up on the other side of the border.

Until 2014, people visited each other as easily and seamlessly as during Soviet times, with no problems. Things later got more complicated when checkpoints acquired barbed wire and special forces employees, and other people crossing were detained or not let through; some even went missing. Most often, though, people were forced to stand in long lines and go through humiliating checks simply to visit loved ones. Until February 2022, however, routes between the Rostov Oblast and the Donetsk and Luhansk Oblasts still continued to operate.

In April 2022, I return to Rostov-on-Don by train for the first time since the war started. Before that, I could fly from Moscow, which took a little under two hours. They built a spiffy new airport in Rostov for the FIFA World Cup in 2018. That airport was closed on 24 February 2022, under an order from Putin, and, at the time of writing, hasn't reopened since.

People now make their way to Rostov primarily by bus and car. Train tickets have tripled in price and are practically impossible to buy. I was simply lucky. As, apparently, were the other passengers. Frightened, knackered passengers curse but they say 'sooner or later, everything will improve'. Those words are uttered somewhat mechanically, without any particular belief in what's said. You have to say something.

'We're alive and thank God,' sighs my chance fellow traveller as she gets off the train at the station in Rostov. 'Unlike them,' she nods, apparently in the direction that implies Ukraine. 'Everything there's basically . . . awful! Their little children . . .' She doesn't finish. She waves her arm and walks away. The little wheels on her suitcase clatter resoundingly on the platform.

Rostov's my homeland. This is where, as before, my parents, teachers and childhood friends live. I feel like a little girl as I walk home from the train station: the street I walked along to school; the park where I strolled with someone I'd fallen for; tram number 10 that brought me to music school.

I see the Don River and realise how much I've missed home.

A river is an important presence in any city that's set on one. Our Don is big, dark and broad-chested. It lies between the Right Bank, where the city lives and works, and the Left Bank, where people unwind.

The Left Bank – LevBerDon, as the locals call it, short for LeftBankDon – consists of tourist resorts, spas, sanatoriums, kebab joints, cafés and expensive restaurants.

As a schoolgirl, I went to LevBerDon for a class outing. The physics teacher led us. He wore a knitted sweater with a high collar, sang songs to guitar music and told amazing stories. Of course we were in love with him.

I later went to LevBerDon with my first boyfriend. We ran along the shore, kissed in the reeds and swam. And he later carried me in his arms through the Don's heavy, cloudy, unctuous water as I threw back my head, squinted at the sun and whispered, *I'm happy, happy, happy.*

I brought my own little children here to fish and look up at the Right Bank from the Don's Left Bank. From the lower to the higher, from the wild to the populated, the urban. I taught them what I myself knew. That this is their motherland, too.

The best vacations of my Rostov childhood took place 200 kilometres away: on the Azov Sea, right next to Berdiansk, not far from Mariupol.

In 2022, my country's troops occupied and destroyed those cities with bombing. A considerable portion of their residents are in Rostov now, as refugees. People deprived of their homes, loved ones and motherland.

I cross the bridge over the Don on my way to one of the largest temporary housing sites for refugees. It was set up on the riverside at the Aelita tourist resort, which comprises a few summer cottages, a heated building, dining hall, laundry and heating plant.

The first refugees – about 50 or 60 people – were brought here around 20 February 2022, meaning a few days before Russian troops' full-scale invasion of Ukraine. They were housed four to six people per room and ordered to wait for the end of a war that nobody had officially announced.

But the war was moving through Ukraine, sowing grief and hatred instead of ending. There are now more than 300 people at the facility. They're fed, clothed and guarded. A policeman patrols the entry to Aelita.

They ask for my documents, jot down my data and lead me to the woman on duty. She takes my passport and is surprised I have permission to spend the day at the facility without an escort. Until me, not one independent Russian journalist managed that. That's how my childhood became a pass into a temporary housing facility for refugees on the Don's Left Bank.

I walk through the resort, looking at the residents. I don't know their views and don't understand who they are or how they ended up at this facility. Who they lost before they ended up here. Or what will become their signal to return home.

There's a smell of bird cherries. I close my eyes and take a deep breath. Damn, I'm at home and I want to go see Mama for lunch, I don't want to talk about the war.

That's all I've been talking about every day for two and a half months. I read about it, watch videos of shelling and bombing, and speak with loved ones from Ukraine whose cities and homes the war came to.

Half my family is being bombed there, in Kyiv. There's my Uncle Sasha who, as a child, taught my mother to play the card game King. When he grew up, he designed the roof over the Boryspil airport; Uncle Sasha received an Honoured Builder of Ukraine award. My brother Andrei is also in Kyiv. I keep his army letters, where he taught me how to understand Pushkin. One time he sent me a 17-page analysis of Pushkin's The Captain's Daughter.

My sister Natasha's there in Kyiv, too. She's very beautiful and as a child I dreamed of looking like her. Natasha has a husband and three children. They don't want to go anywhere. When it's particularly scary, Natasha sends me old photos of our huge family. Yesterday, when Kyiv was being bombed again, Natasha sent a photo of Great-Aunt Katya – our grandfather's sister – roaring with laughter. I was named after her. I set the picture of Great-Aunt Katya as my phone's wallpaper but later took it off, so I wouldn't cry.

Half my family's in Kyiv, the city on which Moscow – where I've lived the greater part of my life and gave birth to my children – declared war.

I'm in Rostov, where my heart is. It's 1,000 kilometres from here to Kyiv. And just as many – 1,000 – to Moscow.

I walk around the facility that's now temporarily housing refugees and hear a voice.

'Can you sense the smell of the bird cherries, child? It's as if nothing happened.'

I turn around. She's standing in rays of spring sun: light, pretty and smiling, as if she's gleaming. I nod. Yes, I hear you.

I say, 'Hello, my name's Katya. I'm a journalist.'

She smiles.

'It's good that you know about yourself, who you are. We no longer do. They've hacked and yanked so much at our lives that nothing's clear at all now. My name's Taisia. Taisia Mikhailovna. We're from Donetsk, meaning they brought us from Donetsk. I'm already in my 86th year, it's possible I no longer want to live. But no, I'm living. See the sun shining? The sun shines and I walk, I stroll. I'll walk to the fence, turn around and walk back. They don't let us beyond the fence. They say we don't need to go there. Why? They say it's dangerous for us. But they don't say what's dangerous or why. They think and decide everything for us. As if we can't make decisions or think for ourselves. Then how did I live my own whole life, with my own mind? I worked on construction projects and tended my husband's homestead, gave birth to children and raised them. I somehow managed. And we didn't have a war. We grew up during the war, we knew we didn't need any war, we needed to live, to raise children.

'I was born in 1936, child. And so I walk, I walk. If you don't walk, you'll sit down, if you sit down you'll lie down, and if you lie down, you'll die. And that's that.

'Although I wonder all the time about why I should even live? If I'd died ten years ago, I would have died happy: husband living, no war, children grown up, grandchildren, great-grandchildren . . . And only joy awaited everyone. Remember how it is in the song? There's only joy ahead.

'But I'm still alive and have lived to a great age. And at the end of my life I've seen so much grief, so much grief. Why take it with me to the other side? I don't know. But for some reason I have to. For some reason I have to. What's the reason?'

Taisia's looking me in the eye, 'What's the reason?' But I don't know the reason.

'I'd like to know myself,' I mutter. But she doesn't hear. She turns away from me, angling her face towards the sun.

She says, 'And my husband died in December. I grieved and grieved. I took to my bed, lay on my bed, waiting for my death, child. And then the medics suddenly come, that's it, Gram, they say, we're evacuating, there's going to be a big war. And I tell them, "And how is it there wasn't war for eight years? Or what was that? What changed that it's now war?"

'War, child, do you know what makes it crafty? It gnaws so much at your heart even if it doesn't wound you. My husband used to work as the head engineer at a big, a very big, site and he retired later but his mind wasn't gone. And he couldn't stand this new wartime because they shoot all the time, they shoot so both the young ones and the old ones die. And who shot first at whom, and why? You can't figure it out now. Basically, his heart started giving up. And his head, too, fog started covering everything. The Lord basically took care of him . . . And he died. And those medics came for me. I asked them, leave me be, young men, what do you need with an old lady like me? Let me die on my own land.

'No, they jabbed me with something. I fell asleep. And when I woke up I was already here, at this tourist resort. And it's as if we're here for rest and recreation. And it works out we're like those ducks they raise for pâté, do you know about that? They feed us three times a day. And don't let us out anywhere. We sit and we'll sit as long as the war goes on in our Donetsk. There you have it.

'Will you walk with me to the pier? The air's good there. And there's a willow tree growing. For some reason I love the weeping willow. It's so nice to just look at it. I look and I think what a tree it is, so similar to me.'

We walk to the pier. Taisia Mikhailovna is wearing white tennis shoes and a knitted dress the colour of milky tea. I ask where all that loveliness is from. She's glad for the question. She straightens the dress – she's as proud of it as a child:

'Take care of the dress from your youth, remember that? I sewed and knitted my whole life. And now I love knitting all the more. It's calming. I had a knitting machine at home, too. And knitting by hand is even better. But my hands are bored here, being idle. A person declines in idleness, in yearning, you know? And we have yearning and idleness all at once.

'I keep asking them to either let me out of here to go to the craft store or to bring me yarn, even one skein, and knitting needles. Even one skein. I'd knit. And I'd leave everybody alone and not pine.

'That's how I calmed myself the whole time at home: they bomb and shoot, and I sit next to my husband and knit. In recent years we didn't go to any bomb shelter. We sat at home, child. Why run from death if it's not coming to you itself? But death was roaming around our city, taking both the young and the healthy.

'The man who lived one floor down from us was so good, so nice, as good-natured as a kitten. He lived with his mother, oh, she loved him. Then he found a wife and things started going better for them. But he was mobilised in the winter. Two came right to his house and took him to fight. He didn't last three weeks, child. They returned him in a wooden coffin, there you go. His mother really grieved him. And his wife was in a dark mood from grief. But I don't see them anymore because they brought me here. Maybe they were taken away, too?'

Taisia Mikhailovna's grey hair flutters in the wind, making her look utterly vulnerable and small. I want to embrace her but I feel shy because we barely know each other. I want to say something consoling to her. But I don't know what can console someone who's in her mid-eighties and has ended up in a temporary housing facility in another country, in a room for six people, with a refrigerator and a television in the building's common lobby. We reach the pier as I'm thinking about that. There are lots of people there and someone's put Verka Serduchka on their phone. The children are dancing to 'Everything Will Be Good'. Their mothers are smoking and milling around. It feels like they'd dance, too, but this isn't the time or place. There's a slight breeze from the Don. It's chilly.

Taisia Mikhailovna introduces me, 'This is a journalist, her name's Katya. She's writing a book about people like us. About victims of the war.'

They shut off the music on the phone. The circle quickly thins out.

Olga, a beautiful, stout woman in a mohair sweater with large orange flowers, is left. Olga's lipstick matches the flowers on her sweater. She says, 'So if you're a correspondent, you tell them that what they're doing, can they really . . . they're inhuman.'

A pause hangs in the air. I look at Olga; Olga glances around.

Women lead their children from the pier as waves from the Don hit the beams underneath and a seagull flies overhead, shrieking loudly and coarsely. Taisia Mikhailovna comes to rescue the conversation with Olga that has hit a dead end.

'Will you explain, sweetheart, what you're talking about?'

Olga's hands are on her hips.

'About the salutes. They boom every day. And my kids lie down on the ground, cover their heads right away. The women go pale and some get sick to their stomach from fear. The whole temporary housing place drops to the ground from any loud noise. What, don't you even understand where we came from?'

It finally gets through to me what she's talking about. Next to the Aelita tourist resort that's been turned into temporary refugee housing, there's a high-end suburban restaurant called Petrovsky Prichal. It came into being in the mid-nineties and seems to be the first place in the city that can claim a Moscow chic. It looks out on the Don, like all the Left Bank restaurants. Petrovsky Prichal has a long pier with two cannons standing at the end. They shoot every day at noon. The restaurant hosts loud weddings and celebrates other occasions every Friday and Saturday; reservations are made months in advance. Those festivities usually end in an opulent cannon salute. Everybody in Rostov knows that. But nobody that settled refugees next to Petrovsky Prichal thought about it.

I ask Olga, 'Have you complained?'

'Who's going to listen to us, we're nobody. We're nobody's people from nobody's land, see what I'm saying?'

Olga lights a cigarette and starts speaking with me using the familiar 'you'.

'So the war started for you in February, right? Do you know how long I haven't seen my husband? I haven't seen him since November. So you count: November, December, January, February, March, April. I've been living without my husband for half a year, see?'

Taisia Mikhailovna touches Olga's elbow. 'Now don't you get worked up, **woman**. We've lived longer than that without husbands, the main thing is that they're all alive. Later you'll meet, get caught up.'

But Olga goes on: 'We didn't ask to join you here. We were living in our own place. I won't speak about how we lived those eight years, that's not what I'm talking about. But I raised two children, one born in 2012, the other in 2010. My kids are from back in peacetime, I wouldn't have thought to have them during a war, I'm not that kind of person. But we held up through all that. And it's like everything even calmed down where we were. Just so you know, I live in Donetsk. So here you go again, with more of this war? Why didn't you leave us any choice? Why'd you take away all our men, who are we going to love and make children with? I don't see my husband; he just sends me pictures. And not of himself, the dear man, but of the bombs and missiles that're falling on our city. Here, look, look, don't turn away, you, too, Gram, you have a look, too.'

Olga opens her phone. There truly are lots of photographs and videos of shell fragments, some of them still smoking. Olga scrolls the pictures; we look.

She says, 'He's a fireman. He shouldn't be fighting. They came and took him, mobilised him, as they announced to us. Could you please tell me what right they have? We've been sitting here four months, not working, not leaving, we can't do anything. The children race around the compound but what about me? I go outside, smoke, go inside, lie down, watch some TV. But there's such dopiness on TV, I can't even convey that to you, what they say, that all this' – and here Olga's eyes look around at the refugee housing facility, children running around a nonfunctional fountain to chase a frog, men playing cards, the Don, the guard in the booth, a three-legged dog sitting by the kitchen waiting for a handout and the wealthy Petrovksy Prichal restaurant – 'is for us. Everything, they say, is at your service. Eat, don't drip it on yourself. Thank you. We've eaten our fill. Do you know when this will all end already? When, huh?'

Taisia Mikhailovna comes to my aid.

'Well, how would she know, child. She's the opposite, a correspondent, she came to talk about us, about how we're living. So why are you mad, huh?'

Olga suddenly deflates. And as she leaves she hoarsely announces, 'I'm tired. I'm fucking exhausted, end of story.'

Taisia Mikhailovna crosses herself. With her cigarette still smoking, Olga takes a step away from her and moves very close to me. And she suddenly says, 'I want to live, I want to go on a scheduled run. I'm a train attendant, see? My life was like this: three days on, five days off. You work three days, have five at home. It's an awesome way for you to live and the husband doesn't get to you. What has all that turned into now? Into me being a refugee. "Help me, good people"? And we never in our lives begged. And I wouldn't have left Donetsk: they brought in those buses for us, crammed everybody in, took us out at night, said, sit tight until we liberate you. What did we need to be liberated for, we're free on our own, right, Gram?'

Grandma Taisia strokes Olga's shoulder. She asks, 'And why can't you work here, daughter? What kind of passport do you have?'

'Whatever kind you want, I have a choice: Russian and Ukrainian and DPR. We took everything they were handing out. But they told me that since I have a DPR passport that means I'm not a refugee but a migrant. And we're not entitled to relocation money and not entitled to housing. We're here "temporarily", we're supposed to go back home later.

'But I can't go to work because even if they let me out of here, which is highly unlikely, who would I leave the little ones with? Everybody here has their own grief, everybody's sitting over it and crying. I'd get on a train now, just call.'

Olga squints and says, 'My carriage is always neat and clean and I even bought a special air freshener, "rose orchids". I had a runner rug, pink, that lay all straight. I preferred distributing the linens myself, I love the smell of laundered linens when they're still a little damp. It smells like snow. I've even happened to make up passengers' bunks myself, I like that.'

'Oh, good heavens,' says Taisia Mikhailovna, suddenly tossing up her hands. 'And I'd forgotten.'

Olga and I turn to her. Grandma Taisia's holding both hands to her cheeks and looking around anxiously,

'Child, I just can't find it. I look and look but I can't find it.'

'What are you looking for? Who?'

'A pillowcase. They gave me a set and I have everything but the pillowcase disappeared. That pillowcase seems like nothing, just silly. But it's gone. And the girls in the laundry scolded me. I went to look for it, I'm thinking maybe it fell out when I was going to my room. But it's not anywhere. And I ran into you and seem to have forgotten myself, I stopped worrying. But now this young woman's talked about bed linens and I immediately recalled the pillowcase. You didn't run across a pillowcase anywhere? When I left my room, I was predicting my future. If I find it – the pillowcase – then everything will end up good for us. But I was walking and walking, looking, and then I ran into you and forgot everything.'

We searched for Taisia Mikhailovna's pillowcase until evening. And didn't find it.

I left.

And I spent the whole evening trying to convince my parents to leave Rostov. If only temporarily, not for ever. They're against it.

In 2014, during the military operation that Russia began in the Donetsk region, black smoke from explosions was visible from the balcony of our apartment, and people in Rostov's southern outskirts heard booming.

Now there's a full-scale war going on just a three-hour drive from my parents' home. Fighter jets scud over their building with furious noise, just as they do over all the other buildings in the city. Here and there, people hear incomprehensible popping and mobile coverage often drops. Residents in the northern district took missile shards out of the asphalt. People in the city started arguing about if it *flew in from them* or if it's *one of ours that didn't make it*. Based on a photograph, they decided it was from us. But there was no official information about that on either the local or national news.

I stand on the balcony and look in the direction where, right now, buildings are blowing up, machine gunners are shooting each other, mines are flying and people are dying.

I can't see anything. Fog.

I leave Rostov.

I return four months later. The city has changed. The war – this is palpable – is approaching Rostov, and it's now simply impossible to miss. The central library, city administration, shopping centre and all public transportation are covered in Zs and Vs, in stripes of brown and red, the colours of the St George's ribbon. They now put on the Russian anthem in the morning at the kindergarten next to my parents' building. It's so loud it's audible in our apartment. There's a poster with the letter Z on the façade. I see it every time I look out the window.

Rostov residents, who previously seemed not to notice the war, are now reacting harshly, even aggressively, to any reminder of it. I hear the word 'war' on public transportation, on the street and in cafés.

I get in a taxi. On the local radio, as everywhere in Russia, they don't call the war a war but they say there are around 200,000 refugees from Ukraine in the Rostov Oblast.

'They're fucking annoying,' comments the cabbie. And he complains that refugees stole his friend's licence plates.

I ask, 'You're sure?'

'I'm sure.'

'What do they need them for?'

'Who knows. But they stole them.'

The topic of finger pointing comes up in all conversations. Life's become harder, more expensive and more unpredictable. People in Rostov most often blame their woes on neighbouring Ukraine and Ukrainian refugees. They're close but Moscow's far.

The cabbie brings me to the Left Bank of the Don. I came to Rostov for family matters but want to visit 'my' refugees. I remember them but for some reason, I think there's no longer anybody at the facility. It's *temporary* housing. I call the duty woman and ask. It turns out *my* people are there.

'And Grandma Taisia?'

'Oh, come on, where's she going?' the woman's cheerful voice answers me.

I'm bringing gifts for Taisia Mikhailovna: knitting needles, yarn, comfortable shoes without heels and a set of cotton hankies.

I ride over the Don and end up at Aelita.

Almost everyone I know and have seen is still here. But there are new ones: from Mariupol, Rubizhne, Kharkiv, Popasna, Volnovakha, Avdiivka . . .

The facility's 'old-timers' introduce me and people approach, show photos and videos of their former homes before the war, and videos of explosions and shelling. They tell stories. We exchange phone numbers. I promise to help whomever I can. I say I'll try. But I'm looking around for Taisia.

I suddenly realise that I miss her and – though I can't yet explain to myself why – that it's very important for me to see her.

They tell me she's at the pier.

I see her from afar. She's standing, both her hands under her cheeks, looking at the Don.

I say hello. She looks at me attentively. Then she says, 'Hello, where did you come from?'

I take her by the hand.

'It's me, Katya. The journalist. Remember we were looking for your pillowcase? I'm back. Do you remember me?'

She smiles.

She says, 'Child, you're so good. You're all so good. You've all helped me so much, you help us so much. May God grant you all health.'

She says, 'I want so much to go home, child, I have a fabulous view from my balcony. I have children and grandchildren, four great-grandchildren. But we didn't see any war. We lived our life

well, friendly. We lived and lived until my husband died, his name
was Viktor Ivanovich. He was a very good person. We lived a long
life. But I just don't understand anything since he died last December, it all went topsy-turvy: there's war, what war? Where did you
come from, child?'

I hold her hand. She speaks and looks past me. And I scrutinise
her: smile, light and clear eyes. The wind's fluttering her white hair,
which has grown out since we last met. Set against the sky, she
becomes transparent: it's as if my Taisia is dissolving, disappearing.

I attempt to remind her. The knitted beige dress she was wearing
the day of our first meeting now looks large on her, as if it were a
hand-me-down. But it still looks good on her. I want to tell her that
but I can't because she's talking nonstop.

She says, 'And we lived, friendly, we didn't hurt anyone, we knew
our place, didn't particularly meddle anywhere, we lived well, very
well, child. And we had plenty of everything. It was in my childhood that things were bad, it was tough, hungry: I was five when
the fascists came and my father died. My mother and I were in the
occupation; she had 12 of us children. But I'm the only one left now.
I so miss them all . . . especially Mama. Mama had such beautiful
hands. With fingers like this, a little knobbly because she worked a
lot. But long fingers and oval nails. But the main thing is her hands
were very warm. I so loved when she hugged me. She never had
time, there were lots of us, and there was lots of work so when
could she hug, but if she did hug, you immediately felt warm. My
Mama, dear Mama . . .'

Taisia Mikhailovna also has long fingers with knots of time and
toil on her joints. Her nails are oval and beautiful, resembling
almonds. She rubs one dry palm against another. Sighs.

She says, 'We, our generation, lived well, we were just always
thinking "so long as there isn't war". And we didn't have a war, see?
That was the contribution of our people and our government. We
overcame hunger, too, and everything else. And I myself was ener-
getic, I worked at a factory and unloaded trains. And people
laughed at me, that I was so strong and healthy. They gave us an
apartment later: you go out on the balcony and see the city, such

beauty. We lived on a high floor, the fifth, and you saw absolutely, absolutely everything. But we didn't see any war . . . Child, can you tell me when they'll bring us back home? I have children there and grandchildren, do you know when they'll bring us? Do you work here?'

I stroke her hand, straighten her hair that the wind has already tousled ridiculously, laughably. The loudspeaker that broadcasts a state entertainment radio station for the whole temporary housing facility sounds with a song that makes her go still.

Lidia Ruslanova, a major popular singer during Taisia Mikhailovna's youth, is singing one of those piercing Russian ballads where tragic lyrics are, incomprehensibly, set to a rollicking melody in a major key. She sings:

> *If I go out to the river,*
> *I'll look at it, swift*
> *If I don't see my dear one*
> *My warm-hearted dear friend.*
>
> *If I don't see my beloved,*
> *My sweet one.*
> *My sweet former one,*
> *My dear boy.*
>
> *Tai-lai-lai-lala*
> *Tai-lai-lai.*
> *Ta-lalalalala*
> *Ta-la-lai-lai-lai*

That song's familiar to me. I know those words but I can't remember why: they're from somewhere in the depths of my childhood. I attempt to recall more specifically but can't. I just can't seem to focus.

Taisia Mikhailovna's next to me, squeezing my hand. And she says, 'I know that song, I've always remembered it . . . I've just started forgetting things. That's our song, a folk song. We always sang it at home. It's about us, about us. About our *grief* . . .'

I stroke Taisia Mikhailovna's shoulder and wrinkled hand and think about how surprising that is: the word 'grief' isn't in the song but the sense of grief is.

Why is that? Nothing comes to mind.

Taisia Mikhailovna whispers, 'It was Mama who sang that song to me. I so want to go to Mama, to Mamochka. I'm so tired, child, take me home to my Mama.'

She cries fast, quiet tears, and nestles against me more firmly. We walk along the path from the pier to building three of the temporary facility for refugees on the Left Bank of the Don in Rostov-on-Don. I bring her to her room and put her to bed. She falls asleep still holding my hand. I quietly kiss her before leaving the room. I don't know if we'll see each other again but I realise she won't recognise me if we do.

I walk down the corridor.

The TV's on in the living room, tuned in to a Russian state newscast. A beautiful presenter is saying that the first traffic light has begun operating in Mariupol.

I know that a third of the 20 people sitting in front of the TV are from Mariupol. I know many of them personally. They've told me about how beautiful their city was before the war: fountains, parks, a theatre.

The TV shows a traffic light blinking in wonder – red, yellow, green, go – at a few cars, set against the backdrop of the charred façades of buildings. The cars go. But there are no other cars at the cross street. Why then is there a traffic light?

And could the beautiful presenter on TV really not have thought about what happened to all Mariupol's previous traffic lights if that's the first?

The item finishes. Everyone's silent. A few women silently go out for a smoke.

I follow them.

There's a scene in the hallway. My acquaintance Olga has slammed the door in her roommates' faces and won't let them in the room.

'Olga, Olga, open up, it's us! Olga, enough stubbornness, Olga. Olga, he'll turn up, Olga, they're scammers, Olga.'

Olga shouts that she doesn't want to see anybody. There's a crash behind the door. It seems like she threw something heavy at it.

They explain: Olga's husband has been out of touch for a long time but now somebody called Olga and demanded money for information about her husband. But the caller didn't tell her if he's alive or not, prisoner or free. Olga held on for a day and then went to pieces.

'He'll turn up,' says one of Olga's roommates.

'She'll calm down,' chimes in her friend.

They sit down to smoke by the entrance to building three of the temporary refugee facility.

He didn't turn up. At least, no new information about her husband turned up during the month Olga and I corresponded. And then Olga took her children, left for Donetsk, changed her telephone number and I know nothing more about her.

In December, just before the New Year holiday, I come to Rostov for the third time in 2022, the gloomiest year of my life.

My visit coincided with the anniversary of the death of my beloved grandmother Roza. I go to visit her grave. The largest cemetery in Rostov is the Northern Cemetery.

My grandmother's grave used to be at the cemetery's edge, close to the road. The cemetery has taken on new graves since I was last here, so it's difficult to find my grandmother.

In mud up to my ankles, I make my way between low fences. It's a winter that initially frightened everybody with killing frosts but then turned out to be slippery and squishy instead of cold. For some reason, I think about how there are soldiers fighting in mud up to their waists 100 kilometres from the cemetery.

I hear a shot nearby. Terrified, I grab at someone's gravestone and look around. A formation of soldiers is shooting in the air over a fresh grave. People lead a crying woman, holding her arms, as two children, twins, about five years old, grasp the hem of her coat. There are few mourners with her. They've already lowered the coffin and the cemetery workers brandish their shovels as they fill. The wet soil sticks to the shovels. The workers are cranky.

The soil sticks to feet, too. I notice that some of the mourners are wearing shoe protectors, so as not to get dirty. The less practical have to wash off the mud in puddles and clean their shoes against the posts of other people's fences.

I walk around the funeral procession in order to have a glimpse of the deceased's photograph. His name is Andrei, 30 years old. Grey eyes. Smiling. Died on 12 December. The place isn't written. A man in a leather jacket is trying to add a plastic orange and black taxi sign to Andrei's cross.

I ask, 'A cabbie?'

'Far from it,' sighs the man. 'He got that Solaris on credit, thought he'd be a "business class" taxi driver but then there was mobilisation, call-up paper and see you later. They identified him with genetics. There's the taxi, young lady. That's what our life is now, holy crap.'

The man moves me aside with his hand as if I were a curtain and walks to the minibus with the other funeralgoers.

I glance at Andrei: smile, cross, the chequered taxi pattern.

When I was a child, I loved to wander around the cemetery when we came here to my grandmother and grandfather's graves. I'd read the dates of birth and death, the inscriptions on the gravestones, and think up stories for the dead, attempting to imagine how they'd lived, what they'd done, who they'd loved and what they dreamed of.

I find my grandmother's grave using the gravestones that helped preserve memories of my childhood.

*Hello, Gram. How are you?*

I, who've missed you so much all my life, have been glad so many times during this last year that you're not here. Because you wouldn't have made it.

*You wouldn't have made it.*

I tell my grandmother about how they're bombing Mykolaiv, the city of her childhood, the city of her pain, the city that sheltered her when she was ten, after her parents were arrested in 1937. They shot her father and sent her mother to a camp for wives of traitors to the motherland. Then the neighbours in Mykolaiv collected money for my grandmother's ticket to Moscow. My grandmother fled, hid with fearless relatives and survived. Everyone she'd known and loved in Mykolaiv was shot in 1941; they were Jewish.

But my grandmother was lucky and returned to Ukraine after the war. She moved to Kharkiv, applied to the aviation institute, couldn't study there, and transferred to the Kyiv Automobile and Highway Institute. Now a qualified engineer, she was part of a mobile team formed from 'politically unreliable' people that came to Rostov to build a bridge over the Don. And she met my grandfather.

According to family legend, my grandfather fell in love with my grandmother when she recited Taras Shevchenko's poem 'My Testament' in Ukrainian at some amateur concert.

Damn, I remember how my grandmother taught me that poem. And how mad she was that I can't say 'милій', for 'beloved', properly. I was always mixing up the vowels, getting them backwards.*

Grandma, how did this all happen? Why?

How good that you're not seeing all this, Grandma.

I buy water at a stall by the bus stop near the cemetery, wash off my sneakers with my hand, wash my hand; nothing washes off. The mud's tenacious, gets under the fingernails, lands on clothes; even my backpack is muddy.

I cry, I'm in a foul mood. I don't know where to go or what to do.

Fuck, I don't know how to live. How to make it through this hatred that's approaching from all sides, how to drown it in love.

What the hell kind of love am I thinking about? It's a war.

A war, Grandma! Can you imagine? We have a war.

Somehow I end up just going to the Left Bank temporary refugee facility. It seems like I'll calm down if I see Grandma Taisia. I think I should go, even if she doesn't recognise me.

I can't get through to the woman on duty and so arrive unannounced.

---

* A short and not very satisfying or scholarly explanation is that the letters and sounds for the vowels in the Ukrainian word 'милій' ('mylii') are very close to those in the Russian word 'милый' ('milyi'). Fortunately, the transliterations show the different order of the letters in both versions of the word. [translator]

The woman on duty, the guards and the temporary refugee facility itself are all gone.

A few of Aelita's cabins have been rented out to vacationers but the rest are empty, awaiting holiday visits.

I go to the kitchen, the laundry and the linen keeper, ask about the people who work at Aelita and what happened to Grandma Taisia, but people don't remember. They're some kind of new people. They say everybody was taken away, settled into various permanent refugee camps. Some went to hotels, some to 'the family place', a family dormitory . . .

'Seems like the old people were moved into the oblast, to a nursing home in Rovenki or Neklinovka, I don't remember, I don't know who you should ask more specifically, lady. There's no longer anybody here who worked on that topic.'

I ask if anybody died at Aelita in the autumn.

The woman answers, 'God forbid, there was none of that.'

I go down to the pier, to the Don. I'm here alone. I watch as a train crosses the Don along the railroad bridge. It whistles. People laugh and clink their glasses in the Petrovsky Prichal restaurant.

The wind blows. Dry, frozen reeds rustle by my feet.

The war's moving farther and farther, gathering up new people underneath itself, leaving behind a dirty, bloody trail of previous life.

But it's quiet here, on the pier. There's nobody. I suddenly hear Lidia Ruslanova's song in my ears, the song Taisia Mikhailovna and I heard a few months ago. The song to which, I now understand, we parted.

> If I go out to the river,
> I'll look at it, swift
> If I don't see my dear one
> My warm-hearted dear friend.

I find the song on YouTube and listen to Ruslanova as I look at the river. She's singing:

*Oy, they said about my beloved,*
*That he is not alive, not well,*
*That he is not alive, not well,*
*As if he went missing.*

I listen, listen, listen . . . When the song comes to an end, I return the cursor to the beginning and listen again. And I suddenly realise that I have never actually heard that song. I just know the lyrics. And the lyrics are different. More specifically, they end differently.

My memory suddenly awakens and hints: I remember those lines in my grandmother's voice. She's the one who recited them to me when I was little, every time we walked or rode or simply ended up by the river. Only these weren't the words; there were different words.

The last time we met, Taisia Mikhailovna told me that song is a folk song. But now, as I flip through dozens of variations of the lyrics on my phone, I see that's not the case. The author of the song is Russian nobleman Yury Neledinsky-Meletsky. He had a great military career in the 18th century, taking part in the siege of the Moldovan village of Bendery, conquering Crimea twice, and earning fame in the Turkish War. Neledinsky-Meletsky eventually reached the rank of privy counsellor under emperor Pavel I of Russia, consulting for the Russian sovereign on, among other issues, questions of war.

Like many people of his circle, Neledinsky-Meletsky thought he knew Russia and its people well. Wishing to confirm that, he wrote 'When I Go Down to the River' to be sung by a female voice, thinking that the people would accept the song as their own, a folk song, rather than recognizing that it was only an imitation.

Which is the way things turned out.

Except that the last lines were different in Neledinsky-Meletsky's original verses:

*I'll go down to the river.*
*Gaze at the swift—*
*Take my grief away,*
*Swift river, away with you . . .*

But the line about grief didn't make it into the folk song. Or maybe it did but didn't take hold. Why? How had the memory of grief ended up being displaced? Why is the one the song's heroine loves and awaits neither dead nor alive but instead 'as if he went missing'?

Nobody will ever answer those questions for me, no matter how much I ask.

And there's nobody here anyway, only the river. It's quiet. Indifferent. I look at it and recall that each time I was at a river with my grandmother – be the river large or small, this one or another – my grandmother would repeat, quickly, like an incantation:

> Take my grief away,
> Swift river, away with you . . .

And she would add, 'You tell the river your grief and the river will take it away.'

I believed my grandmother and told the river my grief. But now I walk away from the pier. The grief that didn't find a place in the song won't find a place in the river either.

It will be with me for ever.

# Acknowledgements

I want to express my eternal gratitude once again to all the figures in this book. I thank them for the trust they showed me after deciding to talk and for the effort that each of them made to be candid.

I believe that these stories are evidence, genuine documents of wartime that mean future versions of us won't forget either the war or the hostility or the violence that were brought upon us.

I'm very grateful to my dear friends Katya Bolotovskaya and Dmitry Muratov, Tatyana Yershova and Ksenia Rappoport, Chulpan Khamatova and Elena Kostyuchenko, Natalia Fishman and Darya Trushkina, Katya Mikhailova and Galina Timchenko, who read this book, either in full or in part, empathising with my interviewees and supporting me at the most difficult points in the work.

Heartfelt thanks to Yana Kuchina, Olga Bobrova and Anne-Marie Rushchina, the editors of the Russian version of the text which, to my deep regret, cannot be published as yet in Russia itself. Not one publisher in Russia has dared to publish the book in Russian. The publishers all patted me on the shoulder and said, 'Oh, you understand.' One of them – who's even a friend – sent me an attorney's 16-page statement instead of a personal response. The attorney's opinion was that the book needed to be shortened by a third, deleting words like war, Putin, Russian soldiers, shot and tank.

Publishing the book in Russian was very important to me. I did, after all, write it in Russian. The book came out in December 2023 with Meduza, a Russian-language independent publisher. Not in Russia. But in Russian.

# Translator's Acknowledgements

Katya's assistance was invaluable to my work translating of *Take My Grief Away*. She read my translation, answered dozens of my questions, answered dozens more questions from our editors, and offered additional background, too. We corresponded about lots of unexpected things. My efforts to get details right led to sending photos of a Starbucks in Hamburg, Germany, so I could decide how to describe an entryway in chapter 21. I also sent a photo of the jacket I thought Danil must have been wearing that day. I always feel an indescribable bond with my authors but this book, anchored as it is by Katya's words about grief as well as our mutual desire to make this English translation of her book read as well as possible, makes me feel I've known her for ever. That, despite the fact that, as of writing this in March 2024, we've never even had a voice-to-voice conversation.

I owe huge thanks to Katya's literary agents, Julia Goumen and Natasha Banke, for asking me to translate a chapter from the book in autumn 2022. I chose what is now chapter 9, 'The Iron', a particularly haunting account that displays Katya's uncanny ability to hold back and listen to her interviewees, granting them the space and silence they need to speak openly.

I also feel particularly fortunate that Julia and Natasha found acquiring editor Suzanne Connelly at Ebury, who purchased English language rights to the book. Suzanne was the first editor to read my manuscript. Her queries and thoughts about *Take My Grief Away* helped Katya and me tremendously: her ear and her ability to tactfully zero in on 'clunky' words and phrases were particularly welcome. As she says, 'many eyes make a book'. It's a privilege to have her eyes and ears involved in *Take My Grief Away*. Editor Amanda Waters of Ebury also made substantial contributions. I'm particularly grateful for her practical decisions on handling footnotes, the glossary, and some of my bad wording. Copyeditor Ian Allen saved me from several gaffes, including an absurd neologism. He, too, reworded some (of my) awkward passages; I'm very grateful for his inspired work. Our legal reviewer, attorney David Hirst, allayed my concerns about all sorts of minutiae. Thank you to our proofreader, Fraser Crichton.

Translators aren't always the solitary beings many people think we are. My regular correspondence and online meetings with colleagues – Anne Fisher, Katherine Young, Marian Schwartz, Alex Shvartsman, Will Evans, and Steve Dodson among them – were invaluable as sources of translation advice as well as positive professional distractions on days when I felt down. Ilona Yazhbin Chavasse deserves very special thanks for offering last-minute suggestions and ideas for translating a few intransigent phrases and words: we discussed foods, illnesses, obscenities, and other tidbits. Alyssa Dinega Gillespie, who translates from both Russian and Ukrainian, helped me with the Ukrainian phrases in the book. Finally, at home, my husband, Park, answered many questions (sometimes many times!) about weaponry and other aspects of war, displaying admirable patience. Our two cats, Edwina and Ireland, spent lots of time in my office, soothing me by letting me pat them as I worked and even pretending to listen when I queried them about word choices. Errors, omissions or clunky phrasings that remain in the translation are, of course, my responsibility.

Finally, I send my gratitude to everyone who will read *Take My Grief Away* in English. Thank you.

Lisa C. Hayden, March 2024

# Text Credits

# Glossary

**ADS**
Air Defence System

**AFU**
Armed Forces of Ukraine

**APC**
Armoured Personnel Carrier

**Azov**
The Azov Assault Brigade, founded in 2014 as a volunteer militia to fight Russian forces, and initially based in Mariupol.

**Banderite**
A term used to refer to a member of the Organisation of Ukrainian Nationalists (established in 1929), derived from the name of Stepan Bandera, who headed up a faction of the OUN. Also used as a derogatory term for Ukrainians.

**DPR**
Self-proclaimed, internationally unrecognised Donetsk People's Republic.

**'Grad'**
A rocket launcher, more formally known as a BM-21. The word град (*grad*) means 'hail' in both Ukrainian and Russian. It can also mean 'torrent'.

**HIMARS**
High Mobility Artillery Rocket System

**IFV**
Infantry Fighting Vehicle

**Kadyrovites**
A term given to the troops from Chechnya who support the Russian war of aggression, derived from the name of Ramzan Kadyrov, Head of the Chechen Republic.

**LPR**
Self-proclaimed, internationally unrecognised Luhansk People's Republic.

**Ribbon of Saint George**
A striped black and orange ribbon that originated in eighteenth-century Russia as a military decoration. It is also known as St George's ribbon or the Georgian ribbon. It has become a patriotic and pro-Russian symbol during the Russo-Ukranian War.

**RPG**
Rocket Propelled Grenade

**Russian World**
Or *Russkiy mir*. A term used by Vladimir Putin since the early 2000s, referring to the Russian sphere of political, cultural and military influence.